Documenting Americans

This is the first and only comprehensive, book-length political history of national ID card proposals and developments in identity policing in the United States. The book focuses on the period from 1915 to 2016, including the post-9/11 debates and policy decisions regarding the introduction of technologically advanced identification documents, including driver's licenses. Putting the United States in comparative perspective and connecting the vital issues of immigration and homeland security, Magdalena Krajewska shows how national ID card proposals have been woven into political conflict across a variety of policy fields. Findings contradict conventional wisdom, debunking two common myths: that Americans are opposed to national ID cards and that American policymakers never propose national ID cards. Dr. Krajewska draws on extensive archival research; high-level interviews with politicians, policymakers, and ID card technology experts in Washington, DC, and London; and public opinion polls.

MAGDALENA KRAJEWSKA is Associate Professor of Political Science at Wingate University in North Carolina. She received her PhD in Politics from Brandeis University and a BSc in Government and Economics from the London School of Economics and Political Science and has lived in Poland, Germany, Great Britain, and the United States. She specializes in comparative and American politics.

Documenting Americans

A Political History of National ID Card Proposals in the United States

MAGDALENA KRAJEWSKA
Wingate University, North Carolina

CAMBRIDGE
UNIVERSITY PRESS

CAMBRIDGE
UNIVERSITY PRESS

University Printing House, Cambridge CB2 8BS, United Kingdom

One Liberty Plaza, 20th Floor, New York, NY 10006, USA

477 Williamstown Road, Port Melbourne, VIC 3207, Australia

314-321, 3rd Floor, Plot 3, Splendor Forum, Jasola District Centre, New Delhi - 110025, India

79 Anson Road, #06-04/06, Singapore 079906

Cambridge University Press is part of the University of Cambridge.

It furthers the University's mission by disseminating knowledge in the pursuit of education, learning and research at the highest international levels of excellence.

www.cambridge.org
Information on this title: www.cambridge.org/9781316510100
DOI: 10.1017/9781108186773

First published 2017

A catalogue record for this publication is available from the British Library

Library of Congress Cataloging in Publication data
NAMES: Krajewska, Magdalena, author.
TITLE: Documenting Americans : a political history of national ID card proposals in the United States / Magdalena Krajewska, Wingate University, North Carolina.
DESCRIPTION: Cambridge [UK] ; New York : Cambridge University Press, 2017. | Includes bibliographical references and index.
IDENTIFIERS: LCCN 2017028903 | ISBN 9781316510100 (hardback : alk. paper) | ISBN 9781316649480 (pbk. : alk. paper)
SUBJECTS: LCSH: Identification cards–Law and legislation–United States–History. | Identification cards–Political aspects–United States–History. | Legal documents–United States–Identification.
CLASSIFICATION: LCC KF4791 .K73 2017 | DDC 342.7308–DC23
LC record available at https://lccn.loc.gov/2017028903

ISBN 978-1-316-51010-0 Hardback
ISBN 978-1-316-64948-0 Paperback

To my mom, Dr. Hanna Bawej-Krajewska

Contents

Tables

Acknowledgments

My family, friends, and colleagues have all made this book possible.

I am grateful to the interviewees who shared with me their time and expertise.

I am grateful to the two external reviewers who wrote the most excellent reviews of my manuscript.

I am grateful to Tom Burke, Rebekka Friedman, and Chappell Lawson for rooting for me and to Richard McCulley at the National Archives for all his help.

I am grateful that my professors at Brandeis University, especially Jytte Klausen, Dan Kryder, and Mingus Mapps, saw the importance of my research.

I am grateful to Tomek and Mikayla, as well as Robert Dougans, for being there at the beginning of this journey and to all my friends who have been there since.

I am grateful to my many great colleagues at Wingate University, especially Joseph Ellis and Bob Billinger, who always believed in me.

Writing a book while teaching a 4-4 course load is not easy, and I thank the Spivey Fellowship for easing my workload for one semester. I will forever be grateful to my Wingate colleagues who voted to award me the Spivey.

My special thanks go to Darin for his support as I was putting the finishing touches on this book.

I am most grateful to my family in Poland. My parents, Hanna Bawej-Krajewska and Zbigniew Krajewski, grandma Apolonia, uncle

Zbyszek, aunt Jola, and cousin Marcin always understood the importance of my work. I spent many holidays working on this book, but I always had their support. Words cannot express the love and appreciation I have for my family. My mom and dad make everything better. My mom has been a constant source of love and optimism and I could not have done this without her.

Abbreviations

AAMVA	American Association of Motor Vehicle Administrators
ACLU	American Civil Liberties Union
ADIS	Arrival and Departure Information System
AFL-CIO	American Federation of Labor and Congress of Industrial Organizations
APIS	Advance Passenger Information System
ARD	Alien Registration Division
BCC	Border Crossing Card
BELIEVE	Biometric Enrollment, Locally Stored Information, and Electronic Verification of Employment
BPC	Bipartisan Policy Center
CBP	Customs and Border Protection
CPR	civil registration number (in Denmark)
CRS	Congressional Research Service
DOD	Department of Defense
DHS	Department of Homeland Security
DMV	Department of Motor Vehicles
DOJ	Department of Justice
DOS	Department of State
DOT	Department of Transportation
EDL	enhanced driver's license
EVVE	Electronic Verification of Vital Events
FACFI	Federal Advisory Committee on False Identification
FAIR	Federation for American Immigration Reform
FAST	Free and Secure Trade

FBI	Federal Bureau of Investigation
FDR	Franklin Delano Roosevelt
FIN	fingerprint identification number
FOP	Fraternal Order of Police
GAO	Government Accountability Office (since 2004)/General Accounting Office (until 2004)
Hauser Files	Box 25, Entry 146, Office Files of Philip M. Hauser, 1942–1947, Records of the Bureau of the Census, RG 29, NAB.
HAVA	Help America Vote Act of 2002
HEW	Health, Education, and Welfare
House Records	Records of the US House of Representatives
H.R.	House bill (in the US House of Representatives)
IAI	International Association for Identification
ICE	Immigration and Customs Enforcement
IDENT	Automated Biometric Identification System
IIRIRA	Illegal Immigration Reform and Immigrant Responsibility Act of 1996
INS	Immigration and Naturalization Service
IRCA	Immigration Reform and Control Act of 1986
IRS	Internal Revenue Service
Knight Papers	Papers of Frances G. Knight, Manuscript Division, Library of Congress, Washington, DC
LPR	legal permanent resident
MALDEF	Mexican-American Legal Defense and Education Fund
MPI	Migration Policy Institute
NAB	National Archives Building, Washington, DC
NCSL	National Conference of State Legislatures
NGA	National Governors Association
NPPD	National Protection and Programs Directorate
NPRM	notice of proposed rulemaking
NRA	National Rifle Association
NSA	National Sheriffs' Association
NVRA	National Voter Registration Act of 1993
NYT	*New York Times*
OBIM	Office of Biometric Identity Management
OECD	Organisation for Economic Cooperation and Development
OMB	Office of Management and Budget
POE	port of entry

Rep.	Representative (member of the US House of Representatives)
RFID	radio frequency identification
RG	record group
S.	Senate bill (in the US Senate)
S.B.	Senate bill (in state legislature)
SCIRP	Select Commission on Immigration and Refugee Policy
Senate Records	Records of the US Senate
SENTRI	Secure Electronic Network for Travelers Rapid Inspection
SFPD	Secure Flight passenger data
SSA	Social Security Administration
SSB	Social Security Board
SSN	Social Security number
SSOLV	Social Security Online Verification
TSA	Transportation Security Administration
TSDB	Terrorist Screening Database
TWIC	Transportation Worker Identification Credential
UMRA	Unfunded Mandates Reform Act of 1995
USCIS	US Citizenship and Immigration Services
US-VISIT	United States Visitor and Immigrant Status Indicator Technology
VRA	Voting Rights Act of 1965
WHTI	Western Hemisphere Travel Initiative
WWI	World War I
WWII	World War II

Introduction

This book examines the politics and history of proposals to introduce national ID cards and other identity policing schemes in the United States. The focus is on the period from 1915 to 2016, including the post-9/11 debates and policy decisions regarding the introduction of electronic and biometric identification documents. This is the first and only comprehensive, book-length political history of national ID card proposals and developments in identity policing in the United States. The data comes from extensive archival work; high-level interviews with politicians, policymakers, and ID card technology experts in Washington, DC, and London; and an analysis of public opinion data.

The task of identifying and documenting citizens and residents, always a challenge for democracies, takes on even greater significance in an era of increasing transnational migration and terrorism. Despite all the post-1989 talk of the end of history, globalization, open borders, and decline of nation-states, the nation-states in today's world are paying increasing attention to policing the identity of people within their territories. This trajectory is not an inflexible trend toward more identity policing but is marked by ebbs and flows.

IDENTITY POLICING

This book introduces the concept of "identity policing" and defines it as efforts of nation-states – primarily governments, police, and other authorities – to collect and record identifying information about individuals who permanently or temporarily reside in their territory; to issue identification documents to those individuals; to require those individuals to identify themselves in interactions with the authorities, with the identification process normally requiring the presentation of identification documents; to recognize those individuals in their fulfillment of responsibilities toward the state; and to authorize those individuals to gain access to the rights and benefits of membership.

Identity policing encompasses registration, identification, authentication, and prevention of fraud. It also encompasses the classification and sorting of people into legal and illegal status. Identity policing can also encompass more sinister activities such as monitoring and control. The focus here is on liberal democracies and on the legitimate uses of identity policing, with the optimistic belief that in liberal democracies the sinister activities of the state are the exception rather than the norm.

Identification documents address an ancient problem: how to designate membership in a nation bureaucratically or officially, beyond familial, local, or tribal membership. Identification differentiates between "us" and "others." States use identification documents – national identification cards (also known as national ID cards) and their functional equivalents such as Social Security cards, alien registration cards, driver's licenses, and, to a degree, passports – to gain effective control over populations and regulate the rights and responsibilities of residents, both citizens and noncitizens. Identification documents and identity policing have become more common just as some observers claim that globalization has eroded the capacity of states to control populations and police territories. Contrary to what some observers argue, the world is neither flat nor borderless, and states remain strong.

IDENTITY POLICING WORLDWIDE: THE FACTS

All countries police the identity of individuals within their territories, but countries use a diverse array of methods to do this; many patch together more than one identity policing method because all methods are imperfect. The most common way to police identity is with a national ID card. At least 170 of the world's nearly 200 countries have some kind of a national ID card or are implementing one.[1] Included in this number are twenty-eight of the thirty-four Organization for Economic Cooperation and Development (OECD) countries. Six OECD countries currently

[1] This data comes from personal data collection. There exists no comprehensive list online; the list on www.identity-cards.net probably comes closest, but it contains mistakes and omissions.

do not have national ID cards: the United States, the United Kingdom, Canada, Australia, Ireland, and New Zealand.

The United Kingdom had national ID cards in the past (1915–1919 and 1939–1952) and recently began to implement them again, only to scrap the project in 2010. Canada and Australia had national ID cards during wartime. Only three OECD countries, the United States, Ireland, and New Zealand, never had national ID cards, not even during wartime.[2] There is no major country outside the OECD that also lacks a national ID card.

The United States, the subject of this book, is among a handful of nations worldwide that lacks a national ID card. The United States and the United Kingdom, which I talk about in Chapter 1 and in the Conclusion, are therefore outliers on the world stage when it comes to identification documents.

REASONS FOR IDENTITY POLICING

The 1990s constituted the heyday of the promise of open borders, visa-free movement of people, free movement of goods in the European internal market, and globalization. Not only has the situation of free travel not fully materialized, but states have on the whole implemented stricter border controls and become stricter in controlling their populations internally with identification documents. Many countries have recently introduced or updated their identification policies, whether in the form of a national ID card, a biometric passport, a new policing initiative, or an e-government initiative. For instance, in 1998, Malaysia became the first country in the world to issue biometric passports. Other countries soon followed, including Australia and Germany in 2005 and Poland in 2006.[3] Most countries have been using national ID cards for decades, but when in 2010 India began the process of issuing national ID cards to its 1.2 billion citizens, it quickly became the world's biggest infrastructural project.[4] Germany has had national ID cards since 1950, but in 2010 it started issuing smart ID cards with encrypted contactless radio frequency identification (RFID) chips containing biometric

[2] Technically, Denmark also does not have national ID cards, but the so-called yellow cards fulfill similar functions.

[3] "Over 60+ Countries Now Issuing ePassports," December 30, 2008, http://findbiometrics.com/over-60-countries-now-issuing-epassports/.

[4] Siddharth George and Arvind Subramanian, "Transforming the Fight against Poverty in India," *NYT*, July 22, 2015.

data – including optional fingerprints. Today, many countries have biometric national ID cards, but in 2011, Mexico became the first country in the world to test the issuance of national ID cards with iris scans.[5] In 2015, Nigerian voters received voter ID cards, which store biometric information such as fingerprints and facial image.[6] In the United Kingdom, the 2006 Identity Cards Act introduced national ID cards for British citizens. The Labour government started issuing national ID cards in 2009, but the new Conservative-Liberal Democrat coalition government scrapped the project in 2010, making all cards invalid by January 2011. British passports have contained RFID chips since 2006. The United States has never had national ID cards, but the REAL ID Act of 2005 legislated significant changes to make driver's licenses more secure. American passports began to include RFID chips in 2006, and the Western Hemisphere Travel Initiative put in place in 2008 requires American citizens reentering the United States from Canada, Mexico, and the Caribbean to present a passport.

It is not particularly surprising that liberal democratic states increasingly police identity of individuals within their territories. As there is no single definition of a liberal democracy, liberal democracy is defined here as a system of representative government by majority rule in which individual rights are protected from interference by the state and cannot be restricted even by an electoral majority, and where the state plays a role in providing a legal framework for society, ensures that law and order prevail, and protects the national territory from external aggression.[7] If we define liberal democratic states as ones that balance the objectives of protecting the individual rights of their citizens with upholding the law and providing security, and if we also assume that liberal democratic states play some role in administering certain scarce resources in the society and providing public goods for its members, then there is nothing paradoxical in states using *some* identity policing as one way to achieve those tasks.

[5] Mexico does not currently have national ID cards, but it has voter ID cards, which are de facto national ID cards. In 2011, some school children received national ID cards as part of a pilot project. "Mexico to Become First Country to Use Iris Scans on ID Cards," *Daily Telegraph*, January 21, 2011.

[6] Giulia Piccolino, "What Other African Elections Tell Us about Nigeria's Bet on Biometrics," March 10, 2015, www.washingtonpost.com/blogs/monkey-cage/wp/2015/03/10/what-other-african-elections-tell-us-about-nigerias-bet-on-biometrics/.

[7] Patrick Dunleavy and Brendan O'Leary, *Theories of the State: The Politics of Liberal Democracy* (London: Macmillan, 1987).

Even if we talk about liberal democratic states that both increase the openness of their borders and increase identity policing at the border and in the interior, there still would be little that is paradoxical about that, regardless of whether the two developments happen simultaneously or whether the increase in identity policing happens in the aftermath of the increase in the openness of the borders.

It is not particularly puzzling why we see an overall increase in the efforts to police identity. The causes are reasonably straightforward: they are the dual forces of global migration and security threats that lead to increased state regulation of access to state borders, state services, political rights, and other citizenship benefits. In western democracies, there are two primary drivers of the new identification schemes, policies, and documents: terrorism and immigration (primarily illegal immigration). Terrorism and immigration provide nation-states, governments, and other authorities with the motivation and desire to regulate population. The security impetus makes identity policing much more comprehensive than a narrower type of policing that focuses solely on access to the welfare state, and where the impetus is more fiduciary: the desire to regulate population for economic reasons.

Identity policing occurs partially because nation-states do not trust that all people will always truthfully say who they are. This does not mean that states invariably police identity due to mistrust, but it does mean that state actors often doubt the honesty of self-identifying statements and put the burden of proof on identification documents. These documents are part of a culture of suspicion in which identification by the state tends to take precedence. States are not unified actors, but, on this issue, multiple components of the state apparatus – primarily the legislators and the bureaucrats, but often also the police – seem to prefer to rely on identification documents. Since many government agencies need to verify the identity of the individuals with whom they have dealings, the logic behind providing a single, government-managed, identity infrastructure is easy to understand. In many countries, each government service has its own ways of verifying the identity of individuals – and each method has different levels of quality – and the government sees benefits to providing a single, high-quality identity service used across the public sector.[8]

The September 11, 2001 (9/11) terrorist attacks in the United States increased demands for identification in the name of security in most

[8] Edgar A. Whitley and Gus Hosein, *Global Challenges for Identity Policies* (New York: Palgrave Macmillan, 2010), 110.

western democracies. Democratic states can and do make use of identity policing without deteriorating into totalitarian states. However, identity policing and national ID cards may infringe on individual liberties, and thus influence the political relations between the state and its citizens. When national ID cards are debated, the debates concern not only the effectiveness and costs of the national ID cards technology, but also the fundamentals of the political relations between the state and its citizens, and the limits of state power.[9] Given that terrorism is one of the biggest problems that many nations face and given that many people – especially in the United States – consider liberty to be the most important value, any possible trade-offs between liberty and security are important ones.

FINDINGS

This book takes a comprehensive look at the past and present of proposals for national ID cards and identity policing in the United States. The United States is an exception on the world stage in that it does not currently have a national ID card scheme. It is also distinctive because it has never had national ID cards.

My study is interesting because its findings contradict the conventional wisdom and debunk some common myths. The most common myth about the politics of identification is that Americans are opposed to national ID cards. The other myth is that American policymakers never propose national ID cards. My narrative history of the politics of identification in the United States debunks both myths.

The first powerful finding of this book is that polling indicates Americans are not particularly opposed to national ID cards. I also show that popular support for national ID cards, as measured by letters to Congress and letters to newspapers, has been significant over the last 100 years. Acknowledging the existence of passionate opposition, my book shows that Americans see national ID cards more positively than is popularly believed. This finding is important because it does in fact debunk the most common myth about the politics of identification in the United States.

The second powerful finding is that over the last 100 years when American policymakers were confronted with the need to strengthen identification, a number of individual policymakers did propose national ID cards.

[9] Jef Huysmans and Alessandra Buonfino, "Politics of Exception and Unease: Immigration, Asylum and Terrorism in Parliamentary Debates in the UK," *Political Studies* 56, 4 (2008): 783.

However, the proposals did not get very far. This is in contrast to pretty much every other nation in the world, including the United Kingdom, which during national crises first created and then repealed national ID cards.

Together, these two findings create a fascinating puzzle. If Americans are not really opposed to national ID cards, why do policymakers repeatedly turn away from this? And if, contra the polling, Americans *are* so troubled by identity policing, why have there been some successful efforts to strengthen existing systems of identification, though often in the form of half-measures, but no national ID card? I address this in Chapter 1 and in the Conclusion.

DATA GATHERING

I gathered research data primarily through archival work and interviews conducted in Washington, DC, and London between 2009 and 2016 and through the examination of legislative histories and opinion polls.

My archival work drew mainly upon primary materials from the Manuscript Division of the Library of Congress and upon primary materials from the National Archives in Washington, DC.

I conducted dozens of in-depth, semi-structured, high-level interviews with politicians, policymakers, and ID card technology experts. Interviewees are quoted anonymously, and only generic details are disclosed: for example, an interviewee may be identified as "a senior Department of Homeland Security (DHS) official."

In addition, I examined legislative histories of identity policing and ID card-related bills, including committee testimony, hearings, and floor debates from the US Congress. I also examined identity policing and ID card–related documents from federal, state, and local governments, interest groups, and police organizations; public statements; any available private communications; historical newspaper accounts; and contemporary media discourse.

I also examined American opinion polls regarding national ID cards. Opinion polls assist in describing the nature of attitudes of the voting public. Interestingly, these polls reveal that a cross-section of American residents say that the United States needs a national ID card. Gallup polls taken in 1983, 1993, and 1995 consistently showed a majority of Americans in favor of a national ID. Immediately after the 9/11 attacks, a Pew Research Center poll found that 70 percent of Americans favored such a card. In the decade since 9/11, the support for national ID cards has remained at around 60 percent.

TERMINOLOGY

In this book, the term "illegal alien" or "illegal immigrant" refers to noncitizens residing in the United States without permission from the federal government. It includes people who entered the United States unlawfully and people who entered lawfully on a temporary basis but remained past their authorized period of stay. Many people increasingly refer to illegal immigrants as "undocumented" rather than illegal, ignoring the fact that many illegal immigrants have fraudulent documents such as counterfeit Social Security cards and forged driver's licenses. Since this book deals with identification documents, it cannot agree with the use of the term "undocumented."

BOOK OUTLINE

Chapter 1 outlines the different types of government-issued identification documents, discusses the historical importance of identification documents, shows where the United States fits in a comparative perspective, and presents key arguments and findings.

Chapters 2, 3, 4, and 5 explore the developments in identity policing and identification documents in the twentieth- and twenty-first-century United States. These chapters focus on proposals, all unsuccessful, to introduce national ID cards in the United States. The chapters fill an important void in the literature since there is no published, comprehensive political history of national ID card proposals and identity policing developments in the United States. The chapters emphasize the role played by the historical crises in the development of identity policing, examine the contemporary drivers of identity policing, assess the obstacles in the development of identification documents and identity policing, and point to the overall incrementalism and patchwork-like nature of identity policing efforts in the United States.

Chapters 2 and 3 focus on the first and second half of the twentieth century, respectively. Chapter 2 explores several partial population registrations (some accompanied by the issuing of identification cards) aimed at certain segments of the population, including aliens (noncitizens) and enemy aliens, during World War I (WWI) and World War II (WWII). Most importantly, Chapter 2 looks at the multiple proposals to introduce national ID cards in the United States. Policymakers and members of the public put forward these proposals mostly during WWII; all the proposals were unsuccessful.

Chapter 3 briefly looks at the development of driver's licenses and Social Security numbers (SSNs) during the twentieth century. Those two in many ways became functional equivalents of national ID cards in the United States. The chapter then looks at the proposals to introduce national ID cards in the United States in the second half of the twentieth century. Public figures and policymakers who put forward these proposals in the 1970s, 1980s, and 1990s primarily did so due to concern about fraud and illegal immigration; all the proposals were unsuccessful.

Chapters 4 and 5 focus on the twenty-first century. Chapter 4 focuses on the post-9/11 political developments regarding identification documents and identity policing. It first outlines the political history of the 2005 REAL ID Act. It then outlines other post-9/11 identity policing schemes, emphasizing the notion of patchwork in identity policing in the United States.

Chapter 5 focuses on the drivers of new identification schemes, especially illegal immigration and terrorism, in the post-9/11 United States. It then focuses on obstacles to these schemes: financial, technological and practical, constitutional and legal, relating to civil liberties and individual freedoms, and stemming from public opinion and resistance.

The concluding chapter summarizes the findings about the past and present of national ID cards and identity policing in the United States. It also talks about the United Kingdom, which is another country that, just like the United States, does not currently have national ID cards. Even though the book focuses on the United States, my research focuses on both countries and allows me to make some important comparisons. The concluding chapter outlines the differences in national reactions to identity policing and national ID cards between the United States and the United Kingdom. The chapter also briefly considers the following question: can identity policing and national ID cards be beneficial to individuals or, as often portrayed by opponents, are they just a threat to individual freedom? The chapter considers the future of identification documents and identity policing, concentrating on the biometric revolution and its costs. The chapter reviews the book's findings, outlines avenues for future research, and spells out the implications of this research for the study of liberal democratic states.

1

Identification Documents and the Book's Findings

An Overview

INTRODUCTION

In this chapter, I first outline the different types of government-issued identification documents, the different types of national ID cards, and the worldwide variation in identity policing. I follow with a few words of caution about the terms "identity" and "identification." I then discuss the historical importance of identification documents and the relationship between identification documents and state-building. I also show where the United States fits in a comparative perspective. I then present key arguments regarding identification documents. After that, I focus on the United States and discuss the book's findings.

TYPES OF GOVERNMENT-ISSUED IDENTIFICATION DOCUMENTS

Sociologist John Torpey divides government-issued identification documents into three broad types: international passports, internal passes (which he calls internal passports), and national ID cards:

> passports and passes share the function of regulating the movements of people within and across delimited spaces, thereby affirming states' control over bounded territories and enhancing their embrace of populations. Identification cards, by contrast, are not normally, or at least not primarily, used to regulate movement, but simply to establish the identity of the bearer for purposes of state administration and of gaining access to benefits distributed by the state.[1]

[1] John Torpey, *The Invention of the Passport: Surveillance, Citizenship, and the State* (New York: Cambridge University Press, 2000), 158–159.

In addition to enhancing bureaucratic domination over persons and territories, the passport vouchsafes the issuing state's guarantee of aid to its bearer while in the jurisdiction of other states. Internal passports or passes, in turn, "may be a state's principal means for discriminating among its subjects in terms of rights and privileges." Internal passes were used in South Africa during apartheid and in the Soviet Union (the *propiska* system). Today, the use of internal passes bespeaks authoritarian governments lording over subdued populations.[2] While in the past internal passes were present even in the cradles of democracy – for example, internal passes for slaves and freed blacks in the United States[3] – by the twentieth century, democratic nation-states have generally abandoned internal passes and the control of internal movements of people, and today internal passes do not exist in democracies.

The national ID card, common to European societies and to those that have experienced European colonialism, constitutes a "mixed" type, lying between passports and internal passes. Torpey deals with national ID cards only in passing as a documentary "gray zone." He notes that ID cards "may be used by the authorities to enforce intermittent checks on movement."[4] However, in democratic states, that is usually not the case with either internal or external movement. Even in the European Union, where ID cards of member states show eligibility for free movement between countries, they cannot as such be used by the authorities to enforce checks on movement. One of the few exceptions exists in the United Kingdom, where authorities can withdraw passports and the right to travel abroad from those with a banning order issued in relation to the Football Spectators Act (1989) and the Football Disorder Act (2000). In addition, in July 2015, British Prime Minister David Cameron announced that parents worried that their children may travel to Syria or Iraq to join the Islamic State will be able to apply to the government to cancel their child's passport.[5]

Countries that have compulsory national ID cards normally require citizens to apply for an ID card just prior to their eighteenth birthday so they can receive it on their birthday and carry it with them from then on.

[2] Ibid., 165.
[3] Allen Parker, *Recollections of Slavery Times* (Worchester, MA: Chas. W. Burbank & Co., 1895); Christian Parenti, *The Soft Cage: Surveillance in America from Slavery to the War on Terror* (New York: Basic Books, 2003).
[4] Torpey, *The Invention of the Passport*, 165.
[5] Patrick Wintour, "UK Parents to Get Power to Cancel Children's Passports over ISIS Fears," *The Guardian*, July 20, 2015.

People are obliged to produce them on the demand of the organs of social order, such as police, and failure to do so can be a punishable offense. Police may use identification documents for arrest and punishment, arguably one of the most consequential functions of ID cards. People are obliged to produce their identification documents to other government authorities, such as electoral commissions or welfare offices, so that they can gain access to certain rights of democratic participation (e.g., voting), public services (e.g., medical care), and transfer payments (e.g., welfare).[6]

I use the following classification of government-issued identification documents. I focus only on identification documents issued by national or local governments, or their agencies:

A. national ID cards for citizens
B. functional equivalents of national ID cards, which may include:
   1. Social Security cards (can be issued to foreigners)
   2. driver's licenses[7] (can be issued to foreigners)
   3. national ID cards for foreigners; alien registration cards; residence permits; Green Cards
   4. other documents of citizenship such as certificates of naturalization and certificates of citizenship[8]
C. state and municipal IDs[9]
D. military IDs
E. national or federal/state/city government employees' IDs
F. IDs for recipients of national/federal benefits (welfare, etc.)
G. birth certificates
H. passports
I. visas

Moreover, government-issued identification documents are further divided into four categories, as shown in Table 1.1: documents issued for one's own citizens; documents issued for foreigners/visitors/temporary residents;

[6] Torpey, *The Invention of the Passport*, 158–167.
[7] Around the world driver's licenses tend to be nationally issued documents while in the United States they are issued by the states.
[8] The US government issues certificates of citizenship to derivative citizens (children of naturalized parents or foreign-born children adopted by US citizens) and to persons with acquired US citizenship (conferred at birth on children born abroad to a US citizen parent or parents).
[9] In the United States, this category includes driver's licenses.

TABLE 1.1 *Four categories of government-issued identification documents*

	Documents for citizens	Documents for foreigners/visitors/ temporary residents
Documents issued by internal authorities for internal use and inspection	National ID cards for citizens; Social Security cards; driver's licenses; state and municipal IDs; military IDs; national or federal/ state/city government employees' IDs; IDs for recipients of national/federal benefits; birth certificates; naturalization certificates; certificates of citizenship	National ID cards for foreigners; alien registration cards; residence permits; Green Cards; visas; Social Security cards; driver's licenses; state and municipal IDs
Documents issued by internal authorities for external use and inspection	Passports; (occasionally) driver's licenses	–

documents issued by internal authorities for internal use and inspection; and documents issued by internal authorities for external use and inspection, where internal authorities are located at the national, state, or local level, and external authorities are located abroad. This depends on who the primary inspectors are and which authorities primarily find given documents legitimate identifying documents.

The focus here is primarily on identification documents issued for citizens, by internal authorities, and for internal use and inspection. Within this subset, of particular interest are national ID cards and their functional equivalents.

TYPES OF NATIONAL ID CARDS

The countries that have national ID cards vary in the kinds of cards they have. Generally, national ID cards contain name, gender, date of birth, and a photograph. Cards around the world normally also contain a national identification number and/or the serial number of the ID card.[10] Most cards also contain some of the following: permanent address, issuing agency, date of issue, place of birth, signature, citizenship, residency, blood group, names of parents, physical characteristics, such as height or eye color, and occasionally also marital status. Most countries issue national ID cards only to citizens, but some countries also issue ID cards to residents. In most countries ID cards are uniform, but in some countries cards make a distinction between different types of people (e.g., residents and nonresidents).

Many countries have replaced their traditional paper or laminated ID documents with plastic cards. Such cards include machine-readable components: chips, magnetic stripes, or optical barcodes. Electronic and "smart" national ID cards have a programmable chip embedded in them for storing some data that can be linked to a central database. Much of the opposition to ID cards concentrates not on cards themselves but on the databases. In the past, there might have been a database but it was a paper one, not easily accessible or retrievable. Now the databases are accessible and retrievable. This connection to a central computer database distinguishes smart ID cards from their paper-based precursors.[11] Chips embedded in "smart" cards have room for additional information, including medical and financial data, and driving records.

"Smart" ID cards can be either "contact cards" or "contactless cards" if they possess RFID tags. These electronic tags utilize tiny inexpensive microchips half the size of a grain of sand to transmit radio signals prompted by a signal from a specialized reader. Some tags can be read from several meters away and beyond the line of sight of the reader. RFID tags are becoming common in passports (where they can store biometric data) and are likely to become more common in national ID cards.

It is already becoming increasingly common for ID cards to include biometric data, where biometrics is the use of data extracted from the body, such as a digital image of the face, a fingerprint, a hand scan, an iris scan, or a retinal scan. A digital image and a fingerprint are the

[10] Denmark is an interesting exception in that it uses a national identification number (civil registration number known as CPR) but does not issue a photo ID. Almost all aspects of Danish life are contingent on possessing the "yellow card" (Sygesikringsbevis; health insurance certificate), which contains the CPR but not a photograph. Danish driver's licenses include both CPR and a photo. Practically everyone has a driver's license.

[11] David Lyon, "Identity Cards: Social Sorting by Database," Oxford Internet Institute, Internet Issue Brief No. 3, November 2004.

most common biometric features of ID cards. Of the twenty-eight OECD countries that have some kind of a national ID card, or are implementing one, some seventeen countries include biometric information on their cards. The recently scrapped British ID scheme also included biometrics.

Biometrics is popular in modern identity policing schemes because it is supposed to be the most accurate method of identification, verification, and authentication, and hence helps reduce fraud. While PINs and passwords may be forgotten or lost, the body is almost always available and provides a direct link between the record and the person. Yet the effectiveness of the enrollment and verification processes depends on the type of biometrics chosen, the quality of the biometrics collected, and the methods used to compare the submitted biometrics with those previously recorded. Different biometrics have different performance parameters in terms of ease of enrollment and likelihood of mismatching or not matching against existing records. At a technical level, the differences between various biometrics can be understood through the following: false match rate (the probability that a person's biometric matches the enrollment template of another person), false nonmatch rate (the probability that a person's biometric fails to match their own enrollment template), and failure to acquire rate (where the submitted biometric is too poor for the system to make a reliable decision).[12]

Traditional ID cards can be used for general identification purposes, voting, travel, proving health care eligibility, certifying right to employment and/or residence, verifying access to banking, and so forth. The more sophisticated biometric and smart IDs can also authorize access to secure areas; act as driver's licenses by containing driving records; contain financial, military, or health records; and enable access to e-government and e-commerce. Passports and immigration papers are used primarily for travel and certifying right to employment and/or residence. Importantly, new ID card schemes challenge conventional distinctions between government and commercial uses, and between domestic and international uses. Modern ID cards can be used for commercial as well as government purposes; internal national purposes of ID cards can be linked with external ones through the passport, and so forth.[13]

[12] Whitley and Hosein, *Global Challenges*, 101–102.

[13] David Lyon, *Surveillance Studies: An Overview* (Cambridge, UK; Malden, MA: Polity, 2007), 127.

WORLDWIDE VARIATION IN IDENTITY POLICING

Worldwide, most countries rely on national ID cards in their identity policing efforts. In these countries, a national ID card becomes a crucial component of identity policing and its highest or "ideal" form as it is supposed to provide a single, authoritative claim of identity. Yet almost no country is alike in the form, laws, and experiences of identity policing. There are significant cross-national differences in the usage of ID documents. National ID cards are one of the components of identity policing, but there is a wide variation in national ID cards worldwide. Sometimes the differences are obvious; sometimes they are nuanced. The frame for worldwide identity policing is therefore more subtle than a simple dichotomy of an "ideal" form based on a national ID card as opposed to schemes that do not contain national ID cards.

There are many differences in identity policies worldwide, including the contexts in which identity policies were introduced, the forms of oversight they involved, the nature of the policy debate that led to the establishment of a policy, the scale of the scheme, and the type of the population (an identity scheme in a country with a small, homogenous population may face issues different from one in a country with a large, heterogeneous, or geographically dispersed population). Countries also vary in the extent to which their cards are voluntary or compulsory (to obtain, carry, or present), the legal frameworks that oversee them, the cost of the card itself, and whether biometrics is used and, if so, if there is one central storage of biometrics or distributed systems that delete the biometrics once a card has been issued. There is also variation in the registration processes: from registering at national ID card offices to registering at police stations, and from requiring the presence of a witness to the submission of a photograph signed by a referee.[14]

There is also variation in the nature of any national identification number used. Some countries use a single ID number for all purposes; others issue sector-specific numbers and even have legislation that explicitly prevents the issuance of a single ID number. The form of the number varies as well. In some countries, the number includes the person's date of birth. Often the last digit is odd for males and even for females (as with the Polish PESEL number). In the United Kingdom, draft secondary

[14] Whitley and Hosein, *Global Challenges*, 20, 23, 70.

legislation claimed that the design of the National Identity Registration Number would prevent the derivation of individuals' characteristics.[15]

Edgar Whitley and Gus Hosein, scholars of information systems, point out that the reasons for such variety are largely attributable to national legal culture. The fact that a country has national ID cards does not mean that its populace supports all forms of identification systems. Identification systems in each country are designed with specific safeguards leading to the variability in design: Sweden refused to make use of the registry; France has not made its card mandatory; and Italian regulators have wide powers to ensure the adequate protection of data. In Germany, data protection law prevents the federal government from creating a central back-end database of biometrics for the ID card (the kind that the British government envisaged for the United Kingdom). Although most Germans readily carry around their ID cards, they are also quite wary (because of past abuses) of the collection of personal information by the government. Any information that is collected for the ID card system is stored locally at the registration offices. A private contractor uses this information to issue the card, but as soon as the document is completed, all personal data is deleted and destroyed. Both Germany and Hungary explicitly ban the use of a single ID number for their citizens, citing data protection concerns.[16] It is misleading to suggest that because so many countries have ID cards there is a strong commonality to their identity policies or identity policing processes, a commonality that implies that ID cards are, in the words of British Prime Minister Tony Blair in 2005, "an idea whose time has come."[17] There is some commonality, but no single design for identity policing schemes.

IDENTITY VERSUS IDENTIFICATION: A FEW WORDS OF CAUTION

It is important to note the often-occurring confusion of terms such as identity and identification. Politicians, policymakers, scholars, technology experts, and ordinary people alike often use the term "identity cards," when it is more accurate (though not more concise) to use the term "identification cards." The term "identity card" is particularly common in the United Kingdom. This book will primarily use the term "identification card," or "ID card," but the term "identity card" will also appear

[15] Ibid., 70–71. [16] Ibid., 70, 147.
[17] "Time Has Come for ID Cards, Says Blair," *Daily Telegraph*, June 27, 2005.

occasionally, especially when used in a historical context, in quotes, or in relation to the United Kingdom.

Failure to make a distinction between identity and identification causes difficulty in discussions of ID documents and identity policing. As sociologist David Lyon points out, there is no way of proving this, but part of the difficulty lies in the fact that the English word "identification" is a six-syllable abstract noun and "identity" is easier to say. Why else would computer scientists talk of "identity management" to refer to ways of managing user credentials? "Identity" there concerns user IDs, passwords, and email addresses. These are "identifiers" used for "identification" and are at best proxies for "identity."[18]

We should understand that the terms "identity policing" and "identity documents" actually refer to identification policing and identification documents. Most sources in the literature provide the same disclaimer, arguing for the convenience of using the term "identity" even though "identification" would be more appropriate.

This terminology can create problems if people perceive governments as trying to establish or verify their identity, rather than identification. After all, identity tends to be very personal and can have philosophical and psychological underpinnings. Identification, on the other hand, is practical and bureaucratic. Identity is a matter of self-identification and often self-expression. For sociologist Erving Goffman, the self or the core identity is forever being "presented" in everyday life. From hairstyles to nicknames, there may be ways of controlling or at least influencing the impressions given to others.[19]

The name, the personal story, and the commitments to places and to people are all matters of identity. Overlapping these, but for different purposes, are the instruments of identification, including ID systems. Lyon gives the example of Portugal, where new parents give their baby a name and at the same time the state issues a number to be used when the child obtains their first citizenship document at age six. The name bestowed by the parents soon becomes part of the baby's identity. The formal identification done by the state, however, is more remote, involving people and systems that the baby will never know. Yet identity and identification should be seen not only in opposition but also in relation to each other. Lyon argues that the "difference between how I identify

[18] David Lyon, *Identifying Citizens: ID Cards as Surveillance* (Cambridge, UK; Malden, MA: Polity, 2009), 9.

[19] Erving Goffman, *The Presentation of Self* (Garden City, NY: Doubleday, 1959).

myself and how I am identified by others – or, today, how a machine system might identify me – is worth maintaining, but it can never be an absolute distinction. The one depends on the other."[20]

The fact that one should distinguish between identity and identification, and that identity documents and identity policing are primarily concerned with identification, does not mean that identification processes are merely practical, technical, or neutral. We should not downplay their social significance. Matters of identity and identification always interact with each other; they are ways of distinguishing certain individuals and groups from others. They establish and signify relationships of similarity and difference. Lyon points out that processes of classification and attachment are always involved, and in the case of national ID cards, both classification and attachment are primarily in relation to the nation-state.[21]

It is also prudent to distinguish between identification and verification/authentication. In today's world, it is often not identification but verification and authentication, or checking that you are who you say you are, that counts. Identification is a process whereby someone's identity is revealed ("This is John Smith"). Identification also involves checking that an individual's record matches the one listed in a relevant database. Verification has to do with checking that the individual is who he or she claims to be. Verification confirms or denies a claimed identity, answering the question of whether a person standing before an immigration official or government official is who he or she says he or she is. Verification and authentication are concerned with qualification: who is qualified and who disqualified from access to resources, privileges, and places. Authentication is a process that results in a person being accepted as authorized to engage in or perform an activity: "I am allowed to withdraw money from this bank account," or "I am old enough to buy alcohol."[22] Most uses for biometrics are not, strictly speaking, for identification so much as for verification or authentication. In fact, most everyday uses, such as using national ID cards for welfare disbursement or border crossing, are, in reality, concerned with verification and authentication.[23]

Emphasis on verification and authentication, in addition to identification, is important given that identity policing encompasses registration, identification, authentication, and prevention of fraud. Fraud, in its

[20] Lyon, *Identifying Citizens*, 8–12. [21] Ibid., 66.
[22] Whitley and Hosein, *Global Challenges*, 2–3. [23] Lyon, *Identifying Citizens*, 115.

simplest form, is the result of improper verification and authentication of identification, and hence a failure of identity policing. Identity fraud may

> turn into a terrorism risk when terrorists are able to get identity documents in the names of other people or travel between countries using multiple identities; into an immigration risk as illegal immigrants can assume the identity of a citizen; into a risk to commerce and e-government as organizations cannot have confidence in the identity of the individuals with whom they are dealing; and into a drop in consumers' and citizens' confidence when their identities are at risk of abuse.[24]

Importantly, a combination of forces, including the state, the private sector, and private individuals, is best at addressing the problem of identity fraud. The responses can include government-issued biometric ID documents, regulations regarding notification of any data breaches, best practice guidelines for secure data handling, and the use of personal shredders.

Legislation in the United States talks not of identity fraud but of identity theft. It defines identity theft as taking place when someone "knowingly transfers or uses, without lawful authority, a means of identification of another person with the intent to commit, or to aid or abet, any unlawful activity that constitutes a violation of federal law, or that constitutes a felony under any applicable state or local law." In the United Kingdom, there is no offense of identity theft per se. Rather, identity crimes arise in conjunction with other offenses (e.g., concealing an existing identity, accruing a financial benefit, or avoiding a financial liability), thus suggesting the use of the term "identity fraud" rather than "identity theft." In the United States, identity theft is the responsibility of the Federal Trade Commission, while in the United Kingdom the main responsibility for identity-related fraud issues resides with the Home Office.[25]

Identity fraud and theft crimes are easier to commit with certain types of identities, and harder to commit with others. The Crosby report (commissioned by the British government to look into matters of identity policy) divides identities into "attributed" (name, date, and place of birth), "biographical" (more detailed personal history, including details of education and employment, and address history from credit records and electoral rolls), and "biometric" (physical attributes associated with the individual). The report argues that attributed identity is the easiest to assume, often based on fabricated or stolen documents, while biographical identity requires much more detailed knowledge of a person's

[24] Whitley and Hosein, *Global Challenges*, 9. [25] Ibid., 11–12.

life history. A biometric identity is the most difficult to assume.[26] It is therefore no wonder that governments and the supplying companies tout biometrics as a key tool in modern identity policing efforts.

We are hence governed by identity, identification, verification, and authentication, or by identity policing that encompasses registration, identification, authentication, and prevention of fraud. It was political geographer Louise Amoore who first used the term "governing by identity" to describe a novel mode of governance indicated by the apparently limitless demands for identification from anyone, from a sales clerk to a security guard.[27] Lyon rephrased this term as "governing by identification" and emphasized how central identification practices have become to determining people's life chances. The infrastructures that permit the processing of personal data depend on ID documents and protocols to mediate between individuals and the organizations with which they relate. The employee authenticates their identity with an access card to enter the workplace, the traveler shows a passport to board a plane, and the patient produces a health card to prove eligibility for medical services. Lyon argues: "Without the card, and the databases on which it depends, identity cannot now be verified. Telling your story no longer suffices. It is displaying your card that counts."[28]

STATE-BUILDING AND THE HISTORICAL IMPORTANCE OF IDENTIFICATION DOCUMENTS

Although historians have long recognized the importance of identification documents in modernizing and modern societies, it took a political scientist, Aristide Zolberg, to call for "a history of paperwork." Zolberg was referring to the need for investigation of the paperwork associated with state regulation of migration, but historians have heeded his call across a much wider range of relations between individuals and the state.[29] Sociologists have incorporated the study of identification documents into the

[26] James Crosby, *Challenges and Opportunities in Identity Assurance* (London: HM Treasury, March 2008).

[27] Louise Amoore, "Governing by Identity," in *Playing the Identity Card: Surveillance, Security and Identification in Global Perspective*, ed. Colin J. Bennett and David Lyon (New York: Routledge, 2008).

[28] Lyon, *Identifying Citizens*, 86, 111.

[29] Jane Caplan and John Torpey, "Introduction," in *Documenting Individual Identity: The Development of State Practices in the Modern World*, ed. Jane Caplan and John Torpey (Princeton, NJ: Princeton University Press, 2001), 12.

growing subfield of surveillance studies.[30] Surprisingly, political scientists have not explored the topic of identification documents and identity policing, even though it sits at the intersection of research on state-building, state power, citizenship, immigration, security, surveillance, civil liberties, and public policy.

Since citizenship is a relationship between a citizen and the state common to one political community,[31] where citizens possess a wide range of civil, political, and social rights as well as responsibilities, national ID cards and passports are manifest signs of citizenship. Citizenship means "membership relations between states and their citizens," and "formal citizenship" is "the legal definition of a close relationship between individuals and one state, usually documented in passports or other citizenship certificates."[32]

The evolution of identification documents links to the general process of state formation and development. Whether it is the need for strong armies, taxation, socioeconomic efficiency, ideological functions (e.g., stimulating national identity), bureaucratic development, rationalization, administrative power, or security, identification documents come into play at all levels. As historian Jane Caplan and sociologist John Torpey point out, establishing the identity of individual people – as workers, taxpayers, conscripts, travelers, and criminal suspects – is increasingly recognized as fundamental to the multiple operations of the state.[33]

For the state to function, its society must be "legible." The concept of "legible people," first outlined by political scientist James C. Scott, refers to people open to the scrutiny of the state or officialdom. Scott regards the state's attempt to make a society legible as a central problem of statecraft. Does the legibility of society and the penetration of it with identification documents have negative or positive consequences? For Scott, the legibility provides the capacity for large-scale social engineering. In addition, he argues that high-modernist ideology provides the desire, the authoritarian state provides the determination to act on that desire, and the incapacitated civil society provides the leveled social terrain on which to build.

30 Lyon, *Identifying Citizens.*

31 Peter Kivisto and Thomas Faist, *Citizenship: Discourse, Theory and Transnational Prospects* (Malden, MA: Blackwell Publishing, 2007), 13.

32 Andreas Fahrmeir, *Citizenship: The Rise and Fall of a Modern Concept* (New Haven: Yale University Press, 2007), 2.

33 Caplan and Torpey, "Introduction," 1.

Legibility is a condition of manipulation, and the greater the manipulation envisaged, the greater the legibility required to affect it.[34]

However, legibility can also have positive consequences. The creation of a "legible people" has become a hallmark of modern statehood, and the paraphernalia and personnel necessary to operate systems of standardized registration have contributed to the character of the modern bureaucratic state. And not only the state; according to Caplan and Torpey, private economic and commercial activities would also grind to a halt unless companies had the ability to identify and track individuals as property owners, employees, business partners, and customers.[35]

In his work on the historical development of passport controls, Torpey uses a metaphor of states "embracing" their populations, which is akin to Scott's idea that states seek to render societies "legible" and thus more readily available for governance. However, the notion that states "embrace" individuals goes further since states hold particular persons within their grasp, while excluding others.[36]

For historian Edward Higgs, the idea of state surveillance, especially for recording population details, often began as a means of reassuring leaders of the "vitality of the nation" rather than necessarily of tying them with a documentary leash. In England, surveillance pre-dated industrialization, and the development of information gathering by state elites had more to do with their own need to preserve their position both within the English polity and international geopolitics, rather than with their desire to reimpose social control over the "society of strangers" created by industrialization.[37]

Meanwhile, the post-9/11 increases in identity policing and in the issuance and dissemination of ID cards speak against the supposed decline of nation-states, which scholars in the 1990s frequently assumed. The nation-state is still the key reference point for citizenship and is likely to remain so. Warnings about the premature declaration of the end of the state are not new. As early as 1981, political scientist Robert Gilpin wrote that the nation-state in historical terms is a rather recent arrival; its success has been due to a peculiar set of historical circumstances, and

34 James C. Scott, *Seeing like a State* (New Haven: Yale University Press, 1998), 5, 65, 183.

35 Caplan and Torpey, "Introduction," 1.

36 Torpey, *The Invention of the Passport*, 12.

37 Edward Higgs, "The Rise of the Information State: The Development of Central State Surveillance of the Citizen in England, 1500–2000," *Journal of Historical Sociology* 14, 2 (2001); Edward Higgs, *The Information State in England: The Central Collection of Information on Citizens, 1500–2000* (London: Palgrave, 2004).

there are no guarantees that these conditions will continue into the future. However, it would be premature to suggest that the nation-state is dying.[38]

It is becoming more obvious that borders and immigration policy alone cannot stop illegal immigration, so many governments turn to internal migration control of illegal migrants.[39] Political scientist Debra DeLaet argues that proposals for a national ID card, a computerized national registry, stronger border control and enforcement measures, are all likely to be significant issues in the perennial debate over US immigration policy.[40] But the fact that many western states have (seemingly) been largely unsuccessful in stopping illegal immigration has spurred a debate on the question of whether or not states have "lost control" on immigration.[41] Political scientists Peter Andreas and Ethan Nadelmann provide a corrective to the perception that states are somehow "losing control" on immigration. While they admit that viewed from a historical perspective, state capacities to detect, deter, and detain transnational law evaders have, if anything, grown substantially and the law enforcement reach of the state has expanded, they also argue that to jump to the conclusion that states are losing control is highly misleading because it falsely implies that states were "in control" in the past. Contrary to popular belief, there has never been a golden age of state control, and cross-border crime is as old as the creation of national borders and the imposition of state controls.[42] Developments in national ID documents and policies speak directly to all these issues. Indeed, the plethora of developments in identity policing and migration control policies, and particularly big changes between 2001 and 2005, point to a homogenizing impact on western countries in the wake of the 9/11 terrorist attacks in the United States, terrorist attacks in Madrid on March 11, 2004, and terrorist attacks in London on July 7, 2005. These attacks made the governments pursue stronger policies on security, immigration control, and ID checks.

[38] Robert Gilpin, *War and Change in World Politics* (Cambridge, MA: Cambridge University Press, 1981), 19.

[39] Dennis Broeders, "The New Digital Borders of Europe: EU Databases and the Surveillance of Irregular Migrants," *International Sociology* 22, 1 (January 2007).

[40] Debra DeLaet, *U.S. Immigration Policy in an Age of Rights* (Westport, CT: Praeger, 2000), 116.

[41] Christian Joppke, *Immigration and the Nation-State: The United States, Germany and Great Britain* (Oxford: Oxford University Press, 1999).

[42] Peter Andreas and Ethan Nadelmann, *Policing the Globe: Criminalization and Crime Control in International Relations* (Oxford: Oxford University Press, 2006), 245–246.

THE UNITED STATES IN COMPARATIVE PERSPECTIVE

My overall interest is in the historical and contemporary developments regarding the adoption of national ID documents and policies in modern industrialized democracies. The historical range covers a century, from 1915 to 2016.

As stated in the introductory chapter, at least 170 of the world's nearly 200 countries (democracies and nondemocracies) have some kind of a national ID card (compulsory or noncompulsory) or are implementing one. Included in this number are twenty-eight of the thirty-four OECD countries (all economically, socially, and politically developed democracies). Those twenty-eight countries are: Austria, Belgium, Chile, the Czech Republic, Denmark, Estonia, Finland, France, Germany, Greece, Hungary, Iceland, Israel, Italy, Japan, Luxembourg, Mexico, the Netherlands, Norway, Poland, Portugal, Slovakia, Slovenia, South Korea, Spain, Sweden, Switzerland, and Turkey. Of the OECD countries that have national ID cards, most introduced them between WWI and the 1950s, though some introduced them only after the year 2000. Norway is in the process of implementing national ID cards.

Six OECD countries currently do not have national ID cards: the United States, the United Kingdom, Canada, Australia, Ireland, and New Zealand. There is no major country outside the OECD that also lacks a national ID card.

This book examines the politics and history of proposals to introduce national ID cards (and other identity policing schemes) in one of the very few countries worldwide that never had national ID cards: the United States. This book provides a deeply contextualized study of developments regarding national ID cards in the United States – both historically and currently.

Sociologist Joseph Eaton argued that in the United States a national ID card is a taboo – an idea regarded by "conventional wisdom" as inherently evil and unacceptable. Specialists "know that American vital statistics records are an open invitation to the fraudulent acquisition of false identity records." However, "many of them fear to express views favorable to comprehensive ID card reform that are apt to be labeled reactionary or insensitive to the risk of preparing the groundwork for totalitarianism."[43]

[43] Joseph Eaton, *Card-Carrying Americans. Privacy, Security, and the National ID Card Debate* (Totowa, NJ: Rowman & Littlefield Publishers, 1986), 66.

The identity policing and national ID card controversies in the United States stand in contrast to the norms in most European countries, such as Germany and Poland, where national identification documents are part of everyday life, most people do not give them a second thought, and, politically, they are a "nonissue." Aristide Zolberg pointed out that in European democracies the public accepts as routine the requirement to have a universal government-issued identification document. It even views it as positive from a civil liberties perspective because it provides some degree of protection against arbitrary police behavior. However, "within the American context," the public would perceive it "to alter profoundly the established balance between freedom and control."[44]

But are the American people as opposed to national ID cards as conventional wisdom suggests? The historical chapters reveal a more complicated story and contradict the conventional wisdom.

While this book focuses on the United States, I also refer, especially in this chapter and in the Conclusion, to the United Kingdom since it is a good comparative case to the United States. After all, both countries are exceptions on the world stage in that they do not currently have national ID cards. The difference, of course, is that the United Kingdom had national ID cards on three separate occasions. The United Kingdom had national ID cards between 1915 and 1919 and between 1939 and 1952. Legislation passed in 2006 introduced national ID cards in the United Kingdom for the third time. The country that until then was one of the last countries without national ID cards now introduced multipurpose, biometric, and technologically advanced cards. However, in 2010, the new coalition government scrapped the project, partially due to cost and efficiency concerns. In the United Kingdom, national ID cards have come and gone despite state-builders' enthusiasm for them. The United States, in contrast, never had national ID cards, just proposals to introduce them.

The fact that neither the United Kingdom nor the United States currently has national ID cards makes each of those two countries outliers. That makes them unusual and intriguing. Both the United Kingdom and the United States have a tradition of respect for civil liberties, and in both countries there is what many regard as healthy skepticism about the claims of benevolence by government; its officials must be watched and constrained by constitutional and legal procedures. Both countries have been challenged by illegal immigration and terrorism. Therefore, in both

[44] Aristide R. Zolberg, "Guarding the Gates," in *Understanding September 11*, ed. Craig Calhoun, Paul Price, and Ashley Timmer (New York: New Press, 2002), 297.

countries the changing perception of threat is creating tension between long-standing legal commitments and the states' perceived needs for security and control of the population. Despite similar political cultures, historical traditions of antistatism, and general respect for civil liberties, the United Kingdom and the United States approach identity policing and identification policies differently.

Interestingly, while in the post-9/11 period the United Kingdom and some other countries have been moving in the direction of supplementing strict external controls with internal ones (including national ID cards), the United States has relatively strict external controls but continues to have lax internal ones. As Zolberg points out, with regard to internal controls, the United States is located "at the extreme liberal end of the continuum."[45] Not only is there no national ID card system, but it is unusually easy to change one's identity. On the other hand, almost all noncitizen entrants to the United States from outside Canada and Mexico now submit fingerprints and digital photographs. In comparison, controls at the land borders with Canada and Mexico may appear relatively lax, contributing to illegal immigration. Historian Andreas Fahrmeir argues that the "contradiction between the production of high-tech passports and identity cards and the generous approach towards immigration which bypasses passport controls reflects a more general contradiction in immigration policies which emerged in the 1970s."[46] The more recent moves toward complex controls at frontiers in both the United Kingdom and the United States, as contrasted with relatively relaxed internal identity policing in the United States, and an ambiguous situation in the United Kingdom, merit further study.

KEY ARGUMENTS

Despite the worldwide prevalence of identity policing, it is actually difficult for a liberal democratic state to implement a comprehensive identity policing scheme – especially one including sophisticated national ID cards – if it did not have one in the past. Nevertheless, some countries, such as the United Kingdom, have tried to introduce such schemes from scratch. There are also countries, such as the United States, that are looking for other ways in which they can police identity that do not

[45] Aristide R. Zolberg, *A Nation by Design: Immigration Policy in the Fashioning of America* (New York: Russell Sage Foundation, 2006), 444.

[46] Fahrmeir, *Citizenship*, 218.

involve a centralized national identification scheme. Instead, they hope to find new uses for and make improvements to existing documents, such as driver's licenses.

Neither the United Kingdom nor the United States has produced or achieved the supposedly highest form of identity policing, one that is based on a comprehensive and centralized register and a national ID card. The United Kingdom tried it on three occasions and was reasonably successful on the first two occasions, both of which were during wartime. The latest national ID card scheme became quite advanced, but ultimately failed. The United States has never attempted this type of identity policing. Why did the United States not develop a national ID card? Why did the last UK project fail?

Both countries, particularly the United States, have used methods other than national ID cards to police identity. The United States is a prime example of a country that has been patching together a variety of methods, at both the federal and state levels, to meet the identity policing objectives that national ID cards are supposed to achieve in other countries. Therefore, while countries around the world are increasingly policing identity and are doing it using technologically advanced databases and ID cards, a small number of countries (primarily the six OECD countries that currently do not have national ID cards) are policing identity but are not doing it with the use of national ID cards. Instead, these countries choose current documents, many far from perfect, and employ them for new uses. They also use partial schemes and patch together different methods. In the United States, when an individual needs to identify him- or herself to certain authorities, he or she often needs to present four different documents issued by four different authorities. For instance, to obtain a Massachusetts state ID card for nondrivers, an applicant must provide four different documents: a valid SSN or an acceptable denial letter, one document to prove Massachusetts residency, one document to prove signature, and one document to prove date of birth.[47] In other countries just one document, typically a national ID card, would be required, or the need to obtain a state ID card would be superfluous because a person would already hold a multipurpose national ID card.

National ID cards and their functional equivalents are means in the identity policing process. Identity policing is a continuous process with an

[47] Massachusetts Registry of Motor Vehicles, "Obtaining a Massachusetts ID," www.massrmv.com/LicenseandID/ObtainingaMassachusettsID.aspx.

upper limit that is movable due to the changing nature of technology. Thus, the upper limit is denoted by efforts of *those* nation-states – primarily governments, police, and other authorities – *that use the most advanced technologies* to collect and record identifying information about individuals who permanently or temporarily reside in their territory; to issue *the most technologically advanced* identification documents to those individuals; to require those individuals to identify themselves in interactions with the authorities, with the identification process *almost always* requiring the presentation of identification documents; to recognize those individuals in their fulfillment of responsibilities toward the authorities; and to authorize those individuals to gain access to the rights and benefits of membership.[48] "The most advanced technologies" and "the most technologically advanced identification documents" mean in this context the most sophisticated and interconnected databases, biometrics, and "smart" cards currently available. This does not mean that those technologies are entirely efficient, reliable, or fully tested, and many critics argue that indeed they are not.

I link national ID card emergence and the expansion of identity policing with political, economic, and security crises and shocks (internal and external), such as wars, revolutions, terrorist attacks, depressions, and demographic shocks (epidemics and large-scale migrations). I argue that crises and shocks induce states to enhance population controls and lead states to argue either for an introduction of national ID cards or for an expansion or an enhancement of existing identity policing efforts.

In the early modern era, up to and including the nineteenth century, states' need for taxation and conscription led to need for increased identification of subject populations. In WWI and WWII, conscription and fear of enemy aliens led to the same need. In the mid-twentieth century, the development of the modern welfare state drove states' needs for increased identification of subject populations, since the state needed to regulate access to employment rights and welfare benefits. In the late twentieth century, and especially since the 1980s, growing migration drove states' needs for increased identification of subject populations. In the twenty-first century, it is the perceived security risks from terrorism and illegal immigration that drive states' needs for increased identification of subject populations.

[48] The emphasis in italics is added to differentiate the general definition of identity policing, outlined in the Introduction, from this one, which emphasizes the upper limits of identity policing.

Never before had we had so many people living in countries where they are noncitizens, yet states seem to care now more rather than less about distinguishing between citizens and noncitizens and about policing identity and entitlements. How should we explain the increased use of identity policing and identification documents in an era of greater openness and fluidity? The dual forces of global migration and security threats lead to increased state regulation of access to state borders, state services, political rights, and other citizenship benefits. The enhanced state regulation is coupled with otherwise open societies resulting in the increased contestation of the nature of the national subjects. Terrorism and immigration (primarily illegal immigration) are two primary drivers of the new identification schemes, policies, and documents. These two drivers are interconnected.

In addition to the larger crises and shocks, there are other possible "triggers" for the development of identity policing, such as moral panics. Sociologist Stanley Cohen coined the term "moral panic" to describe widely held and media-promulgated beliefs that a particular group is a menace to social stability. The threat may be a real one, such as terrorism, but it is exaggerated, or it may be an imagined one. Political scientist Jytte Klausen points out that moral panics are a cause for concern because they pose obstacles to sensible and pragmatic solutions to societal problems.[49] Importantly, moral panics, as opposed to conflicts with deeper institutional and structural roots, often simply settle down as the public moves on to other issues.

Table 1.2 presents an overview of the contemporary drivers, obstacles, and realization of identity policing schemes and initiatives in the United States. The contemporary identity policing schemes are analyzed in Chapter 4 and the drivers and obstacles are analyzed in Chapter 5.

Scholars have long argued that states use existing capacities and enhance them at moments of crisis.[50] The 9/11 attacks have given an impetus to the expansion of state power, possibly at the expense of individual liberty. Coupled with global migration, cheaper transportation, and transcontinental family networks, states are at a historical

[49] Jytte Klausen, *The Islamic Challenge: Politics and Religion in Western Europe* (Oxford: Oxford University Press, 2005), 128–129.

[50] Jytte Klausen and Louise A. Tilly, "European Integration in a Social and Historical Perspective," in *European Integration in Social and Historical Perspective: 1850 to the Present*, ed. Jytte Klausen and Louise A. Tilly (New York: Rowman & Littlefield Publishers, 1997).

TABLE 1.2 *Overview of the contemporary drivers, obstacles, and realization of identity policing schemes and initiatives in the United States*

Drivers	Terrorism Illegal immigration Preventing identity fraud/theft (a limited motivation and one analyzed primarily in connection with illegal immigration)
Obstacles	Financial costs Technological obstacles and practical constraints Constitutional and legal obstacles Civil liberties and individual freedom concerns Public opinion and resistance
Realization	The REAL ID Act of 2005 Other (often voluntary and partial) identity policing schemes including federal initiatives (WHTI, EDLs, trusted traveler programs, TWIC, US-VISIT, Secure Flight, E-Verify), legislative proposals (BELIEVE), and state initiatives (Arizona S.B.1070, voter ID laws)

crossroad weighing the use of new technologies to control cross-border population movements, and their populations internally.

According to realists, states seize whatever means they have to protect their security interests. In terms of domestic politics, the primary concern for any ruler is stability, for without internal stability it is difficult to pursue other political, economic, or social objectives. Wars, revolutions, and other crises cause states to increase their demands for identity policing. When these threats go away, states often become more lax about identification documents. The need for identity policing rises and falls with various threat levels, producing historical ebbs and flows in identity policing, yet the overall trend is toward more identity policing.

Identity policing helps build state power, and states often take advantage of technological innovations, but a trend toward more identity policing does not apply evenly across countries or is met everywhere with approval. While identification documents are an enduring aspect of the modern state, obstacles such as public resistance make it hard for liberal democratic states to increase their identity policing efforts.

Whereas some states around the world are part of a trend toward approaching the upper limits of identity policing (Hong Kong, Malaysia), many others (United Kingdom, United States) encounter significant obstacles in their ability to implement, execute, and gain acceptance for identity policing efforts. These obstacles are financial costs, technological obstacles and practical constraints, constitutional and legal obstacles, civil liberties and individual freedom concerns, and public opinion and resistance. They can "act as a grounding mechanism, bringing policymakers with lofty dreams of new technological infrastructures down to reality when faced with detailed implementation challenges."[51] Dreams of combating terrorism through the use of biometric passports and ID cards are easy to come up with, yet the implementation of these documents takes time and effort as governments grapple with building biometric enrollment centers and securing information, to name just a few of the difficulties.

Importantly, domestic political circumstances influence how the government, media, and public opinion react to the proposals. While terrorism and illegal immigration are the big drivers in the development of identification policies, certain governments may choose not to emphasize prevention of terrorism and illegal immigration as the features of their new ID policies. They may choose to use other selling points for such policies. Governments may argue instead that the desired outcomes of new identification policies are establishing secure employment verification and access to entitlements, as well as crime and fraud prevention, e-government, and convenience. Alternatively, unsure how to sell their ideas, they reach for convenient arguments rather than well-thought-out ones. The list of drivers may have little to do with the actual reasons for introducing policy change. Terrorism and illegal immigration can be the primary drivers of identification policies, while crime and fraud prevention, e-government, convenience, and establishing employment verification and access to entitlements can be the specific selling points and desired outcomes of these policies.

As David Lyon points out, today the pressure is on to find identity policing schemes that work for several purposes – border crossing, e-government, security access, and commercial activities. New ID schemes tend to create citizens in the image of the leading motifs of the societies that give birth to them. In societies dominated by consumption, citizenship is recreated in terms of consuming. With e-government, the client mentality is apparent. If the leading motifs informing citizenship are ones designed to outlaw certain groups, then identification processes will reflect such attitudes. If these motifs operate at the same time, they could turn out to be mutually supporting.[52]

Some observers of identity policing schemes around the world point out with irony that when devising identity policies, policymakers often

[51] Whitley and Hosein, *Global Challenges*, 17.

[52] Lyon, *Identifying Citizens*, 81.

have a clear vision of what the resulting scheme will accomplish: just about everything. Whitley and Hosein point out that the purpose of the 2005 REAL ID Act in the United States was to prevent another 9/11; national ID cards in the United Kingdom were to combat identity and benefits fraud, terrorism, and crime; and biometric passports were to prevent bad people from traveling. They conclude: "All these years later it is often easy to look back with fondness at that era of simple solutions such as identity cards to complex problems like global terrorism."[53]

However, an important point is in order. While many governments and companies are guilty of repeatedly claiming that biometric ID cards, passports, and enhanced driver's licenses will cure all the world's ills, the dishonesty of those claims has only helped to galvanize opposition to these supposedly miraculous solutions. Although national ID cards may help address problems of illegal immigration, and may even have some national security and terrorism-prevention benefits, some governments worldwide have lost public support by arguing for an introduction of ID cards as a panacea for all evils. Identification documents are not in and of themselves a solution to the complex problems of today's world. No system is fool-proof.

Nevertheless, if properly designed and implemented under suitable oversight, national ID cards have the potential to help address at least some of the problems. Provided that they do not simply becamc yet another element of the "security theater" (the adoption of useless or nearly useless security measures to provide the reassuring appearance of a response to perceived risks), well-functioning identity policing schemes can become a successful part of a "layered security" approach, a practice that combines different security layers to find networked solutions to security problems.

In relying on a patchwork of various instruments of policing identity, certain countries are "satisficing." The concept of "satisficing," coined by the Nobel Laureate Herbert Simon, describes a decision-making process in which one takes the shortcut of defining what is acceptable and then settles on the first alternative that meets those minimum requirements. It is a play on the words *satisfy* and *sacrifice*, meaning that one sacrifices the best alternative for one that adequately satisfies one's demands. *Satisficing* is a decision-making strategy that aims for a satisfactory or adequate result, rather than an optimal solution. In decision-making, satisficing

[53] Whitley and Hosein, *Global Challenges*, 209.

explains the tendency to select the first option (or one of the first options) that meets a given need or to select the option that seems to address most needs. Satisficing can be a very pragmatic and necessary approach in many cases, so one does not have to experience the "paralysis of analysis." Often it simply is not worth it to examine every single option.

Moreover, ad hocism (the tendency to establish temporary, chiefly improvisational policies and procedures to deal with specific problems) can creep into identity policing. Identity policing can emerge in a piecemeal and haphazard fashion, and not part of a large concerted effort. Frequently, it has been specific needs that have generated a quest for identification schemes. Many systems for crime control, colonial administration, and conscription have been partial and limited to specific population groups, at least at first.[54] More general identity policing efforts have built up on those and have developed sporadically and patchily. However, this is not only specific to identity policing. In general, infrastructures are always built on an installed base, on the basis of what existed previously. They are almost never built from scratch. As political scientists Karen Orren and Stephen Skowronek argue, the construction of new edifices always occurs on existing sites.[55] New order is simply layered atop prior patterns.

In addition, infrastructures can never be changed all in one go. The introduction of any new infrastructure is normally phased in over a period of months or years, as new equipment and processes are introduced, with associated periods of retraining and organizational adjustment. As Whitley and Hosein point out, no infrastructure development project will ever cover the whole of the infrastructure, but rather will have to be developed in conjunction with the constraints arising from existing aspects of the infrastructure. Moreover, once large infrastructures become established, path-dependency kicks in, with self-reinforcing mechanisms often preventing much-needed change. For instance, the inefficient QWERTY keyboard layout has been retained despite being designed to slow down the process of typing. Once the infrastructure is initialized, unless it is carefully designed and managed, it will be increasingly difficult to make changes to it.[56] In particular, the start-up costs help determine the path a project will take. When financial and social costs are incurred early on, it is difficult to justify a change later on. The historical institutionalist literature points

54 Lyon, *Identifying Citizens*, 37.

55 Karen Orren and Stephen Skowronek, *In Search of American Political Development* (New York: Cambridge University Press, 2004).

56 Whitley and Hosein, *Global Challenges*, 112–113.

out that institutional development is characterized by relatively long periods of path-dependent institutional stability and reproduction. The institutional development is occasionally punctuated by brief phases of institutional flux, critical junctures during which more dramatic change is possible. These choices close off alternative options and lead to the establishment of institutions that generate self-reinforcing path-dependent processes.[57] According to political scientist Paul Pierson, junctures are "critical" because they place institutional arrangements on paths or trajectories, which are then very difficult to alter.[58]

However, if "satisficing," "ad hocism," and "path dependency" are such strong patterns, how is it that most of the rest of the world seems to have escaped them by creating new things, such as national ID card schemes, leaving the United States as an outlier? Why do proposals for national ID cards or increased identity policing efforts not necessarily lead to the same outcomes across different countries? While the focus of this book is on telling the political history of national ID card proposals in the United States, rather than explaining the patterns of ID card adoption and nonadoption across countries, it is worth pointing out that scholars have long noted that all states, including advanced capitalist states, exhibit considerable unevenness in capacity across functions and jurisdictions.[59] David Lyon and Colin Bennett say that the patterns of adoption of ID card systems are likely to vary according to structural factors and that comprehensive national ID schemes tend to be the product of strong states that have the institutions and resources to penetrate and regulate society. Such schemes might also reflect the efforts by weaker states to render society legible and thus to become strong. Lyon and Bennett argue that structural attributes of the strong state model, such as the hierarchical integration of state bureaucracy, the centralization of state functions, and the extent to which states are permeable to private sector influence, might help us understand the patterns of ID cards adoption and nonadoption[60] and the extent of identity policing efforts.

[57] Giovanni Capoccia and R. Daniel Kelemen, "The Study of Critical Junctures: Theory, Narrative, and Counterfactuals in Historical Institutionalism," *World Politics* 59, 3 (2007): 341.

[58] Paul Pierson, *Politics in Time* (Princeton: Princeton University Press, 2004), 135.

[59] Theda Skocpol, "Bringing the State Back In: Strategies of Analysis in Current Research," in *Bringing the State Back In*, ed. Peter B. Evans et al. (Cambridge: Cambridge University Press, 1985).

[60] David Lyon and Colin J. Bennett, "Playing the ID Card: Understanding the Significance of Identity Card Systems," in *Playing the Identity Card*, ed. Bennett and Lyon, 15–16.

FOCUS ON THE UNITED STATES

Up until now, no one told the comprehensive story of national ID card developments in the United States. Rather than just accepting as given the oft-repeated refrain that national ID cards are "un-American," we should get to know the complex and nuanced story about how policymakers and the public have viewed proposals for national ID cards over the last century.

The focus here is on a number of historical and contemporary episodes during which policymakers in the United States put forward proposals for national ID cards or put forward proposals for (and in some cases implemented) other identity policing schemes and initiatives. The primary focus is on national ID card proposals and other identity policing schemes put forward in WWI, WWII, the 1970s, 1980s, 1990s, and the period after 2001.

Some may question the value of looking at schemes that never materialized. Yet there are many reasons to look at schemes that never came to be, whether or not we consider them failures. For a start, success and failure are slippery concepts, often highly subjective and reflective of an individual's goals, perception of need, and even psychological disposition toward life.[61] One person may argue that a policy has failed, while another person might look at it as a tentative first step toward a larger goal.[62] Moreover, even if a policy is indeed a failure, it provides an opportunity to learn from mistakes. Citizens expect government officials to learn from failures and prevent them. Failure to learn from experience is particularly embarrassing to members of government if they repeat the mistakes of the past. If the political system fails to learn from these events, the public can plausibly claim that the system is dysfunctional.[63] Blundering governments do not command universal respect, with implications for democratic processes in other areas. Finally, paths considered but not taken also teach us a lot about the nature and character of the country. Even though the United States lacks a national ID card, its efforts at policing identity – and the hurdles, limits, and obstacles it encounters – are worth analyzing.

[61] Helen M. Ingram and Dean E. Mann, "Policy Failure: An Issue Deserving Analysis," in *Why Policies Succeed or Fail*, ed. Helen M. Ingram and Dean E. Mann (Beverly Hills: Sage Publications, 1980), 12.

[62] Thomas A. Birkland, *An Introduction to the Policy Process: Theories, Concepts, and Models of Public Policy Making*, 2nd ed. (Armonk, NY: M.E. Sharpe, 2005), 190.

[63] Thomas A. Birkland, *Lessons of Disaster* (Washington, DC: Georgetown University Press, 2006), 29.

THE BOOK'S FINDINGS

This book presents a comprehensive political history of national ID card proposals and identity policing developments in the United States. That detailed and practical narrative, previously missing from the scholarship, can help us fill existing gaps in our understanding of the identity policing landscape.

The United States has never had national ID cards, but it had several partial population registrations (some accompanied by the issuing of identification cards) aimed at certain segments of the population during wartime. Most people are not aware that there were multiple proposals to introduce national ID cards in the United States during WWII, in the 1970s, 1980s, 1990s, and after 9/11. All of these proposals were unsuccessful. However, authorities have been implementing and continue to implement other identity policing schemes, with varying degrees of success. For instance, in 2005, the REAL ID Act legislated significant changes to make driver's licenses standardized and more secure.

The United States is unlikely to introduce national ID cards in the future, yet it already faces important challenges regarding the harmonization of state driver's licenses in accordance with the REAL ID Act, the issuance of driver's licenses and municipal IDs to illegal immigrants, Arizona S.B.1070-type immigration enforcement laws, fraud in SSNs, employment eligibility verification, and voter ID laws. While in other countries around the world national ID cards help ensure the legitimacy of the voting process, confirm work eligibility, and provide access to government services, American policymakers are not currently considering national ID cards, and there is little informed public debate on the subject.

My book, while scholarly, is not intended as a theoretical contribution to citizenship theory, American political development, or a particular theoretical argument in political science. Instead, it explores historical episodes involving proposals and actions to introduce new or improve existing identification documents in the United States, and it draws on those historical episodes to debunk some common myths: that all Americans are staunchly opposed to national ID cards and that American policymakers never propose national ID cards. Moreover, should there be a political reform of identity policing in the United States, the book can help to furnish a "usable past": a narrative that would make sense of American history in terms that would be useful for the present. The book does not have a normative message, nor is it predictive, but by providing a coherent record of events it should help us understand where we have been, where we are now, and where we might go in the future.

Americans are largely unaware of the identity policing plans from the past. This is important, since these plans would have a significant impact if authorities put them in place. This book is largely a history of the past and present developments, rather than an exposé on how national ID cards would impact the United States. In fact, the United States is unlikely to introduce national ID cards in the future, but will surely see continuing challenges to identity policing, and changes in identification practices.

The conventional wisdom is that the American people and policymakers are staunchly opposed to national ID cards and that American policymakers never propose national ID cards, but the historical evidence I examined reveals a more complicated story. I show that policymakers and the public often support the proposals for introducing national ID cards and for improving existing identification documents. This is particularly the case in times of war, when the country is under attack, or when it is experiencing a crisis. Passionate opposition to national ID cards has been and remains present in the United States, but many policymakers and members of the public see national ID cards more positively than conventional wisdom would let us believe.

The first powerful finding of this book is that polling indicates Americans are not particularly opposed to national ID cards. This happens across several different historical and public policy settings and different wording of poll questions. I show that popular support for national ID cards, as measured by opinion polls, letters to Congress, and letters to newspapers, has been significant over the last 100 years and has frequently represented a majority view. Acknowledging the existence of passionate opposition, my book shows that Americans see national ID cards more positively than is popularly believed.

The second powerful and fascinating finding is that over the last 100 years when American policymakers were confronted with the need to strengthen identification, a number of individual policymakers did propose national ID cards. However, the proposals did not get very far, and policymakers as a whole have repeatedly turned to some existing system of identification tied to other policy fields (Social Security cards, driver's licenses) rather than opting to create a free-standing national ID card. This is in contrast to pretty much every other nation in the world, including the United Kingdom, which during national crises first created and then repealed national ID cards.

Together, these two findings create a fascinating puzzle. If Americans are not really opposed to national ID cards, why do policymakers repeatedly turn away from this? And if, contra the polling, Americans *are* so troubled by identity policing, why have there been some successful efforts to strengthen existing systems of identification, though often in the form of half-measures, but no national ID card?

Why would the "path dependency" dynamics, which places institutional arrangements on paths that are then difficult to alter, be particularly powerful in the United States? The comparison with the United Kingdom only magnifies this question. Both countries have had exogenous shocks that have stimulated increased identity policing; both countries have values and groups that support strengthening identity policing and oppose it. When proposals to create a national ID card have arisen, in both nations daunting practical issues have been raised. Yet the United Kingdom has on three occasions enacted a national ID card, whereas the United States has never once come close to doing so.

While the focus of this book is on telling the political history of national ID card proposals in the United States, rather than examining the structure of the US political system, it seems likely that political structure, especially the large number of veto points in the US system, likely has influenced the outcome. The United States has a system with an unusually large number of veto points, whereas the United Kingdom has just one veto point, parliament. This disparity in veto points creates differing opportunities for policymakers. As is well known, in parliamentary systems with few veto points there is tendency toward major changes in public policy, sometimes including (as in the case of a national ID card system) adoption followed by quick repeal. In this respect the British outcome is not so surprising. On the other side of the spectrum, in systems with many veto points, there is a tendency toward incrementalism because many groups need to come together to make policy change, and some will have investments in current arrangements.[64] The price of policy change, then, is a bargain in which elements of the existing system are kept in place. Thus path dependency is not an equal force in all political systems; it is far stronger in systems with multiple veto points. This may by itself provide a sufficient explanation for the difference in pattern between the United Kingdom and the United States.

[64] George Tsebelis, "Veto Players and Institutional Analysis," *Governance* 13, 4 (2000); Terry M. Moe, "Political Institutions: The Neglected Side of the Story," *Journal of Law, Economics, & Organization* 6 (1990).

Steven Teles's "Kludgeocracy in America" demonstrates that this pattern of adopting half-measures tied to existing systems is widespread in American public policy and is rooted in the distinctively large number of veto points in American government. The need to gain consent from multiple actors makes attaining any degree of policy coherence difficult at best, which means that kludges – ill-assorted, clumsy, but temporarily effective solutions to a particular problem – remain in place.[65] The story of identity policing in the United States seems like a textbook example of "kludgeocracy" in action, the tendency in public policy to build on existing systems, whatever their weaknesses, rather than to replace them with better alternatives. The result of relying on a patchwork of various instruments of policing identity is that the United States is characterized by a genuine identification assemblage.

SUMMARY

The United States has never had national ID cards, and is unlikely to introduce national ID cards in the future, but will surely see continuing challenges to identity policing and changes in identification practices. The topic of identity policing is of public relevance, since identification documents feature in many current controversies, including those over the REAL ID Act, immigration reform, and voter ID laws. The future of identity policing in the United States is in question and is likely to remain so. Thankfully, for the purposes of this analysis it does not matter whether the United States implements national ID cards or, if it does, when that happens. The broader topics of identity policing and the related questions of state power, individual rights, liberty, and security are of perennial significance. With developments continually unfolding, the analysis can only gain importance.

My book fills an important void since there is no published, comprehensive political history of national ID card proposals and identity policing developments in the United States. Written work on national ID cards in the United States tends to come not from objective scholars but from engaged critics. Instead of focusing either on philosophical reflections on the desirability of the ID schemes or on the technical intricacies of the schemes, my book's focus on the political history of proposals results in a detailed and practical narrative.

[65] Steven Teles, "Kludgeocracy in America," *National Affairs* 17 (2013).

2

Identification Documents in the United States in the First Half of the Twentieth Century

INTRODUCTION

Chapters 2, 3, 4, and 5 explore the developments in identity policing and identification documents in the twentieth- and twenty-first-century United States. In particular, the chapters focus on proposals, all unsuccessful, to introduce national ID cards in the United States. They fill an important void in the literature by providing a comprehensive political history of national ID card proposals and identity policing developments in the United States. The chapters emphasize the role played by the historical crises in the development of identity policing, examine the contemporary drivers of identity policing, assess the obstacles in the development of identification documents and identity policing, and point to the overall incrementalism and patchwork-like nature of identity policing efforts in the United States.

This chapter explores several partial population registrations (some accompanied by the issuing of identification cards) aimed at certain segments of the population, including aliens (noncitizens) and enemy aliens, during WWI and WWII. Most importantly, this chapter looks at the multiple proposals to introduce national ID cards in the United States. Policymakers and members of the public put forward these proposals mostly during WWII; all the proposals were unsuccessful.

The history of national ID card proposals in the United States overlaps with that of census, birth certificates, passports, driver's licenses, SSNs, immigration reforms, employer sanctions, employment eligibility documents, criminal and police registers, and fingerprinting. This chapter does not attempt to deal with most of these, and refers to them only insofar as they are directly relevant to the development of ID card policies and attitudes. The chapter pays more attention to fingerprinting, since it was a crucial element of national ID card proposals during WWII.

IDENTIFICATION DOCUMENTS PRIOR TO WWI

Until the late nineteenth century, if life events of American people were recorded at all, they were more likely to be entered in a family's Bible or a church register than registered by a clerk in a government office. It was mainly the development of the public health movement and the advancements of medical science that propelled the demand for official vital statistics in the United States. In 1900, 40 percent of the country's population had their deaths recorded; in 1915, it was 67 percent; and by 1925, it was 88 percent.[1]

A great stimulus for acquiring birth certificates came from the Social Security Act of 1935 and WWII. Many people had not considered a birth certificate to be of importance until old age assistance, unemployment insurance, and other ramifications of the Act necessitated this official proof of their existence. One way to get people to register was to use the public schools to instruct the upcoming generation about the importance of public health and the necessity of cooperating with governmental authorities for such purposes.[2] At the start of WWII, many Americans of working age lacked a birth certificate, but those who sought work in defense industries as the war progressed soon learned the importance of acquiring one. By 1950, the Census Bureau estimated that officials were registering 97.9 percent of all births in the United States.[3]

Author Carl Watner points out that the success of the federal and state governments in "accomplishing the feat of legitimizing itself in the minds and bodies of its citizenry has been phenomenal." In the span of a few generations, "Americans have moved from a situation of quasi-voluntarism (of having their lives largely unregulated by

[1] Carl Watner, "The Compulsory Birth and Death Certificate in the United States," in *National Identification Systems: Essays in Opposition*, ed. Carl Watner and Wendy McElroy (Jefferson, NC: McFarland & Company, 2004), 72–75.

[2] Ibid., 76.

[3] James Rule, Doug McAdam, Linda Stearns, and David Uglow, "Documentary Identification and Mass Surveillance in the United States," *Social Problems* 31, 2 (December 1983): 224.

government) to one of near-total government control over all their activities (literally, from birth to death)." Now, a person "has no real legal proof of existence in the eyes of the state without a proper birth certificate."[4]

An important question arises: why did we not observe a similar shift toward a national ID card? This is especially interesting given that, contrary to popular opinion, America was no stranger to written passes, identification tags, discs, and other identification devices, which elsewhere in the world were often precursors of national ID cards. In the United States, those were tools of oppression: demanded of slaves and freed blacks, but not of the others. It is not surprising that many Americans have subsequently had negative views of identification documents if they associate them with dehumanizing practices from the past.

During his visit to the United States in 1833, Alexis de Tocqueville reflected on the ease with which people with checkered pasts could begin anew and the impact this had on the penal system. He argued that where passports do not exist, "nothing is easier than to change one's name; if therefore a delivered convict commits a new crime under a fictitious name, he can very easily conceal his relapse" as "there is no central power to which the police officers might refer to obtain information regarding the previous life of an indicted person."[5]

As Craig Robertson's history of the American passport reveals, passports were the first government-issued identification documents in the United States. In the early years, a variety of officials, including state governors and mayors, had issued passports. In August 1856, Congress gave the secretary of state the sole authority to issue passports. It became illegal for others to issue passports or documents in the nature of a passport. Congress also declared that only US citizens were eligible for US passports.[6] According to John Torpey, the issuance of passports by state and local authorities before 1856 confirms that, during the antebellum period, the central government of the United States had, in the words of political scientist Richard Bensel, "only a token administrative presence in most of the nation and [its] sovereignty was interpreted by the

[4] Watner, "The Compulsory," 80.

[5] Gustave de Beaumont and Alexis de Tocqueville, *On the Penitentiary System in the United States and Its Application in France*, trans. Francis Lieber (Philadelphia, 1833), 72.

[6] Craig Robertson, *The Passport in America: The History of a Document* (New York: Oxford University Press, 2010), 141.

central administration as contingent on the consent of the individual states."[7] Importantly, though, nineteenth-century passports were not equivalent to modern passports, in that they were not used as ID cards at the time. Rather, between the eighteenth and the twentieth centuries, the US passport transformed from something like a letter of introduction to a certificate of citizenship to an identification document.

Other official identification documents in America had their origins in anti-immigration sentiments. The nineteenth century witnessed an influx of Chinese workers during the 1848 gold rush and transcontinental railway building boom. It also witnessed a development of Sinophobia, which by the mid-1870s reached boiling point. The Chinese Exclusion Act of 1882 aimed at restricting the immigrant flow except in the case of workers who returned to China temporarily. The question was how to identify them – and fingerprinting seemed to be preferred to physical descriptions because officials claimed to find it difficult to recognize one individual from another.[8] The Geary Act of 1892 (which extended the Chinese Exclusion Act for another ten years) required that all Chinese laborers in the United States carry a photo identification card (a "certificate of residence"). Historians examined special identification documents for the Chinese in America, such as "certificates of identification" ("return certificates"), "431 papers," and "Section Six certificates" ("Canton certificates"), and the development of the so-called paper families. They gained fascinating insights into the hostility aimed at the Chinese, the exploitation of American stereotypes about the Chinese (like the belief that all Chinese looked alike) by the Chinese people themselves, the practice of buying and selling documents, the ever-increasing levels of government surveillance, and the development of the US immigration apparatus as a result of the need to enforce the laws aimed at the Chinese.[9] Again, it is no wonder that many Americans have subsequently had negative views of identification documents if they associate them with hostile attitudes or sketchy practices.

[7] Torpey, *The Invention of the Passport*, 95; Richard Bensel, *Yankee Leviathan: The Origins of Central State Authority in America, 1859–1877* (New York: Cambridge University Press, 1990).

[8] Lyon, *Identifying Citizens*, 31–32.

[9] Torpey, *The Invention of the Passport*; Parenti, *The Soft Cage*; Estelle T. Lau, *Paper Families: Identity, Immigration Administration, and Chinese Exclusion* (Durham: Duke University Press, 2006).

REGISTRATION AND IDENTIFICATION DOCUMENTS FOR ENEMY ALIENS DURING WWI

Just as the second half of the nineteenth century witnessed resentment toward the Chinese, the two world wars in the twentieth century witnessed resentment toward German-Americans, Japanese-Americans, and Italian-Americans, and the creation by the US government of special identification documents for these groups. In WWI, following America's declaration of war against Germany on April 6, 1917, public sentiment began to build against German-Americans, and Congress debated various measures of registering them to prevent espionage and subversion.

On April 6, 1917, President Woodrow Wilson's proclamation placed significant restrictions on the activities of enemy aliens. Wilson's proclamation on November 16, 1917, placed additional restrictions on the movement of nonnaturalized males of German origin, fourteen years of age or older. Based on that November proclamation, in early February 1918, Attorney General Thomas Watt Gregory issued regulations regarding the registration of German enemy aliens. All male subjects of the German Empire (i.e., those who were German citizens or natives, but were not actually naturalized as American citizens) who were within the United States and who were over fourteen years of age or older were required to register as enemy aliens. Women were exempt. The registration lasted from February 4 to 9, 1918. In more populous municipalities registration took place at police stations. In less populous communities, registration took place at post offices. Gregory argued that the "persons required to register are, by doing so, giving proof of their peaceful dispositions and of their intention to conform to the laws of the United States,"[10] an argument that would be repeated, almost verbatim, in both 1940 and 1942.

Once German-American aliens reported for registration, they had to fill out personal information forms and supply several photographs of themselves. They also had to submit fingerprints. They received an alien registration card with their name, address, photograph, and thumbprint, and were required to carry it at all times. Aliens had to report to officials if they changed their address and had to acquire special certification if they needed to enter, work, or reside in or near certain war-sensitive areas, such as harbors or industrial parks. As scholar Pamela Sankar points out, officials believed they could identify possibly hostile German-American

[10] "Gregory Defines Alien Regulations," *NYT*, February 2, 1918.

aliens before they acted by reviewing their alien registration/identification cards. Officials then could deport or incarcerate these people, or at least keep them away from vital resources. The registration process proceeded without incident, and estimates based on the 1910 census indicated a near total compliance of the target population. Within a few months, nearly 500,000 German-Americans had reported to registration centers.[11]

Earlier debates over the establishment of government surveillance capabilities in the form of a Department of Justice (DOJ) detective bureau had raised strong opposition, but the bill to fingerprint and monitor German-American aliens passed with only moderate criticism. Sankar argues that those who did have reservations made clear that only the threat of sabotage and espionage had moved them to act. Although some congressmen favored the generalization of registration to all aliens at all times, the words of another summarized the majority position when he described the act as "purely an emergency measure." Others made clear that the government would lift these restrictions when the war ended. Critics also feared that officials would extend registration to the entire US population. Some perceived such monitoring as un-American. One congressman summed up this position: "when people come here from other countries they have the idea that this is a free country and they do not want to feel that the police are tagging after them."[12]

The alien registration program had at least one major flaw in that unless laws required all those in the United States to carry an ID card, failure to produce one was without clear meaning. A questionable individual could as easily be a German spy as a loyal American. Still, Sankar argues, the flaw did not undercut completely the system's effectiveness. If a person detained could not present an alien registration card and if authorities later established such person was a German-American alien, such person was automatically guilty of a crime: failure to carry an ID card. This infraction was punishable by a fine of up to $2,000 and imprisonment of up to five years, as were most violations of the registration act. ID card checks helped to generate information about the people required to follow the ID card rule. The rule distinguished compliant from noncompliant (and thus potentially dangerous) German-American aliens. Although an ID card violation might mean little in the short term, it could lead to opening a file and initiating a record for an individual. Authorities

[11] Pamela Sankar, "A National Fingerprint System for the United States," in *National Identification Systems*, ed. Watner and McElroy, 94–95.

[12] Ibid., 95.

would no longer consider any subsequent violation, also entered into this record, as an isolated event but as part of a pattern of resistance.[13]

Nearly all German-American aliens reported swiftly and without complaint to registration centers. During the war, they dutifully carried their ID cards containing photographs and thumbprints, and they produced them on demand. Their willingness to help the government keep track of possible wrongdoers and facilitate administration of the war effort helped fingerprinting become associated with conformity. The registration ended with WWI.[14]

IDENTIFICATION AND FINGERPRINTING IN THE INTERWAR PERIOD

In the interwar period, there were some interesting debates regarding the desirability of the universal registration of all aliens.[15] However, the focus in this period was on the potential universal fingerprinting of US citizens.

Prior to the mid-1920s, the government's fingerprint requirements applied mainly to criminals. In 1905, the DOJ created a Bureau of Criminal Identification to provide a centralized reference collection of fingerprint cards. In 1907, officials moved the collection, as a money-saving measure, to Leavenworth Federal Penitentiary, where convicts staffed it. Suspicious of this arrangement, police departments formed their own centralized identification bureau, maintained by the International Association of Chiefs of Police, which refused to share its data with the Bureau of Criminal Investigation. In 1924, Congress merged the two collections in Washington, DC, under Bureau of Investigation administration, thereby establishing the central repository for criminal fingerprints. Law enforcement agencies across the country began contributing fingerprint cards to the Bureau of Investigation by 1926.[16]

In the mid-1920s, starting with the establishment of the Identification Bureau (later renamed the Identification Division) at the Bureau of Investigation (renamed the Federal Bureau of Investigation, or FBI, in 1935), the government began to extend fingerprint requirements beyond the criminal population to include military enlistees, immigrants, and federal employees. The government also started a vigorous campaign for voluntary contributions from civilians, including schoolchildren and private

[13] Ibid., 96. [14] Ibid., 97.
[15] "Alien Registration Urged by J.B. Trevor," *NYT*, March 14, 1932.
[16] FBI, "A Brief History," www.fbi.gov/about-us/history/brief-history.

sector employees. By 1939, the Bureau's collection numbered nearly 11 million, representing a ten-fold increase in little more than a decade. Within another ten years, the collection swelled to over 110 million. Sankar points out that as with the German-American alien program, peacetime fingerprint programs targeted individuals not because of some past criminal act, but because of their membership in broad social groups: workers, immigrants, and youths. Under these new programs, people submitted fingerprints during common procedures, such as applying for a job. This helped to establish fingerprinting as an ordinary occurrence.[17]

While there were suggestions for a universal US fingerprint requirement as early as 1911, they did not gain popularity until after WWI. According to Sankar, WWI radically altered both public and government perceptions of the necessity of domestic surveillance and the utility of fingerprinting to enact that surveillance. Previously, officials had perceived fingerprinting narrowly as a measure to help control criminals. However, during the decade following the war officials began to envision fingerprinting as a tool of routine civil administration. Officials realized they could use it against political dissenters.[18]

During the 1910s, enthusiasm grew for civilian applications, such as fingerprinting children. In 1919, New York City Deputy Police Commissioner Joseph Faurot, claiming that the wealthy already fingerprinted their children as a provision against kidnapping, urged middle-class citizens to submit fingerprints voluntarily. In 1921, President Warren G. Harding had his fingerprints publicly taken. In Michigan, brothers Edward and James Murphy operated a private bureau that charged citizens $2 to register their fingerprints and $3 for a pocket identification card with leather case.[19]

Meanwhile, J. Edgar Hoover, envisioning the FBI as a domestic surveillance agency, wanted the ability to track as many citizens as possible, not just those who passed through the criminal justice system. He launched a campaign for universal fingerprinting. The national trauma over the kidnapping of the Lindbergh baby in 1932 helped popularize the notion that all citizens should be fingerprinted for their own protection. A universal fingerprinting campaign in Massachusetts collected 500,000 noncriminal fingerprint cards between 1928 and 1935. In 1936, the Berkeley Police Department, under the leadership of police reformer

[17] Sankar, "A National Fingerprint System," 97. [18] Ibid., 88.

[19] Simon A. Cole, *Suspect Identities: A History of Fingerprinting and Criminal Identification* (Cambridge, MA: Harvard University Press, 2001), 197–199.

August Vollmer, set up stations for voluntary fingerprinting where compliant citizens were rewarded with an "I have been fingerprinted" button. Berkley's police collected 50,000 prints in this campaign. In February 1938, the American Civil Liberties Union (ACLU) characterized the attempts at securing voluntary fingerprints from Americans as part of the general scheme for the compulsory regimentation of the entire population and as inevitably leading to the establishment of a domestic passport system.[20]

REGISTRATION OF ALL ALIENS DURING WWII

Putting aside the registration of Americans subject to draft in 1917–1918 and thereafter, Americans as a group have not been subject to any universal wartime registration during the twentieth century. The same has not been true of aliens. The term "aliens," which appears throughout the book, comes from historical and contemporary discourse and is the official term used by the US government to describe noncitizens, including legal permanent residents, temporary nonimmigrants, and illegal aliens.

During WWI, only enemy aliens (i.e., Germans) who were male and over the age of fourteen were subject to registration. However, after WWII began, and before Japan even attacked the United States at Pearl Harbor, the US government ordered registration of all aliens, through the Alien Registration Act of 1940.

Historian Lorraine Lees argues that by the time the United States entered WWII, the American public had become used to equating immigrants and exiles with concerns about national security. She claims that concern about ethnicity was not a phenomenon unique to the 1940s, but its persistence during a war waged against racial extremism by liberals dedicated to freedom and tolerance illustrated that at least part of the country's definition of national security rested firmly on a nativist base.[21]

Support for alien registration manifested itself among several local and national organizations and among state and federal officials. For instance, the Chamber of Commerce of the State of New York adopted an alien registration resolution in 1922, and on at least five occasions since then – in 1925, 1926, 1931, 1934, and 1936 – the Chamber reaffirmed the action it took in 1922. On June 6, 1940, the Chamber unanimously

[20] Ibid., 246–249; Sankar, "A National Fingerprint System," 87.

[21] Lorraine M. Lees, *Yugoslav-Americans and National Security during World War II* (Urbana and Chicago: University of Illinois Press, 2007), 11, 53.

adopted a resolution approving the objectives of H.R.5138, which was soon to become the Alien Registration Act of 1940. The Chamber saw it "as a vital part of the national defense plan."[22]

Several states passed alien registration laws. For instance, the Commonwealth of Pennsylvania passed an Alien Registration Act in 1939. The Act required every alien eighteen years or over, with certain exceptions, to register once each year and provide the information outlined by the statute. The alien would then receive an alien identification card and carry it at all times. The alien would have to show the card whenever any police officer or agent of the Department of Labor and Industry demanded it. The alien would also need to exhibit the card to register a motor vehicle or obtain a driver's license. Nonexempt aliens who failed to register were subject to a fine of no more than $100, imprisonment for no more than sixty days, or both. For failure to carry an identification card or failure to show it on demand, the punishment was a fine of no more than $10, imprisonment for no more than ten days, or both.[23]

Yet the most interesting developments regarding alien registration took place at the federal level. Congress endorsed alien registration in legislation, and the president approved it in June 1940 in the form of the Alien Registration Act.

Some contemporaneous accounts claimed that Attorney General Robert Jackson suggested alien registration.[24] While Jackson came to support alien registration, it is unlikely that the plan originated with him as anti-immigrant sentiments evident in the United States at the time deeply troubled him. Jackson, who was convinced about the need to protect both individual liberties and national security, urged restraint when it came to controlling aliens. Jackson knew that authorities should supervise aliens more strictly, but he was "utterly opposed to a new policy of persecuting or prosecuting aliens just because of alienage."[25]

Much of the push for alien registration came from several members of Congress who introduced alien registration, fingerprinting, and deportation bills in 1939 and 1940. While some members of the public opposed the bills, and described them as "anti-alien," others supported the bills.[26]

[22] H.R.5138, Boxes 272–274, Records of the US House of Representatives (House Records), 76th Congress, Record Group (RG) 233, National Archives Building, Washington, DC (NAB).

[23] *Hines v. Davidowitz*, 312 U.S. 52 (1941)

[24] Frank L. Kluckhohn, "Aliens Now Face a Closer Watch," *NYT*, July 7, 1940.

[25] Lees, *Yugoslav-Americans*, 26–27.

[26] H.R.5138, Boxes 272–274, House Records, 76th Congress, RG 233, NAB.

A Gallup poll in January 1939 revealed that 87 percent of the population favored requiring all noncitizens to register with the government.[27]

However, none of the bills attracted as much attention as H.R.5138, an omnibus bill proposed by Rep. Howard Smith (D-VA) in March 1939. While in later years, many observers would identify Smith with his opposition to civil rights and his support for gender equality, he will always be primarily associated with H.R.5138, which became the Alien Registration Act of 1940, also known as the Smith Act.

Ironically, in April 1939, Smith said he had "no pride of authorship" of H.R.5138. "The drafting of the bill is not my work, other than a codification of measures that have been offered from time to time, some of them many times. I have tried to bring them altogether in a comprehensive bill, and I have tried to eliminate from the bills that have been offered on the subject those which seemed to me would cause much controversy."[28]

An overwhelming majority of congressmen supported H.R.5138, which provided, among other things, for the registry and fingerprinting of all aliens in the United States, and of those seeking admission to the country hereafter. As he spoke on the House floor on June 22, 1940, Rep. Clarence Hancock (R-NY) expressed what many of his colleagues felt about the provision to register and fingerprint all aliens in the country. He said that although it will cause them some inconvenience, "honest aliens should not object to proper identification." Hancock noted that back in 1939

> this provision in the bill might have been rejected, but we now know that the modern technique of war involves "fifth columns." Aliens come from foreign countries illegally or under one pretext or another to organize espionage, sabotage, and subversive movements. We regard it as a measure of self-defense to provide for the fingerprinting and registration of all aliens in the United States. We also regard it as a safeguard to know something about their activities and their movements here.[29]

The Senate passed the bill with a voice vote on June 15, and the House passed it by an overwhelming margin of 382 to 4 on June 22. Following President Franklin Delano Roosevelt's signature, the Alien Registration Act became law on June 29, 1940.

[27] Michal R. Belknap, *Cold War Political Justice: The Smith Act, the Communist Party, and American Civil Liberties* (Westport, CT: Greenwood Press, 1977), 21.

[28] Hearing on H.R.5138, Subcommittee no. 3, Judiciary Committee, House of Representatives, 76th Congress, April 12 and 13, 1939, 71.

[29] H.R.5138, Boxes 272–274, House Records, 76th Congress, RG 233, NAB.

Much of the law's focus was on the prohibition of certain subversive activities. Title I made it a criminal offense to advocate the overthrow of any government in the United States or to be a member of any group devoted to such advocacy. As such, Title I reinstated the sedition crime of the WWI era, criminalizing a wide range of constitutionally protected political behavior. Throughout the 1940s and 1950s, anti-Communists used the Act against those with a real or suspected association with the Communist Party.[30] Title II allowed for the deportation of aliens who were abetting illegal immigration or had weapons violations.[31]

Title III of the Act focused on the issuance of visas and on the registration and fingerprinting of aliens. Section 30 stated that authorities should not issue a visa to any alien seeking to enter the United States unless said alien has been registered and fingerprinted in duplicate. The consul shall retain one copy of the registration and fingerprint record. The second copy shall be attached to the alien's visa and shall be taken up by the examining immigrant inspector at the alien's port of arrival in the United States and forwarded to the DOJ. The law excluded from admission any alien seeking to enter the United States who did not present a visa (except in emergency cases), a reentry permit, or a border-crossing identification card.

Most importantly, section 31 mandated every alien now or hereafter in the United States, whom authorities have not registered and fingerprinted under section 30, and who remained in the United States for thirty days or longer, to register and submit fingerprints before the expiration of such thirty days. The law applied to aliens fourteen years of age or older. Parents or guardians had to register alien children under fourteen years, but children had to submit fingerprints only after they reached their fourteenth birthday. While women were exempt from the enemy alien registration in 1918, they were subject to the alien registration of 1940. Only foreign government officials and their families were exempt from the registration and fingerprinting requirement.

Section 33 stated that aliens had to make all applications for registration and fingerprinting under section 31 at post offices. Every postmaster had to promptly forward the registration and fingerprint record of every alien he registered and fingerprinted to the DOJ. Section 35 stipulated that any alien who resided in the United States, and was subject to the

[30] David Cole, *Enemy Aliens: Double Standards and Constitutional Freedoms in the War on Terrorism* (New York: New Press; distributed by W.W. Norton & Co., 2003), 139–144.

[31] The Alien Registration Act of 1940, Public Law 76–670.

registration requirement, had to notify the Commissioner of Immigration and Naturalization in writing of each new address within five days.

Section 36 stated that any alien who willfully failed to apply for registration and fingerprinting was, upon conviction thereof, subject to a fine up to $1,000, imprisonment up to six months, or both. Any alien who failed to give written notice of change of address was, upon conviction thereof, fined up to $100, imprisoned up to thirty days, or both. Any alien who filed an application for registration containing false statements or who procured or attempted to procure registration through fraud was to be fined up to $1,000, imprisoned up to six months, or both. In addition, any alien so convicted within five years after entry into the United States was, upon the warrant of the Attorney General, to be taken into custody and deported.

In signing the Act, President Franklin Delano Roosevelt (FDR) argued that the law "should be interpreted and administered as a program designed not only for the protection of the country but also for the protection of the loyal aliens who are its guests." He argued that the registration and identification of approximately three and a half million aliens did not carry any stigma or implication of hostility toward those who, while they may not be citizens, were loyal to this country and its institutions. Roosevelt further stated:

> I ask that citizens and non-citizens alike cooperate with a full sense of the responsibilities involved so that we may accomplish this task of registration smoothly, quickly and in a friendly manner, our aim being to preserve and build up the loyalty and confidence of those aliens within our borders who desire to be faithful to its principles. With those aliens who are disloyal and are bent on harm to this country, the government, through its law enforcement agencies, can and will deal vigorously.[32]

Roosevelt also warned that the only effective system of control over aliens in this country must come from the federal government alone, and any attempts by the states or communities to deal with the problem individually "will result in undesirable confusion and duplication."[33]

Solicitor General Francis Biddle also made clear that state and local governments had to leave control of aliens to the federal government. While he welcomed the cooperation of states and local governments in the forthcoming alien registration drive, control of aliens was the duty of the federal authorities. Biddle said that the lack of uniformity in local

[32] "Roosevelt Signs Bill to List Aliens," *NYT*, June 30, 1940. [33] Ibid.

regulations would be one reason to avoid local alien control. If the regulation of one locality should be stricter than that of another, it would lead to migrations. Such migrations would not solve any alien problem but merely shift it from one locality to another.[34]

Alien registration became the responsibility of the DOJ. This was so since in May 1940 Roosevelt recommended that Congress shift the Immigration and Naturalization Service (INS) from the Department of Labor to the DOJ. This reorganization showed that the federal government increasingly thought of immigration as relating less to employment and more to national security.[35] Still, the *New York Times* argued that federal officials made it clear that "no alien who accepts the American form of government and respects American laws has anything to fear from the new set-up." Immigration would not be turned over to the FBI, "which may have implied that every alien was a suspected criminal."[36]

The *New York Times* stated that organizers were yet to work out the mechanics of the registration. "We may learn something from Great Britain," proclaimed the newspaper, noting that in Great Britain aliens remaining longer than three months had to register at the central police stations, get ID cards, and have facts about them go into special files. The government at all times had track of any given alien. "By the same token, his card is his protection as long as he behaves himself." The *New York Times* argued that the local police forces in American communities did not receive training for this kind of function, but INS officers could carry them out "kindly, efficiently, and firmly."[37]

While INS had its own Commissioner of Immigration and Naturalization, the authorities placed the entire INS under the direct supervision of Solicitor General Biddle, who was responsible in turn to Attorney General Jackson. The *New York Times* declared that both Biddle and Jackson "are known as liberals to whom the oppression of the foreign-born would be an outrage." To administer the provisions of the Act, INS established the Alien Registration Division (ARD), whose personnel "has been selected with infinite care."[38]

The person in charge of alien registration was Earl G. Harrison, a compassionate Philadelphia lawyer. Attorney General Jackson, a Democrat,

[34] "Biddle Opposes State Alien Rule," *NYT*, July 8, 1940.

[35] Vernon M. Briggs, Jr., "The Administration of U.S. Immigration Policy: Time for Another Change," *The Social Contract* (spring 1994): 194.

[36] "Alien Registration," *NYT*, May 25, 1940. [37] Ibid.

[38] Delbert Clark, "Aliens to Begin Registering Tuesday," *NYT*, August 25, 1940.

appointed Harrison, a Republican, as the Commissioner of Alien Registration at the suggestion of Solicitor General Biddle, also a Democrat. In his article reflecting on Harrison's life, Lewis Stevens, a member of the Philadelphia Bar, concluded that Harrison, while starting from scratch and with no precedents to guide him, "so brilliantly administered the project that instead of antagonizing the nation's future citizens, he actually achieved a better understanding between citizens and non-citizens." He even preferred the word "noncitizens" to that of "aliens." It was Harrison who "imaginatively suggested the use of the post offices" for registration and fingerprinting instead of police stations.[39]

Indeed, while the ARD at the DOJ had to carry out the job of registering and fingerprinting aliens, the Post Office Department had also helped in the massive undertaking. The two departments, in cooperation with the Census Bureau, had worked out the plans.[40] The Postmaster General was James A. Farley, a prominent national figure and Roosevelt's close political adviser up until their fallout in the run up to the 1940 election. Farley left the position in September 1940. Frank C. Walker, one of Roosevelt's closest advisers, replaced Farley. It was Farley's and then Walker's postmasters who greatly aided the registration.

In June 1940, Solicitor General Biddle announced that before actual registration, there would be an intensive education campaign to acquaint the aliens with what the authorities demanded of them. This would involve more than 1,000 foreign-language newspapers; hundreds of other publications, clubs, and churches having alien membership; radio stations that broadcast in foreign languages; and English-speaking groups that had contact with aliens. Biddle said that he would make an appeal for help to service groups such as the Lions, Rotary and Kiwanis Clubs, Chambers of Commerce, and the American Legion.[41]

The authorities estimated that the registration effort would cost the government $3.1 million.[42] They also estimated the number of aliens subject to the registration requirement at approximately 3.6 million.[43] One *New York Times* article found it strange that the government had no conclusive numbers on the number of aliens. "Odd as it may seem, the government has no accurate knowledge of how many aliens are actually in the country." The government had precise figures for many aliens, but

[39] Lewis M. Stevens, "The Life and Character of Earl G. Harrison," *University of Pennsylvania Law Review* 104, 5 (March 1956): 596–597.
[40] "Roosevelt Signs Bill." [41] Ibid. [42] Kluckhohn, "Aliens Now."
[43] "Alien Registering to Cover 3,600,000," *NYT*, July 31, 1940.

not for those who entered before 1924, the year when the present immigration laws went into effect. For them, there was no count at all.[44]

Government officials based the 1940 registration estimates in part on the 1930 census data, since the data from the census conducted in April 1940 was not available until May 1943.[45] The 1930 census revealed that the foreign-born population of the United States was 14,204,149. This comprised all persons born outside the country, except certain persons whose parents were American citizens. Of those, 7,919,536 were naturalized citizens and 6,284,613 were noncitizens. Of the 6,284,613 noncitizens, officials classified 4,518,341 as "alien," 499,853 as having an "unknown" status, and 1,266,419 as "having first papers." The "first papers" were the declaration of intention to become a US citizen. Any eligible alien eighteen years of age or older could make such declaration at any time after arrival in the United States. However, aliens usually could not complete the process of naturalization until at least two years (but no more than seven years) had elapsed after the declaration of intention, nor until the applicant had resided at least five years continuously in the United States.[46]

INS thought that the number of noncitizens shrank from 6,284,613 in 1930 to 3.6 million in 1940 due to naturalizations, deaths, and departures. INS estimated that 3.6 million would be subject to registration under the 1940 Act.[47] In the end, upward of 4.7 million people registered.[48] The 1940 census ultimately revealed that, as of April 1, 1940, there were 4,314,631 noncitizens in the United States. It also revealed that the foreign-born population of the United States was 11,594,896 people: 7,280,265 were naturalized citizens and 4,314,631 were noncitizens. Of the 4,314,631 noncitizens, officials classified 2,555,128 as "alien (no papers)," 834,979 as "foreign born, citizenship not reported," and 924,524 as "alien (first papers)."[49]

At a press conference on July 30, 1940, Harrison revealed the details of the vast undertaking. Authorities expected noncitizens to appear for

[44] Clark, "Aliens to Begin."

[45] Letter from J. C. Capt, Director of the Census, May 28, 1943, www2.census.gov/prod2/decennial/documents/33973538v2p1.pdf.

[46] 1930 Census, Volume II, General Report. Statistics by Subjects (Washington, DC: GPO, 1933), chapters 5 and 8.

[47] "Alien Registering."

[48] "Alien Total So Far Is Put at 4,741,971," *NYT*, January 13, 1941.

[49] 1940 Census, Volume II, Characteristics of the Population – Part I (Washington, DC: GPO, 1943), chapter 2.

registration and fingerprinting voluntarily. However, since the process was compulsory, officials were to seek out those failing to comply. On further refusal, such noncitizens were to be subject to the Act's penalties. Harrison reiterated the government's attitude that the registration and fingerprinting carried no stigma and that no "witch hunt" would result.[50]

Although the Act never mentioned the FBI, section 34 specified that persons or agencies designated by the Commissioner, with the approval of the Attorney General, should have access to all registration and fingerprint records. At a press conference on July 30, Harrison and Biddle announced that, as a measure of precaution, they were to forward millions of fingerprints to the FBI (at the DOJ) for retention in a separate file, where it would be possible to check them against FBI's own fingerprint file to discover criminal records or false statements of any kind. However, Harrison made it clear that he deemed most of the aliens to be law-abiding, peaceful people, and thought the disclosures would be comparatively few.[51]

Registration lasted from August 27 until December 26, 1940. Starting in mid-August, organizers made sample alien registration forms (AR-1) available at all 45,000 post offices. The four-page forms contained two pages of instructions and two pages of questions. The aliens had to take them home, fill them out, and return them to one of the 7,300 post offices designated as registration centers where they completed the actual forms (AR-2), swore to the truth of their statements, and submitted fingerprints for complete identification.

At the time, the press reported that an alien would later receive by mail "an identification card," which would be "protection to the alien" if he for any reason later ran afoul of the police.[52] One contemporary scholar writes that the card the aliens received "was tantamount to internal passport."[53] However, the document in question was simply an alien registration receipt card (AR-3). Once INS reviewed the registration documents and found them acceptable, it issued and mailed a receipt card bearing the registrant's name and address, their registration number, a signature, and a right index fingerprint.[54] Each alien who had complied

[50] "Alien Registering." [51] Ibid. [52] Ibid.; Clark, "Aliens to Begin."

[53] Roger Daniels, *Guarding the Golden Door: American Immigration Policy and Immigrants since 1882* (New York: Hill and Wang, 2004), 83.

[54] GAO, "Homeland Security. INS Cannot Locate Many Aliens Because It Lacks Reliable Address Information," November 2002, 31.

with the law received such alien registration receipt card as proof of compliance.[55] This card served as evidence of registration.

The card contained the following message from Earl Harrison: "Your registration under the Alien Registration Act, 1940, has been received and given the number shown above your name. This card is your receipt, and is evidence only of such registration. In writing to the Department of Justice about yourself, always give the number on this card." The card also reminded all resident aliens to report each change of address within five days. Other aliens, including visitors and students, were to report their address every three months whether they changed their address or not. The message continued: "Prepared forms for such address changes and reports may be obtained at any post office. A penalty of fine and imprisonment is provided by law for failure to make the reports … When reporting, give both your number and name." The aliens were told to send address letters and reports to the ARD at the DOJ in Washington, DC. Moreover, the alien registration receipt card should be sent there if it is found or if the person named on it departs from the United States, becomes naturalized, or dies.

Importantly, all aliens were required to have, but not to carry, a registration card. In contrast to the 1939 Pennsylvania Alien Registration Act, which required every alien over eighteen years old to carry an alien identification card at all times, the 1940 federal law embodied no requirement that aliens carry a registration card and show it to police. Under the 1940 Act, aliens did not need to carry registration cards, and authorities could not punish them for not carrying the cards.[56]

The 1940 Act made a willful failure to register and to give written notice of change of address a criminal offense. It was also an offense to file information known by the applicant to be false or to procure registration through fraud.

As part of the registration process, aliens had to answer fifteen detailed questions, most of them routine (name, age, physical facts, places and dates of arrival in the United States, employment and present citizenship status). However, the registration form also required each alien to list their membership or activities in all clubs, organizations, and societies in the past five years. Moreover, the form asked if an alien was engaged in influencing or furthering the political activities, public relations, or public policy of a foreign government. Other questions dealt with information

[55] "Alien Registration Reaches End Today," *NYT*, December 26, 1940.

[56] *Hines v. Davidowitz.*

on any past criminal record (except minor traffic violations), relatives, and military service for any country.[57]

The *New York Times* reported that even though registration was free, fraudsters were offering to "help" the foreign-born for suitable fees. Since many foreigners would be ignorant of what officials expected of them, Harrison announced that organizers would translate the fifteen questions into at least six foreign languages. Dissemination through the foreign-language press would carry the information into thirty languages in all.[58]

The *New York Times* speculated that the fact that it was common in most European countries to require universal registration and the carrying of ID cards should be of assistance in obtaining cheerful compliance with this law. The paper claimed, "it would, conceivably, be infinitely harder to accomplish a peaceable registration of all our citizens, although some advocate this on the ground that the registration of one group alone is discriminatory."[59]

Just as in 1918 the DOJ talked about WWI identification cards for German enemy aliens having a protective value, authorities now applied the same argument to all aliens. INS stressed from the start that the registration "would be in the nature of protection rather than surveillance" and would benefit the alien. "By the simple act of voluntarily registering and identifying himself, the alien is now safeguarded from bigoted persecution."[60]

Speaking on August 25, New York's Governor Herbert Lehman (D) said that the officials designed the registration process to protect the loyal aliens. "We intend to so act as to earn their trust and maintain their loyalty. They must so conduct themselves as to merit our trust and confidence." Lehman pointed out that the architects of the Act designed it so that the United States could determine exactly how many aliens were in the country, who they were, and where they were. Its proper execution would be a tremendous undertaking that would require the cooperation not only of all noncitizens but also of a great many citizens as well. Lehman added that it was his "sincere hope that the registration will be made the basis for a broad program of Americanization – a program designed to win and keep the loyalty of the three and a half million aliens in this country and eventually make them good American citizens."[61]

On August 24, New York City Mayor Fiorello La Guardia (R) issued a proclamation stressing that fingerprinting did not carry any stigma.

[57] "Alien Registering." [58] Ibid. [59] Clark, "Aliens to Begin." [60] Ibid.
[61] "Alien Registration Lauded by Lehman," *NYT*, August 26, 1940.

He said that the real purpose of fingerprinting was "to protect all law-abiding persons in the United States." He continued, "Fingerprinting is not degrading or humiliating. It is the most modern and scientific means of accurate identification." In his words, fingerprinting was no different from the recording of a signature, only more accurate.

The entire staff of the mayor's office had their fingerprints taken on August 27, the first day of registration. The mayor pointed out that facilities would be available throughout the city to citizens who wanted to record their fingerprints voluntarily. For added convenience, groups of ten or more people could request a visit of a fingerprinting expert at a time and place of their choosing.[62]

The mayor also pointed out that several million citizens had already voluntarily recorded their prints. The *New York Times* reported that at mayor's request, Lewis J. Valentine, the New York City Police Commissioner, prepared a report showing the value of fingerprinting for civilian identification. According to the *New York Times*, Commissioner Valentine pointed out that, unfortunately, newspapers have always associated the use of fingerprints only with criminals. Valentine stressed that civilian fingerprints do not connect to criminal records. According to him, people have overlooked and disregarded the many other useful purposes they serve. He listed the many instances in which the New York City departments took fingerprints. He also pointed out that banks have been using the fingerprint system to ensure positive identification of depositors who are unable to write, while the postal savings division of the post office has been using fingerprints as a means of identification of depositors for some time.[63]

Also on August 25, Solicitor General Biddle gave a radio address in which he tried to reassure aliens about the registration. He said, "It was not the intention of Congress to start a witch hunt or a program of persecution of peaceful and law-abiding aliens." He added that the Alien Registration Act calls for fingerprinting "because it is the most accurate and dependable method of identification known to science."

> Many people still feel that there is a stigma attached to being fingerprinted. I have been fingerprinted, as have millions of others who served in the armed forces of the United States. All Federal civil service [employees] are fingerprinted. Even postal savings depositors are fingerprinted. I assure you that there is no stigma attached to being fingerprinted in this day and age.
>
> We who are citizens view the law-abiding non-citizen of this country as a guest of the United States. You who are not as yet citizens should not consider

[62] Ibid. [63] Ibid.

registration as an imposition, but as a measure vital to the security of the United States – a measure designed to safeguard the national household in which you and your family make your home and livelihood. Consider registration in this light and you will interpret it not as an ordeal but as a patriotic duty.[64]

Government asked citizens to help encourage noncitizens to participate. Even the *American Journal of Nursing* contained a call for help:

[The INS] asks for the cooperation of all citizens in carrying out the Alien Registration program in a friendly manner so that our large foreign population is not antagonized. Citizens may be of great help to their non-citizen neighbors or relatives by explaining to those who do not speak English well what the registration is, where aliens go to register, and what information they must give.[65]

Government officials continued their efforts to reassure the aliens by continuing to stress that thousands of citizens submit to voluntarily fingerprinting every year. All members of the US Army and Navy had been fingerprinted, as had many government workers. Many hospitals established the practice of taking footprints of newly born babies.[66]

Noting that all Americans were at some point immigrants, Biddle made clear that he wanted officials to apprehend disloyal foreigners, but also to make sure that people did not unjustly condemn "loyal American aliens" for the disloyal behavior of the few. "Our legislation will be their protection from persecution."[67]

Registration proceeded smoothly. In Los Angeles, on the first day of registration, long before the doors of the local Alien Registration Center opened at 9 a.m., the first people arrived to tell Uncle Sam all about themselves in compliance with the law. Some foreign community leaders wanted journalists to photograph them as they were submitting fingerprints, as that would set a good example for their respective communities. The leaders believed that if the communities showed they were willing to cooperate with the government, the government would treat them fairly. By late afternoon on the first day, more than 500 aliens had registered. They included Mexicans, Japanese, Chinese, Poles, Germans, English, and Canadians. By late November 1940, some 80,000 of Los Angeles' estimated 125,000 aliens had already registered.[68]

64 Ibid.

65 "Alien Registration Required," *American Journal of Nursing* 40, 9 (September 1940), 985.

66 Ibid. 67 Ibid.

68 "Alien Registration Act of 1940," *Los Angeles Times*, February 14, 2012, http://framework.latimes.com/2012/02/14/alien-registration-act-of-1940/.

A *New Yorker* article in November 1940 described the registration procedure as simple and brief. While a few people were embarrassed to have their fingerprints taken, most dressed in their best clothes for the event and were quiet, cheerful, and cooperative.[69]

On January 12, 1941, the DOJ announced that the preliminary hand count of registration forms and fingerprint cards that poured into the Washington headquarters showed that 4,741,971 aliens had registered so far. Harrison pointed out that the figure was 1,141,971 above the preliminary estimate of 3,600,000. He also noted that "for a time" post offices were continuing to accept registrations. Officials were to conduct a machine count of registration cards in the spring.[70]

However, the registration process was not entirely without faults. One problem had to do with the citizenship status of people subject to registration. Apparently, people who were unsure of their status were required to register even if it was later determined that they were US citizens.[71] However, the Alien Registration Act contained no such language, and I have seen no evidence that US citizens registered under the Act. Nevertheless, in July 1940, the *New York Times* announced that those whose citizenship was doubtful despite their claims must register pending settlement of the facts.[72] In a January 1941 letter to the *New York Times*, Rosetta Oppenheimer of the New York Section of the National Council of Jewish Women wrote that her organization, which gave naturalization aid, found that many people "who are definitely citizens" had nevertheless registered as aliens "to be on the safe side." She argued that this was partially because it was difficult for derivative citizens to prove their status. Apparently, many of the derivative citizens had followed the advice of well-meaning but ill-informed friends, who argued, "if you haven't papers to prove citizenship, you are certainly an alien." According to Oppenheimer, these people were not aware that a person who derived citizenship through a parent or a husband did not necessarily have to have their own papers. She also pointed out that the instruction sheet and specimen form completely omitted any questions that might have brought out the fact of derivative citizenship, and thus help these people to understand their status more clearly.[73]

69 Lees, *Yugoslav-Americans*, 30. 70 "Alien Total."
71 USCIS, "Alien Registration Forms on Microfilm, 1940–1944," www.uscis.gov/history-and-genealogy/genealogy/alien-registration-forms-microfilm-1940–1944.
72 "Alien Registering." 73 "Unnecessary Alien Registration," *NYT*, January 17, 1941.

Another problem had to do with the mailing of registration receipt cards. In January 1941, the *Christian Century* revealed that organizers failed to send out in a timely fashion some of the receipts to those who had registered. Therefore, aliens could not prove that they had complied with the law. The magazine saw this as a violation of the government's pledge that it would not treat aliens with anything but tolerance and forbearance.[74]

Yet another problem had to do with the "change of address" requirement. All resident aliens, after registration, had to give notice within five days of any change of address, using change of address cards available at post offices. This requirement technically provided INS with the means to track and locate resident aliens while they were in the United States. INS considered the requirement important because it provided the only statutory method for keeping these aliens' locations current. However, as time progressed, this proved difficult.[75]

Initially, the process seems to have worked well. By February 1943, INS received 1.85 million notifications of changes of address. In 1943, the INS Commissioner reported that the information collected by the Alien Registration Program had been essential to preserving the nation's internal security.[76]

The INS was initially able to determine if an alien had complied with the change of address requirement because it maintained all address verification cards in the ARD headquarters. Hence, INS staff could review the change of address records to determine if an alien had provided a change of address. If no change of address card for a specific alien was in INS's centralized file, the INS could determine that it did not have a record showing that the alien had reported a change of address.[77]

However, by 1944, the ARD was increasingly unable to maintain current address information for aliens who were in the country. An estimated 5 to 40 percent of the registered aliens had moved without filing changes of address, and the US attorneys had generally refused to prosecute these violations. In addition, the Alien Registration Act did not require card owners or their relatives to report aliens' deaths and departures to the ARD,[78] even though the alien registration receipt card contained a message that the card "should be sent" there if the owner departed from the United States, naturalized, or died. Still, many aliens' deaths and departures went unreported, and hence it was impossible to

[74] Lees, *Yugoslav-Americans*, 220–221, fn. 83. [75] GAO, "Homeland Security."
[76] Ibid., 31. [77] Ibid., 18. [78] Ibid., 31–32.

maintain a file of aliens' address cards with any degree of accuracy. The government disbanded the ARD in December 1944.[79]

Despite those later problems, and despite some initial opposition to the program from certain civil liberties groups, most press accounts about the program (and the motivation behind it) were supportive. Even conservative *New York Times* correspondent Frank Kluckhohn wrote: "That a procedure should be adopted which hitherto always has been scorned as out of line with the American way of life is indicative of the seriousness with which the government regards the threat to its integrity and security" growing out of Nazi victories in Europe. Kluckhohn added that it was the knowledge of the part that "fifth columnists" played in Hitler's conquest of European countries that led Washington to take steps to deal with any subversive alien activities that could arise. The open objective of the registration program was to get a line on spies, saboteurs, and "fifth columnists" believed to be a small but important factor among the aliens. In addition, the government wanted to know which aliens were living near plants producing materials for national defense and near defense establishments and strategic points.[80]

By mid-1940, press accounts were full of items about "fifth columns," and many people supported registration of aliens. In a Gallup poll taken in 1939, 84 percent replied "yes" when asked whether they thought aliens should be registered and fingerprinted.[81]

In the minority opposing the registration were the ACLU and the Common Council for American Unity. In the spring of 1940, Alan Cranston, who served as the Council's Washington representative, wrote in the *Contemporary Jewish Record* that he feared that Congress would use the alien as "an official scapegoat for the nation's ills." Cranston predicted that alien registration would lead to a "domestic passport system," with citizens having "to produce evidence of citizenship or face arrest as suspected unregistered aliens." If even a few of these measures became law, he said, Congress "may one day be held in part responsible for the decline of American democracy."[82]

Once the administration declared registration "a necessary defense measure," Cranston's organization dropped its opposition to the program and he later praised Harrison, Biddle, and Jackson for developing a program that was educational and represented "Americanization at its best, aiming to draw the alien to America."[83]

[79] GAO, "Homeland Security," 31–32, 37. [80] Kluckhohn, "Aliens Now." [81] Ibid.
[82] Lees, *Yugoslav-Americans*, 23–24. [83] Ibid., 30.

One example of the educational efforts related to alien registration was a radio program, "Good Guests of America," produced by the DOJ, in which an alien of distinction advised other aliens about the merits of the registration program. In the first broadcast, in September 1940, novelist Thomas Mann eased the fears of a "Mr. Kirsch," who claimed the registration program signaled that he was not welcome and that American authorities were "angry with me," and possibly suspected that aliens belonged to the Fifth Column and were spies. Mann responded that America asked little of its guests other than registration, and in return provided "security and peace." He also explained the misuse of the term "fifth column." The "fifth column" of civilians who had brought victory to the fascists in Spain had been natives of the countries in question, not aliens. In any case, Mann speculated that aliens such as himself, who had fled tyranny in their native lands, might be more conscious of American freedoms and "anxious to defend them" than native-born citizens who accepted these rights "as a matter of course." Kirsch at last agreed with Mann and declared himself, as a member of the American community and an aspiring citizen, happy to register so "that democracy may be saved."[84]

In administering the alien registration program, Harrison did much to create a program that would safeguard America for both the foreign- and native-born. However, he never intended his official public service to be long term. When Jackson appointed Harrison in July 1940 to undertake the first national registration of the foreign-born, there was an understanding that he would remain only for six months. In January 1941, after serving for six months as Director of Alien Registration, Harrison resigned to return to private practice in Philadelphia.[85]

IDENTIFICATION DOCUMENTS FOR ENEMY ALIENS DURING WWII

Following the universal registration of all aliens in 1940, in late 1941 and early 1942 the United States imposed a new set of requirements aimed specifically at enemy aliens, namely, aliens residing in the United States who were nationals of countries with which the United States was now at war.

On December 7, 1941, immediately after the Japanese attack on Pearl Harbor, President Roosevelt invoked the Alien Enemies Act of

[84] Ibid., 29–30. [85] "Resigns Alien Registry Post," *NYT*, January 22, 1941.

1798 against Japanese nationals, and issued Presidential Proclamation 2525, designating Japanese aliens residing in the United States as enemy aliens and authorizing officials to detain those who were potentially dangerous. The next day he issued Presidential Proclamations 2526 and 2527, extending those regulations to German and Italian aliens. The government was to regulate individuals based on their enemy alien status, rather than based on evidence indicating sedition, espionage, or disloyalty. The DOJ took on the running of the Enemy Alien Control Program, and DOJ officials asked Earl Harrison to return to government. On December 7, Harrison agreed to work with the new Attorney General, Francis Biddle.[86]

After the United States declared war in December 1941, federal authorities used data gathered from the 1940 alien registration to estimate the number of enemy aliens. Of the close to 5 million aliens present in the country, the government estimated the number of enemy aliens at between 990,000 and 1,100,00, consisting of 90,000–92,000 Japanese, 300,000–315,000 Germans, and 600,000–695,000 Italians.[87]

Presidential Proclamations 2525, 2526, and 2527 banned enemy aliens from possessing firearms and ammunition and made clear that all such property found in the possession of any enemy alien would be subject to seizure and forfeiture. Attorney General Biddle ordered enemy aliens to surrender their firearms, radio transmitters, shortwave radio receivers, and cameras by January 5, 1942. In addition, the government curtailed freedom of travel of Japanese, German, and Italian nationals. The government allowed enemy aliens to travel in their local communities and engage in daily activities. It also allowed them to travel between their homes, places of employment, and government agencies. Before taking any other trips, enemy aliens had to give a week's notice to the US Attorney for their district, who could prohibit any such travel if it was "potentially dangerous to public safety." The government also prohibited enemy aliens from air travel.[88]

The alien registration of 1940 provided the DOJ with data that contributed to the roundup of some enemy aliens it considered dangerous. The government took 2,971 of them into custody by the end of December

[86] National Archives, "Brief Overview of the World War II Enemy Alien Control Program," www.archives.gov/research/immigration/enemy-aliens-overview.html; Stevens, "The Life," 597.

[87] Daniels, *Guarding the Golden Door*, 87.

[88] "Orders Axis Aliens to Give Up Arms," *NYT*, January 2, 1942.

1941. However, Attorney General Biddle stated that so long as an enemy alien conducted himself in accordance with the law he need fear no interference by the DOJ. "They may be assured," he declared, "that every effort will be made to protect them from any discrimination or abuse. This assurance is given not only in justice and decency to the loyal non-citizens in this country but also in the hope that it may spare American citizens in enemy countries unjust retaliation." The *New York Times* reported that in furtherance of this tolerant ideal, the DOJ discouraged alien registrations and roundups ordered by local police and municipal authorities in certain cities throughout the country as soon as the war broke out.[89]

The *New York Times* declared, perhaps sarcastically, that aside from the fact that the government asked all enemy aliens in the country to turn over firearms, radio transmitters, shortwave radio receivers, and cameras, and made them subject to certain requirements regarding travel, enemy aliens were "as free as the American born citizen of the country." Only those aliens who were disloyal to their adopted country should fear arrest, questioning, temporary custody, and possibly internment camps.[90]

Biddle pointed out that no one should discriminate against aliens in private employment. Such discrimination was shortsighted, wasteful, and un-American. It would create disunity. He also pointed out to employers who discharged men with foreign-sounding names that many of the "foreigners" they discharged had "sons serving in our Army and Navy" and that many American soldiers killed at Pearl Harbor had foreign-sounding names.[91]

On January 14, 1942, FDR issued Presidential Proclamation 2537, requiring every enemy alien of fourteen years of age or older to apply for and acquire a certificate of identification. He authorized the Attorney General to provide for the receiving of such applications and for the issuance of appropriate identification certificates. The proclamation stated that after the date fixed by the Attorney General for completion of such identification procedure, "every alien enemy within the United States, Puerto Rico, or the Virgin Islands shall at all times have his identification card on his person."[92] The proclamation interchangeably referred to a "certificate of identification," an "identification certificate," and an

[89] Robert F. Whitney, "Only 2,971 Enemy Aliens Are Held," *NYT*, January 4, 1942.
[90] Ibid. [91] Ibid.
[92] Presidential Proclamation 2537, January 14, 1942, Code of Federal Regulations, NAB; "For Enemy Alien, Listing," *NYT*, January 15, 1942.

"identification card," but there was no doubt that all enemy aliens were now required to apply for and carry the document in question at all times.

Following Roosevelt's proclamation, the DOJ issued instructions that all Japanese, German, and Italian aliens (i.e., those who had not yet acquired US citizenship) who were fourteen or older had to apply for certificates of identification. Enemy aliens were required to apply for certificate of identification at the post office nearest to their place of residence.[93] Aliens residing in California, Oregon, Washington, Montana, Nevada, Arizona, Utah, and Idaho were required to file their applications for certificates at their nearest post office between February 2 and 7, while those in other states were required to file between February 9 and 28.[94]

When applying, enemy aliens had to present their alien registration receipt card (which they received after they registered as aliens in 1940) and three recent 2 by 2 inch photographs.

Aliens did not have to incur any expenses other than obtaining the photographs.[95] At the post office, each enemy alien filled out an application form and submitted fingerprints.

The 1940 alien registration receipt card contained the registrant's name and address, their registration number, a signature, and a right index fingerprint. The 1942 certificate of identification contained not only the registrant's name and address, their alien registration number,[96] a signature, and a right index fingerprint, but also a photograph, date and place of birth, citizenship, length of residence in the United States, height, weight, hair color, and a note of any distinctive marks. The certificate also contained a signature of the Identification Official, date of issue, and a note that the application was filed in the ARD and a copy was filed with the local FBI office.

Enemy aliens received their certificates of identification at their place of residence.[97] Each holder of the certificate had to carry it and had to produce it if required by any police officer or another accredited official.[98]

The DOJ argued that the identification certificate would "protect an alien." An argument familiar from DOJ statements in 1918 (on

93 "Told to Get State Cards," *NYT*, January 26, 1942.

94 "Axis Aliens Warned on Identity Cards," *NYT*, January 25, 1942.

95 "Told to Get."

96 On the 1940 documents for all aliens, the number is called a "registration number," while on the 1942 documents for enemy aliens, the number is called an "alien registration number."

97 "Told to Get."

98 USCIS, "A-Files Image Gallery," www.uscis.gov/history-and-genealogy/genealogy/files-image-gallery.

identification cards for German enemy aliens) and from Roosevelt's and INS statements in 1940 (on registration for all aliens) was repeated, this time about enemy aliens. The DOJ again claimed that the new cards were to give evidence of aliens' peaceful disposition and of their desire to conform to American laws.[99]

Officials also argued that identification certificates were as vital for protection of the individual as for the government. According to Lawrence Camp, the US Attorney for the Northern District of Georgia, identification cards would aid in preventing disturbances arising from prejudice and would clarify the holder's status.[100] The *Atlanta Constitution* followed up by arguing that in times of peace as well as war, such cards would be valuable. "On the surface the plan may smack of authoritarian methods, but no conscience-clear man or woman should object. Its advantages would, apparently, far outweigh any small inconvenience involved."[101]

In a radio speech on February 1, 1942, Attorney General Biddle urged people not to persecute enemy aliens, and reminded them: "The alien of today is the citizen of tomorrow. Large numbers of those people we classify as alien enemies have American-born children – perhaps future leaders of our country." He explained that the DOJ's program of personal identification of enemy aliens "means adding vital information to the record we already have of these aliens. It means establishing their identities through signatures and photographs. And to each alien of enemy nationality so registered, it means the possession of a certificate of identification to be used at all times and in all places, for the duration of the war." Biddle described the identification program "as another part of the job of making America safe – safety for the nation against the small minority of alien enemies who may be contemplating trouble, and safety for the great majority of aliens who are above suspicion." He added: "because of the disloyal few, the many must be inconvenienced."[102]

Biddle warned enemy aliens that if they did not apply for certificates of identification by February 28, they faced possible internment. He noted a mistaken impression by some enemy aliens that registration under the 1940 law was sufficient. He emphasized that it was not.[103]

[99] "All Axis Aliens Must Get Certificates Next Week," *Los Angeles Times*, January 29, 1942.

[100] "Enemy Aliens Must Register," *Atlanta Constitution*, February 8, 1942.

[101] "Identification Cards," *Atlanta Constitution*, February 8, 1942.

[102] Francis Biddle, "Identification of Alien Enemies," Washington, DC, February 1, 1942, www.justice.gov/ag/aghistory/biddle/1942/02-01-1942.pdf.

[103] "Biddle Warns Aliens to Register by Today," *NYT*, February 28, 1942.

Yet not all aliens required to register were quick to do so. In New York, registration was proceeding more slowly than elsewhere in the country, according to Harrison, who became a Special Assistant to the Attorney General for issuing certificates of identification to enemy aliens.[104] In Fulton County, Georgia, in the first eight days of registration, with just thirteen days left to go, only 106 of 391 people subject to the registration had complied with the requirements. Postmaster Lon Livingston stated that once the registration period was over at the end of February, "aliens of the three countries we're fighting will be in a bad way if they don't have the identification cards." Interestingly, when the registration effort began in Georgia on February 9, special quarters were set up at the Old Post Office in Atlanta to shield the registrants from casual eyes. Newspapers pointed out that this was the fourth registration for Atlanta aliens: previously they were required to go through similar registrations with the state patrol, the city and police, and the first federal registration of August–December 1940.[105]

In early 1942, the government successfully completed the task of issuing certificates of identification to the roughly 1,100,000 enemy aliens. In July 1942, Harrison became the Commissioner for Immigration and Naturalization, a position he held until July 1944. Referring presumably to both the 1940 alien registration and the 1942 issuance of identification cards to enemy aliens, Attorney General Biddle said that registration "had first created a sense of terror," but because of Harrison's work registration "was finally looked upon as a sort of American Club." He added, "in many towns there was a waiting list to see who could register first." In recognition of his administration of alien registration and other successes, the American Committee for Protection of Foreign Born awarded Harrison its annual medal in 1943.[106] President Truman revoked the Presidential Proclamation 2537 in December 1945.

However, the issuing of certificates of identification to some 1,100,000 enemy aliens was only one part of the government's activities in early 1942. On February 19, FDR issued Executive Order 9066, which laid the foundation for the Japanese internment program on the West Coast. The order did not mention the Japanese by name, but it authorized the

[104] "Enemy Aliens Warned on Identity Card Delay," *NYT*, February 20, 1942; Stevens, "The Life," 597.
[105] "Fulton Aliens Are Slack in Registration," *Atlanta Constitution*, February 17, 1942.
[106] Stevens, "The Life," 597–598.

removal of any persons from designated military zones. Eventually, the order enabled the government to intern some 120,000 men, women, and children of Japanese ancestry, two-thirds of whom were US citizens. The government sent them to one of ten internment camps. Some of the interned stayed in confinement for almost four years. In 1942, the government established special identification tags with family number for persons of Japanese ancestry. People of all ages were required to hang the special tags from the lapel of their outer clothing. The government discontinued the tags by 1946. It was not until 1976, the thirty-fourth anniversary of FDR's internment order, that President Ford issued a proclamation revoking the order.[107]

Interestingly, the US government was not the only entity that issued identification documents for aliens and enemy aliens during WWII. The Japanese American Citizens League started issuing certificates of identification to its members, who were all US citizens. The certificates contained a photograph, basic biographical information, a right index fingerprint, and an accompanying oath of allegiance to defend the United States.[108]

Even those not classified as enemy aliens felt that having identification documents might be useful. Following the December 7, 1941, Pearl Harbor attack, Chinese-Americans anticipated that hostility toward the Japanese may be directed toward them so they went to great lengths to not be misidentified as Japanese. On December 8, T. K. Chang, the Chinese consul in Los Angeles, said that the Chinese in America were designing a lapel button that would show the nationality of the wearer. Dr. Kiang Yiaseng, the Chinese consul in Seattle, had ordered ID cards for all Seattle Chinese to distinguish them from the Japanese.[109]

PROPOSALS FOR NATIONAL ID CARDS AND UNIVERSAL FINGERPRINTING OF US CITIZENS DURING WWII

During WWII, several congressmen, organizations, and private citizens introduced proposals for national ID cards and universal fingerprinting,

[107] Roger Daniels, "Incarceration of the Japanese Americans: A Sixty-Year Perspective," *The History Teacher* 35, 3 (May 2002): 297–310.

[108] Densho Encyclopedia, "Primary Source," http://encyclopedia.densho.org/sources/en-denshopd-p25-00015-1/.

[109] "Chinese in U.S. Want No Identification Errors," *Atlanta Constitution*, December 9, 1941.

though none of the proposals was ultimately successful. Despite modern-day claims that the American people despise national ID cards, the historical evidence suggests that ID card proposals have generated not only significant opposition, but also significant support.

Many people wrote letters to Congress and to newspapers either in support of or in opposition to ID card legislation during WWII. This book is the first to analyze the letters. Those letters show us the side of the story we have not seen before, namely, what regular Americans thought about identification documents.

My examination of the legislative histories of the relevant bills reveals a true range of attitudes toward national ID cards and universal fingerprinting. The records of the House and Senate Judiciary Committees, to which the bills were referred, are helpful in understanding those attitudes. Since most of the WWII bills on national ID cards and universal fingerprinting originated in the House, the letters sent to Rep. Hatton W. Sumners (D-TX), Chairman of the House Judiciary Committee between 1931 and 1947, are of particular importance.

The first attempts to introduce universal fingerprinting (though not national ID cards) occurred in the 76th Congress (1939–1941). On January 13, 1939, Rep. William Miller (R-CT) introduced H.R.2554, a bill to provide for universal fingerprinting. If the bill passed, it would have become the Universal Fingerprinting Act of 1939. The bill required every person residing in the United States not attending a primary or grade school or below the entrance age to such school to report to the post office nearest to their place of abode for fingerprinting within sixty days of the Act's approval. The superintendent of every primary or grade school was to arrange with the Director of the FBI to have the fingerprint record of all schoolchildren made at their school buildings.[110]

H.R.2554 also proposed what the Smith Act ultimately implemented in June 1940, namely, that officials should not issue immigrant visas to aliens seeking to enter the United States unless the aliens submitted fingerprints. Aliens who procured their visas before this Act became effective would have to submit fingerprints at the port of entry.

Failure to the comply with the Universal Fingerprinting Act would have been punished by a fine of no more than $10,000, imprisonment of no more than five years, or both. In case of an alien, the punishment would also involve deportation.

110 H.R.2554, Box 268, House Records, 76th Congress, RG 233, NAB.

The National Archives contain just a handful of documents regarding H.R.2554. These documents show that the idea of universal fingerprinting generated both opposition and support.

Opposition to H.R.2554 was apparent in a March 1939 letter from the Acting Postmaster General, W. W. Howes, to Chairman Sumners. Howes did not like that the measure would require postal employees to record fingerprint impressions of practically the entire adult population of the country, within the limited period of sixty days. His letter stated:

> In view of the short time within which the fingerprinting at post offices is to be accomplished, of the limited personnel which could be properly assigned to such work without interference with the functions of the postal office, and of the fact that no provision is made by the bill for reimbursing the Post Office Department for the services to be performed by its personnel, we are opposed to the enactment of this measure.[111]

It is interesting that the focus here was just on practical difficulties of implementing universal fingerprinting. The National Archives file on H.R.2554 contains no letters criticizing the bill for being anti-American or detrimental to civil liberties. Such opinions must have been present (similar bills at other times during WWII generated plenty of them), but, for whatever reason, no letters containing them have been preserved.

Support for proposals embodied in H.R.2554 was evident in a letter from Mr. W. Innes Forbes, the Commander-in-Chief of the Military Order of the Loyal Legion of the United States, a post–Civil War fraternity. In January 1939, just a few days before Rep. Miller introduced his bill, Forbes wrote to Chairman Sumners to notify him of the resolution adopted by the Order at its October 1938 meeting. The resolution urged Congress to enact legislation requiring registration by fingerprinting of all persons in the United States for record in a noncriminal file (unless there was disclosure of criminal associations). Such registration should take place under the direction of the DOJ. The resolution argued that "universal fingerprinting and registration of all persons in the United States would not only greatly facilitate enforcement of law, but also definitely tend to prevent lawlessness through fixation of individual responsibility and the enhancement of the danger of detection."

In the end, nothing came out of H.R.2554. Materials at the National Archives indicate that the 76th Congress saw another effort to introduce universal fingerprinting, but it also failed: in June 1940, the Federal

[111] Ibid.

Grand Jury Association of the Southern District of New York proposed a bill on registration and fingerprinting, but it did not get through Congress.[112] In June 1942, the Associated Press reported that an attempt to enact mandatory fingerprinting legislation was defeated in 1940 "chiefly because of the cost of the project."[113]

While the 76th Congress saw efforts to introduce universal fingerprinting, the 77th Congress (1941–1943) saw efforts to introduce both universal fingerprinting and national ID cards. Shortly after Pearl Harbor, on December 17, 1941, Rep. Carter Manasco (D-AL) introduced H.R.6256, a bill to require all US citizens over the age of sixteen to carry identification cards and be fingerprinted. The bill was referred to the House Judiciary Committee. If it passed, it would have become the Citizen Identification Act of 1942.[114]

Also on December 17, Manasco introduced H.R.6258, a bill to require all aliens in the United States to carry identification cards and be fingerprinted. If the alien was too young to make application for an identification card, the nearest kin or legal guardian had to make the application. The rest of the bill read just like H.R.6256, but since it concerned aliens, H.R.6258 was referred to the Committee on Immigration and Naturalization. If the bill passed, it would have become the Alien Identification Act of 1942.[115]

Nothing ultimately came out of either bill, but the bill concerning US citizens generated a lot of attention. H.R.6256 would have applied to anyone who on or after the date of the enactment was sixteen or more years old and who was either a US citizen or a citizen of an insular possession of the United States. Every person subject to this legislation would have to apply for registration and fingerprinting, and would have to submit under oath the information required for identification. The president would issue to every such person an identification card that would contain a general description of such person, including his name, sex, and date of birth; his fingerprints; and whether he was a native-born or naturalized citizen and, if naturalized, the time and place of naturalization. People would have to carry the identification cards with them at all times when away from home.

[112] S.313, Box 12, Records of the U.S. Senate (Senate Records), 78th Congress, RG 46, NAB.

[113] H.R.6256, Box 149, Senate Records, 77th Congress, RG 233, NAB.

[114] Ibid.

[115] H.R.6258, Box 149, House Records, 77th Congress, RG 233, NAB.

Even though the bill was introduced right after the shocking attack on Pearl Harbor, many people wrote to Chairman Sumners asking him to defeat H.R.6256. Most of the preserved letters and postcards date to June 1942. Even though it was at the height of the US war effort, and one would think Americans would universally support a legislative proposal aimed at helping in the war effort, many people strongly opposed the measure.

Some people gave no reasons for their opposition. Other people said the bill would set up two classes of citizenship. Others still wrote that the bill is "very undemocratic and un-American," and they are "very much opposed to placing all our people under such restrictions." Miss Rose Kerrett of New York City wrote that "fingerprinting of every person in this country might lead to restriction of our liberty." She added that mass fingerprinting "might bring in its wake extortion and blackmail. People who were trying to lead decent, upright lives would live in constant fear and misery." She did not explain why. One unique argument came from a woman in Brooklyn who wrote to Sumners that she opposed H.R.6256 because identification cards would enable employers to discriminate against older job seekers upon learning their true age. Some described any new bill as "Hitler's."[116] While references to Hitler were rare, the notion that ID cards were "un-American" was one that was brought up by opponents repeatedly not only during WWII, but also earlier, during WWI, and later, for the rest of the twentieth century; and it is still being brought up today.

However, there was also significant support for H.R.6256. The International Association of Chiefs of Police, headquartered in Washington, DC, gave its unequivocal approval for universal fingerprinting and compulsory identification cards for all US citizens. In March 1942, Edward Kelly, the Executive Secretary, wrote letters to Chairman Sumners and to members of the House of Representatives, saying that for over forty years the Association had been urging legislation along similar lines. Such legislation "would permit the immediate and positive identity of persons losing their lives in disasters and afford some means of identifying the great number of unknown dead reported each year."

The Association added, "H.R.6256 is of particular importance at this time when there is great possibility of enemy air raids. The resulting causalities would include a large number of maimed bodies, the

[116] H.R.6256, Box 149, House Records, 77th Congress, RG 233, NAB.

identification of which would be impossible at the present time because of lack of national file of fingerprints of all citizens." The Association made a very important point that "the Alien Registration Act extends this protection of assured identity to aliens, and our citizens should be permitted to enjoy the same security." Stressing that aliens had a protection that the citizens lacked was a persuasive argument.

The International Association of Chiefs of Police felt so strongly about national ID cards that it urged Congress to support H.R.6256 "not only as a vitally needed emergency measure but also as a statute which would be of equal value in times of peace." Support for peacetime national ID cards was also evident among members of Congress. For instance, Rep. Philip Traynor (D-DE) expressed his support for H.R.6256 in a March 1942 letter to Sumners, in which he said that "this worthwhile measure" should be supported "especially for the duration of the war, and also afterwards."

Individual police departments also wrote in support of H.R.6256. In February 1942, Mr. B. C. Bridges, Superintendent of the Bureau of Identification, Alameda Police Department, in Alameda, California, wrote to Chairman Sumners that the bill "is one of the most excellent contributions to war-time efficiency." He claimed that in addition to the large social and economic importance of fingerprinting, "the identification of subversive persons is a requirement vital to your safety and mine, and to our country's welfare. Sporadic fingerprinting can never accomplish this. It is plain that such identification is possible through all-inclusive registration only. Fingerprinting is a national necessity at this time."

Another voice of support for H.R.6256 came from the International Association for Identification (IAI), the world's leading forensic science identification association, established in 1915. The IAI first expressed hope for universal fingerprinting in a resolution adopted in 1927. On September 11, 1942, the IAI unanimously passed a resolution in support of H.R.6256. In sending the copies of the 1942 resolution to the President of the United States, the Secretary of War, the Attorney General, the Chairman of the House Judiciary Committee, and the Director of the FBI, among others, the IAI offered its services in a consultant capacity should the government plan and execute the universal fingerprinting project.

Yet another letter in support of H.R.6256 came from the American Legion, a veterans' organization. Mr. June Valiant, adjutant for the organization's Oregon Department, wrote in February 1942 that there is no better way of providing security for this great nation than through universal fingerprinting. He even suggested fingerprinting those below sixteen years of age. The fingerprinting would be primarily for the protection of the fingerprinted individual. Valiant added that in his many years of Legion work he found fingerprints to be of inestimable value in apprehension of criminals and identifying unknown deceased persons and amnesia victims. He concluded that fingerprinting of individuals "is not in any sense interfering with civil liberties and the opposition to this plan is fostered primarily by persons with ulterior motives."

Police professionals, forensic experts, veterans, and members of Congress were not the only ones favoring universal fingerprinting and national ID cards. Some ordinary people did, too.

One such example was Mrs. Brimmer from Jacksonville, Florida. In November 1942, she wrote, "With everyone being fingerprinted, there will be no stigma. And surely the right kind of people will not object to being fingerprinted when it means so much to our country."

A more striking example of an ordinary person's support for universal fingerprinting and national ID cards came from Mrs. Lucille Tull Kopp of Cos Cob, Connecticut. In February 1942, she wrote to Sumners urging not only the passage of H.R.6256, but even the bill's enlargement. Kopp told Sumners that before she even knew of the bill, she devised a plan that "goes even further and will not only serve as means of identification, but as a continuous check up on the movements of everyone" in the United States and would also "help eliminate the undesirable." She even sent her plan to President Roosevelt.

Kopp's plan was to register and fingerprint all residents of the United States, regardless of age. She saw her plan as a way to "fine-comb the entire nation and help rid our country of all the vermin and rats, whether we call them Fifth Columnists, Enemy Aliens, Spies or by any other name." If a person goes away (to visit to a private household or a hotel) and remains there for more than twenty-four hours, he or she would have to be registered with local police. In addition, all employers would have to verify credentials of all employees, and schools and colleges would have to do the same for students. While nothing came out of Kopp's plan, it is interesting to think that despite her incendiary talk of "vermin and rats," she was decades ahead of her time in her proposals for employment verification.

Other people also felt passionate about issues of universal fingerprinting and personal identification. Herman Doepner of St. Paul, Minnesota, who had been interested in fingerprinting for the previous sixteen years, wrote to the House Judiciary Committee on March 13, 1942.

In the letter, Doepner discussed the technicalities of fingerprinting, and, while supportive of universal fingerprinting, he pointed out many potential obstacles.

One of the obstacles would be the FBI's inability to fingerprint more than 100 million people. Doepner insisted such inability was evident in a report of the committee on universal fingerprinting made to the 1940 convention of the IAI. The report admitted that the FBI system could not handle the nation's prints in the event of adoption of universal fingerprinting. It recommended a system of registration by states.

Doepner also pointed out a huge backlog currently at the FBI. Apparently, at the 1941 convention of the IAI, an FBI representative reported that the Bureau had a staff of seventy-five experts devising means of expanding the system to cope with the normal intake of prints. The representative also reported that about half of the prints of WWI soldiers remained unclassified after twenty-five years.

Another obstacle was the popular association of fingerprinting with criminals. Doepner wrote that the public's prejudice to fingerprinting in the past rose because authorities used fingerprinting exclusively with criminals. Any system of personal identification in the United States "can and should be adopted primarily because there are more social benefits to non-criminal identifications than in criminal ones." Therefore, neither the FBI nor the DOJ should oversee universal fingerprinting. Doepner also warned against using post offices for taking fingerprints, as they were not technically prepared for it. Rather, the government should create a separate department.

Those were not the only obstacles. Doepner estimated that it would take six months to train new fingerprinting experts, and then it would take a year for some eight thousand clerks to classify 100 million prints. He even pointed out that universal fingerprinting would require "miles upon miles of steel filing cabinets." With the war on, obtaining steel for filing cabinets would be a significant problem.

Doepner made another important point: "Because personal identity records in years to come will be a vast national asset, the department should be located away from the national capital, to avoid capture in time of war. It would be difficult to transport them in cases of emergency, and to destroy them would be expensive and foolish."

Doepner summarized, "There are many benefits to be derived from universal fingerprinting, and many advocates for it. However, the problem is so complex and vast that it would take at least a solid year of preparatory work after passage of the law to make it effective."

Until a national universal fingerprinting law could operate efficiently, Doepner advocated for a temporary system where all citizens were fingerprinted in duplicate and required to carry one identification card on them and leave the other one at home with the head of the family.

In another letter, on March 19, 1942, Doepner claimed, "The profession is quite unprepared for universal fingerprinting." He wrote:

> I cannot be too emphatic in cautioning extreme foresight in fingerprint legislation. I as much as anyone else in this country appreciate personal identification needs along national lines, but I also realize that there are prerequisites which must first be met if we are to establish universal fingerprinting upon technically sound foundations, instead of risking a national fiasco of great proportions.

Doepner continued his warnings: "Correspondence schools and police organizations have been unremitting in fostering and advocating universal fingerprinting, motivated mostly by desires to advance their own interests, but their technical theories and practices are not quite equal to the demands." Doepner concluded his second letter: "A fingerprint law is necessary, but its contents should be carefully considered."

While nothing came out of Manasco's bill, H.R.6256, the press expectations, as late as June 1942, were that there was "a strong possibility" that Congress would make universal fingerprinting "mandatory for every man, woman, and child in the country." The Associated Press made such prediction in June 1942, after an official disclosure that a big percentage of the nation's population already submitted fingerprints because of the war.

In testimony made public by the House Appropriations Committee, S. A. Andretta, an administrative assistant at the DOJ, said that the Bureau had "continued to receive a tremendous number of fingerprint records," resulting chiefly from Army and Navy demands that all employees in war industries were fingerprinted. He added that fingerprint records were pouring in at the rate of 60,000 a day. In anticipation of continued demand, the FBI purchased 48 million fingerprint cards in 1942.

One legislator, unnamed by the Associated Press, concluded: "With the boys in the Army and those in the war industries being fingerprinted, there can be no valid objection from the rest of the population. Besides, it would prove extremely valuable as a civilian defense measure in the event of an aerial attack."

Attorney General Biddle also stressed the growing importance of fingerprinting. In a July 1942 letter to Sumners, Biddle emphasized the tremendous growth of the central repository for criminal fingerprints established by the FBI only eighteen years prior, in 1924. The criminal fingerprint files grew to 11,670,008 by June 30, 1942. The value of fingerprinting for identification purposes became recognized so that instead of being limited to its use in the enforcement of the criminal law, it was gradually extended for other purposes to large groups of the civilian population. Thus, the entire personnel of the US armed forces had been fingerprinted, and persons joining the armed forces were fingerprinted as they were inducted, enlisted, or commissioned. All government employees had been fingerprinted. All aliens in the United States were fingerprinted pursuant to the requirements of the Alien Registration Act. More recently, at the request of the War and Navy Departments, the fingerprinting of all employees of national defense plants was undertaken. In addition, numerous individuals, either singly or in groups, deposited their fingerprints with the FBI for purposes of individual identification. There were 42,874,078 fingerprints on file in the FBI on June 30, 1942. FBI received additional fingerprints at the rate of over 100,000 a day.

Despite stressing the growing importance of fingerprinting in the letter, Biddle failed to support Manasco's bill. He said that fingerprinting the remainder of the population of the United States at one time and the issuance of identification cards to all persons who were or would be fingerprinted would be a "stupendous task." It would require a large staff, a great quantity of equipment and supplies, and a great amount of building space to store the records. He pointed out that no attempt had been made to calculate the cost of the proposed undertaking, "but it is safe to say that it would aggregate a very large sum of money." Biddle added that the Director of the Bureau of the Budget advised him that the enactment of the legislation would not be in accord with the program of the president, at least at the time.[117]

In the end, nothing came out of H.R.6256. Despite support of police professionals, forensic experts, veterans, and congressmen, this attempt to introduce universal fingerprinting and national ID cards for all Americans over the age of sixteen died in 1942.

In the 78th Congress (1943–1945), there were more national ID card bills and more evidence of how much passion some of the ID card proposals started to generate. January 1943 saw the introduction of two identical national ID card bills: one in the House (H.R.1032) and one in the Senate (S.313).

117 Ibid.

On January 11, 1943, Rep. Raymond Springer (R-IN) introduced bill H.R.1032, which would require all US citizens over the age of sixteen to carry identification cards and be fingerprinted. Springer was a judge, WWI veteran, and unsuccessful candidate for governor of Indiana in the 1930s. He served in Congress from 1939 until his death in 1947. He pushed for identification cards for all US citizens over sixteen years old with at least three separate bills, and with perfect regularity: in January 1943, January 1945 (H.R.601), and January 1947 (H.R.318).

We know little about the fate of H.R.1032, other than that it was referred to the Committee on the Judiciary. Documents preserved at the National Archives reveal that several people and organizations subsequently wrote to Chairman Sumners about the bill. Some, like the Sorosis Club of Topeka, Indiana, a professional women's club, asked Sumners in November 1943 to move H.R.1032 out of committee so that congressmen could fully discuss it on the floor of the House. Others expressed interest in any developments with respect to the bill and asked Sumners to keep them informed of future hearings, but they did not express either support or opposition to the bill. This was in great contrast to S.313, a bill identical to H.R.1032, but introduced in the Senate. It is unclear if S.313 truly generated more opposition than H.R.1032 or if the documents showing the opposition to S.313 were simply preserved at a greater rate.[118]

On January 11, 1943, Senator Monrad Wallgren (D-WA) introduced bill S.313 that, just like H.R.1032, would require all US citizens over sixteen years old to carry identification cards and to be fingerprinted.[119] Wallgren was good friends with Harry Truman and would later become the governor of Washington.

If the Senate and the House enacted H.R.1032 or S.313, the legislation would have become the Citizen Identification Act of 1943. This legislation would apply to all those who were citizens of the United States (including citizens of US territories and possessions and the Panama Canal Zone) over sixteen years old.

Bill S.313, just like H.R.1032, read that the identification card shall contain a general description of the holder, including name, sex, date of birth, and whether the person was a native-born or naturalized citizen and, if naturalized, the time and place of naturalization. The identification

118 H.R.1032, Box 106, House Records, 78th Congress, RG 233, NAB.
119 S.313, Box 12, Senate Records, 78th Congress, RG 46, NAB.

card would also contain a person's fingerprints. Any person subject to the legislation would have to carry the identification card "on his person at all times while away from his home."

In addition, bill S.313, just like H.R.1032, read that application for identification cards should be made within sixty days after the date of the enactment of the Act. Every person who became subject to the Act after the date of its enactment should apply for identification and fingerprinting. Such person would need to apply within 120 days of becoming subject or within 120 days after the date of the enactment, whichever is later. Anyone convicted of failing to comply with the Act would be subject to a fine of up to $1,000, imprisonment of up to six months, or both. Each day of failure to comply would constitute a separate offense. Individuals would have to submit all information under oath. If authorities found that anyone made false statements knowingly, and if they convicted them, such person would be subject to a fine of up to $1,000, imprisonment of up to six months, or both. Anyone convicted of reproducing or forging an identification card would be subject to a fine of up to $5,000, imprisonment of up to five years, or both.[120]

Bill S.313 was referred to the Senate Committee on the Judiciary, chaired, between 1941 and 1945, by Senator Frederick Van Nuys (D-IN). Many individuals and organizations subsequently sent letters to Chairman Van Nuys about S.313.

In late April and throughout May 1943 multiple letter writers asked for S.313 to be defeated in committee. Many people did not give any reasons for their opposition, but others said they opposed the Wallgren bill since "such proposals are un-American." Miss Ida Hyman of New Jersey wrote that the bill un-American, undemocratic, and "against everything for which we are now fighting." Another person felt the bill was "reminiscent of the methods used in the old Czarist Russia and revived under the Gestapo of Germany," and she felt that such a law should not exist in a democracy. Another woman said the bill smacked "of the Gestapo surveillance." Miss Rose Leonard from Pennsylvania wrote that the ID law would be "contrary to the free spirit of our democratic land." Mrs. Magen of Philadelphia wrote that this bill represented "a bigoted and reactionary outlook" and was "a definite infringement on our Bill of Rights." She added, "Our boys are fighting for a better world and we at home should do our very utmost to achieve their and our ideals." Passage

[120] Ibid.

of the Wallgren bill "would be a step backwards." This set of letters is a great example of the kind of arguments historically used against national ID cards.

Most of those who wrote were women; many were from Pennsylvania, New Jersey, and New York. Some identified themselves as members of the Women's Division of the American Jewish Congress. At least one of the male writers also identified himself as a member of the American Jewish Congress. Interestingly, some of the letters came from rather random places, including a department store and a hardware store, both in Tupper Lake, New York. In May 1943, even the New Haven Fruit and Vegetable Peddlers' Protective Association wrote to Chairman Van Nuys to oppose the S.313 bill.[121]

Interestingly, the National Archives file concerning S.313 contains only one letter in support of S.313, and about sixty letters against it. Mixed responses to similar bills indicate that it is unlikely that there was simply more opposition to the bill than support for it. More likely, officials were selective in saving the letters.

The one letter in support of S.313 came from the Federal Grand Jury Association of the Southern District of New York. Their motto was "fewer and better laws" – some may argue that it was ironic that an organization with such a motto would support this bill, while others would argue the opposite. In an October 1943 letter to Chairman Van Nuys they recommended passage of the S.313 bill, claiming that it "generally follows and gives effect" to a similar bill that they proposed in June 1940.

On June 9, 1943, Senator William Langer (R-ND) introduced a bill that was almost identical to Wallgren's S.313 bill. The Langer bill, S.1191, would also require US citizens to carry identification cards and be fingerprinted, but it would require it from those over twelve years old, rather than sixteen. Like S.313, S.1191 was referred to the Senate Committee on the Judiciary. If Congress enacted it, the bill would have become the Citizen Identification Act of 1943.[122]

The Langer bill read that people would have to apply for identification cards within 90 (rather than 60) days after the date of the enactment. Everyone who became subject to the Act after the date of enactment would have to apply for identification and fingerprinting within 30 (rather than 120) days of becoming subject or within 90 (rather than

[121] Ibid. [122] S.1191, Box 42, Senate Records, 78th Congress, RG 46, NAB.

120) days after the date of the enactment, whichever is later. Some fines in the Langer bill were less strict, while others were stricter than in the Wallgren bill. Anyone failing to comply with the Act would upon conviction be subject to a fine of up to $500 (rather than $1,000), imprisonment of up to a year (rather than six months), or both. Each day of failure to comply would constitute a separate offense. Individuals would have to submit all information under oath. If authorities found that anyone made false statements knowingly, and if they convicted them, such person would be subject to a fine of up to $1,000 (same as in the Wallgren bill), imprisonment of up to two years (rather than six months), or both. Anyone convicted of reproducing or forging an identification card would be subject to a fine of up to $1,000 (rather than $5,000), imprisonment of up to two (rather than five) years, or both.

Langer's legislation that provided for the fingerprinting of every American twelve years of age or older proved unsuccessful. Controversies surrounding him might have had something to do with this. Opponents accused Langer of political corruption while he was governor of North Dakota in the 1930s. A US Senate committee even found him guilty of "moral turpitude." He remained a controversial figure, though some of his positions, like his support for implementing affordable health care for everyone, were also ahead of his time.[123] While the biography of Langer does not talk about the fingerprinting bill, Langer's support for a national ID card for the United States could not have happened because of an emulation of the United Kingdom. He was an isolationist and had "a hatred of England that was almost a phobia."[124]

The National Archives contain little documentation regarding the public's feelings toward the Langer bill, but the remaining documents show that at least one organization was in favor of the bill. In May 1943, the Disabled American Veterans created a draft statement in which they listed the benefits of fingerprinting and identification cards. The organization claimed that "no law-abiding citizen is fearful of having his fingerprints recorded with a federal agency." The organization expressed support for legislation similar to the Langer bill and, pending the enactment of such proposed legislation, urged all national veteran organizations

[123] U.S. Senate, "The Expulsion Case of William Langer of North Dakota," www.senate.gov/artandhistory/history/common/expulsion_cases/123WilliamLanger_expulsion.htm.

[124] Agnes Geelan, *The Dakota Maverick: The Political Life of William Langer, also Known as "Wild Bill" Langer* (Fargo: Kaye's Printing Company, 1975), 112, 116.

and other patriotic, social, and civil organizations to conduct local campaigns to bring about the voluntary fingerprinting of all persons within their respective communities. It even seems that the North Dakota chapter of the group drafted S.1191 for Langer, or at least they assisted each other in drafting it. While having a stake in S.1191, the Disabled American Veterans also cared about the earlier ID card bills. In June 1943, they informed Chairman Van Nuys of their interest in testifying about the S.313 bill. They also informed Chairman Sumners of their interest in testifying about the H.R.1032 bill.[125]

Bills H.R.1032, S.313, and S.1191 did not indicate which agency would administer the Citizen Identification Act. On September 7, 1943, Attorney General Biddle wrote to Chairman Van Nuys regarding S.1191, and on October 15, 1943 Biddle wrote to Van Nuys regarding S.313. Both letters expressed exactly the same opinion on each bill. Biddle wrote that he would not be expressing any views as to the merits of the proposed legislation, but he wanted to call attention to the fact that the bills entirely overlooked the existence of the Identification Division at the FBI, which was a central depository for millions of fingerprints. He further claimed that the bills overlooked the fact that throughout the United States there were law enforcement officers who were thoroughly familiar with the technique of taking fingerprints. He added, "Any attempt on the part of inexperienced individuals to take fingerprints is apt to create confusion and delay." Biddle suggested that if the bills were to receive favorable consideration, legislators would have to amend them to vest in the FBI the duty of taking, classifying, and filing fingerprints, and the issuance of identification cards. Legislators would also have to authorize the Bureau to designate state and local law enforcement officers as agents for the taking of fingerprints and receiving applications for identification cards.[126]

Very importantly, however, Biddle added that, according to the Director of the Bureau of the Budget, this legislation was not in accord with the program of the president. Since there seems to have been some bad blood between FDR and Chairman Van Nuys dating back to the 1930s,[127] one can wonder if that could have played a role in Roosevelt's opposition.

125 S.1191, Box 42, Senate Records, 78th Congress, RG 46, NAB.
126 Ibid.; S.313, Box 12, Senate Records, 78th Congress, RG 46, NAB.
127 New Netherland Institute, "Frederick Van Nuys," www.newnetherlandinstitute.org/history-and-heritage/dutch_americans/frederick-van-nuys/.

This, however, was not the end of ID card proposals during WWII. Rep. Springer was the author not only of H.R.1032 from 1943, but also of two additional bills. In the 79th Congress (1945–1947), on January 3, 1945, Springer introduced H.R.601, which, like his bill H.R.1032, would have required all US citizens over the age of sixteen to carry identification cards and to be fingerprinted.

We know little about the fate of H.R.601, other than that it was referred to the Committee on the Judiciary. In April 1945, the Federal Grand Jury Association of the Southern District of New York wrote to Springer to support H.R.601. However, while in the 78th Congress they supported S.313, which would have required all US citizens over the age of sixteen to carry identification cards and to be fingerprinted, this time they were only in favor of fingerprinting but opposed the provision that every person should carry an identification card when away from home. "A person always carries his fingerprints and that would seem to be sufficient if the proper record is kept by the authorities."[128] H.R.601 was yet another national ID card and universal fingerprinting bill that did not get through Congress.

Springer's last attempt to introduce national ID cards and universal fingerprinting occurred after WWII. In the 80th Congress (1947–1949), on January 3, 1947, Springer introduced H.R.318, which, again, would have required all US citizens over the age of sixteen to carry identification cards and to be fingerprinted.[129] This bill was also referred to the House Committee on the Judiciary, now chaired by Earl Michener (R-MI).

As was the case with previous bills on national ID cards and universal fingerprinting, H.R.318 generated both opposition and support. Most letters of opposition came from New Jersey in May and June 1947. Rep. Mary Norton (D-NJ), a labor advocate and the first female Democrat to serve in the House, was the recipient of those letters. She passed them to Chairman Michener. The opposition came primarily from two groups in Jersey City: the Jewish War Veterans of the United States at Post No. 377 and the Hudson County Bar Association. The latter group argued that H.R.318 would be detrimental to the American people, would result in the violation of cherished American rights, and "would lead inevitably to the practices of oppression, intimidation, regimentation, and other evil aspects of totalitarian governments."

[128] H.R.601, Box 140, House Records, 79th Congress, RG 233, NAB.
[129] H.R.318, Box 3, House Records, 80th Congress, RG 233, NAB.

However, there was support, too. H.R.318 had the support of the American Legion (just like Manasco's H.R.6256) and the Hearst newspapers. Ordinary people supported it, too. Some even wanted the fingerprinting and ID cards to begin at an earlier age. Walter Barrett of Tampa, Florida, wrote in April 1947 that the United States should not stop at fingerprinting just the schoolchildren and the people over sixteen years of age: "we need everybody's prints." Fingerprinting, he argued, could help locate wanted criminals and amnesia victims, prevent juvenile crime, and help during natural disasters.

Harvey Ekerdalen of Newfolden, Minnesota, wanted fingerprinting to start before the age of sixteen, and proposed fingerprinting all persons over the age of twelve. He wrote that universal fingerprinting would enable identification of victims of foul play, sudden death from sickness, and accidents. It would also prevent the impersonation of people who are deceased in order to collect money or property.

Ordinary people supported more than just fingerprinting. Some felt passionate about national ID cards. The folder relating to H.R.318 at the National Archives contains another plan to make everyone in the United States carry compulsory identification cards. The plan, devised by F. O. McPhail of Denver, Colorado, would have required the fingerprinting and registration of all citizens and legal entrants (over the age of eighteen), and the carrying of ID cards (with the right thumbprint). In addition, the plan would have prohibited employment of individuals not legally within the United States. The plan would have banned firms from employing anyone over eighteen who did not have an ID card. Every alien arriving on a limited visit to the United States would receive a visitor's permit ID card bearing the date of its expiration.

Chairman Michener seems to have personally read all the letters and thanked most authors (including bill supporters). In the end, H.R.318 did not get through Congress, sharing the fate of previous national ID card and fingerprinting bills for US citizens.[130]

Criminologist Simon Cole is not discussing the bills I have analyzed here, but in his discussion of the history of fingerprinting he points out that although Americans were susceptible to demagoguery aimed at immigrants and dissidents, they remained steadfastly protective of their own privacy. They saw the universal fingerprinting movement "for what

[130] Ibid.

it was: an effort by the state to establish a comprehensive surveillance system over its own citizens."[131]

SELECT PARTIAL IDENTIFICATION SCHEMES FOR US CITIZENS DURING WWII

Yet while efforts to legislate ID cards for the whole nation were unsuccessful, members of Congress were happy to start using ID cards themselves. On December 25, 1941, the *New York Times* announced that all members of the House and the Senate as well as congressional employees were to be required to carry an identification card bearing a photograph as they moved about the Capitol and congressional office buildings between the hours of 4:30 p.m. and 8 a.m. The *New York Times* added that, thus far, no congressmen had any complaints. On the contrary, "many of them welcome the move and look forward to the day when they could carry identification cards, not only around the Capitol and office buildings, but around the departments and agencies of the Executive branch." This is the case since for many weeks "in visiting various departments and agencies, members of both the House and the Senate have found difficulty, or at least delay, in reaching their objectives."[132]

Other segments of the population also got their identification cards. In 1941, John Baylis, then captain of the US Coast Guard and subsequently of the Port of New York, started the Coast Guard's ID card system. By June 1942, 700,000 people had applied for the cards (in a similar system during WWI officials issued 500,000 cards). The cards contained photographs, fingerprints, and other identifying data. The cards were strictly for identification purposes and did not entitle holders to enter any waterfront area unless they carried legitimate passes. Baylis started the ID system with full security authority granted by FDR to Coast Guard officers in every port of the country. In a June 1942 assessment, Baylis judged that he was "well satisfied with the system, and was convinced that it had kept many subversive agents from the waterfront" and had contributed to the security of the Port of New York.[133]

[131] Cole, *Suspect Identities*, 249.
[132] "Congress to Use Identity Cards," *NYT*, December 25, 1941.
[133] "Identity Cards Issued to 700,000," *NYT*, June 21, 1942.

SECRET CONSIDERATIONS OF NATIONAL ID CARDS AND A GENERAL REGISTRATION DURING WWII

There is evidence that in 1942 both military and civilian officials were secretly considering a general registration and national ID cards for all inhabitants of the United States. The evidence exists in the papers of Philip Hauser, Assistant Director at the Bureau of the Census, preserved at the National Archives.[134] Letters from February 1942 indicate that J. C. Capt, Director of the Census Bureau, and Calvert Dedrick, a Census Bureau staff member, were considering a general registration of all inhabitants of the United States.[135]

In May 1942, Forrest Linder, then Assistant Chief Statistician for Vital Statistics at the Census Bureau, prepared a thirty-five-page report on the technicalities of such registration. The report was called "Memorandum Relating to a General Population Identity Registration for Military Purposes." It was prepared at the requests of both Colonel Karl Bendetsen, then Assistant Chief of Staff, Civil Affairs Division, Wartime Civil Control Administration at the Western Defense Command and Fourth Army, and Dedrick, who, in addition to his Census Bureau work, was Chief of the Statistical Division at the Wartime Civil Control Administration under Bendetsen.[136]

Linder's report outlined some of the major problems of designing and administering a population identity registration for military purposes. Linder began his report by stating that a general population identity registration is a technical and administrative operation. Authorities should not undertake it without most careful study and consideration. He said that the identity registration of a single individual could be a very simple procedure, but the difficulties of repeating it millions of times were invariably underestimated.

Linder pointed out that the costs of collecting data for a US population census were approximately $0.10 per person, excluding tabulation costs. However, the costs of an identity registration would exceed this amount

[134] Box 25, Entry 146, Office Files of Philip M. Hauser, 1942–1947, Records of the Bureau of the Census, RG 29, NAB (Hauser Files).

[135] William Seltzer and Margo Anderson, "After Pearl Harbor: The Proper Role of Population Data Systems in Time of War" (paper presented at the annual meeting of the Population Association of America, Los Angeles, March 2000).

[136] Forrest E. Linder, "Memorandum Relating to a General Population Identity Registration for Military Purposes," and covering letter to Calvert L. Dedrick, both dated May 9, 1942, Hauser Files.

since a registration involves providing each individual with a distinct registration card and establishing a relationship between each issued card and the corresponding record filed in the registration offices.

Linder's report made it clear that an identification card would be an integral part of any universal registration. He described both a minimum and an optimum system of identity registration. In both, it would be compulsory to carry an identification card at all times.

The report pointed out that in the United States there have been a very large number of partial registrations, including the selective service registration, the sugar rationing registration, alien registration, etc. Linder dismissed the idea that the government could organize some form of omnibus registration that would replace all of these various separate registrations. He also rejected the suggestion that the government could collect the information contained in the existing records and files and organize it into a central identity file. Instead, he concluded, "if military necessity or national policy requires that each person carry an identification certificate, then a new registration must be had for this purpose."

The report went on to describe some advantages of a general population registration for identity purposes, and the technical and administrative difficulties of such an undertaking. Linder mentioned also the "political and psychological dangers." He stressed that traditional American thinking regarding freedom of action and thought might consider a mandatory identity registration as an infringement of that liberty and as the beginning of an American "gestapo." The political implications or effects of a compulsory identity registration might be considerable, unless a substantial part of the public clearly saw the necessity for it. In addition, the possibilities of a "blacklist" inherent in an identification system were certain to arouse the opposition of labor groups. He added that such considerations may matter less in wartime, but during peacetime, they "have appeared to be effective barriers in the minds of population statisticians who have always been interested in creating a population register."

Linder believed that if the government establishes a population registry sometime in the future, it would probably be the result of some rather drastic change or anticipation of change in the industrial, military, or political situation. For Linder, the creation of a registry was not a foregone conclusion. The objectives of the possible system were not clear, either. In a May 9, 1942, letter, which accompanied the memorandum, Linder wrote to Dedrick that "the techniques and procedures for a registration can be planned only in general terms until a policy regarding the extent and the objectives of the system is more clearly formulated."[137]

On May 9, 1942, upon receipt of Linder's report, Dedrick wrote to Bendetsen to give his opinion on the general registration of the civilian population. He stressed that he had not yet had the opportunity to discuss the report with his superiors at the Census Bureau or the Department of Commerce (the Bureau's parent department), and therefore did not have their endorsement. Still, Dedrick's own opinion was that "a general registration of population would go far in meeting many military as well as civilian needs." It would give "a definite registration record of the population" and "a basis for the issuance of certificates of identification, for example, those necessary for the granting of exemptions from curfew or military regulations." It would also provide "quantitative population data on a current basis." Dedrick wrote that registration of the population residing in defined military areas appeared "to be administratively feasible." He added that the government could conduct a general registration with what Linder called "low level identification," accompanied by the issuance of "high level identification" to only certain classes of persons, at a relatively low cost. Dedrick concluded:

> It would not be advisable to have uncoordinated local registrations for individual cities, counties, sectors, corps areas, or even Defense Command Areas. If a general registration of military areas is undertaken, each of the local units should follow policies and utilize forms and procedures that fit into a national plan so that, if necessary, the registration might ultimately include the entire population of the United States in one integrated system. To accomplish this will require consultation with other agencies in Washington and may require Presidential or Congressional approval.[138]

The public did not see any of these considerations. On July 4, 1942, Colonel Bendetsen wrote to J. C. Capt, Director of the Bureau of the Census, saying that although Linder's report was "a real contribution in this field" and was prepared for Bendetsen, "no publicity should be given which would in any way indicate that we are or were at any time considering a general registration."[139]

It seems that the country had to deal with more pressing tasks. One job that needed particular attention of vital records officials stemmed from a

[137] Ibid.

[138] Calvert L. Dedrick, Memorandum for Colonel Karl R. Bendetsen, "Plans for a general registration of the civilian population," May 9, 1942, Hauser Files.

[139] Colonel Karl R. Bendetsen, Letter to J. C. Capt, July 4, 1942, Hauser Files.

huge burden placed on the existing local and state registration offices by the thousands of native-born Americans who were attempting to establish their citizenship by seeking a delayed certificate of birth. Proof of citizenship was now required for most war-related work. Since most births went unregistered prior to 1935, large numbers of adults were filing applications for the delayed registration of their birth. Introducing improvements in the system of vital records took priority, and in June 1943, the Bureau of the Budget formally abandoned the proposal for a general population registration and national ID cards.[140]

PUBLIC OPINION ON IDENTIFICATION DOCUMENTS DURING WWII

Shortly after the Pearl Harbor attack, a Gallup poll revealed that 69 percent of Americans believed that "everyone in the United States should be required to carry an identification card containing, among other things, his picture and his fingerprints." Of those polled 25 percent opposed the idea of a national ID card and 6 percent were undecided.[141] Even though the Gallup data from that period comes from a skewed sample of the mass public,[142] it is still helpful to realize the strength of the public support on this particular issue.

George Gallup, director of the American Institute of Public Opinion, wrote that the large favorable vote "is undoubtedly explained by the fact that for many years the public has been ready to accept universal fingerprinting." Already in 1937, a Gallup survey found more than two-thirds of voters with opinions on the subject in favor of starting fingerprint records for everybody in the United States – a plan that FBI's J. Edgar Hoover had been advocating for many years.

George Gallup argued also that any opposition to the ID card proposal came from a feeling that it is "un-American to be so regimented" and that

[140] Seltzer and Anderson, "After Pearl Harbor."

[141] George Gallup, "Gallup Poll Reveals: Identification Cards Favored," *Atlanta Constitution*, February 4, 1942.

[142] As Berinsky et al. point out, polls conducted before the 1950s relied on quota-controlled sampling methods, in which pollsters sought to interview certain predetermined proportions of people from particular segments of the population. George Gallup was most interested in predicting elections, so he drew samples representing each population segment in proportion to the votes that segment usually cast in elections. Because Southerners, African-Americans, and women turned out at low rates, these groups were deliberately underrepresented in polls. Adam J. Berinsky, Eleanor Neff Powell, Eric Schickler, and Ian Brett Yohai, "Revisiting Public Opinion in the 1930s and 1940s," *PS: Political Science and Politics* 44, 3 (July 2011): 516.

the plan was not necessary. However, those who favored the idea pointed out two advantages that they thought it would have. First, it would aid police authorities in catching spies and saboteurs. Second, it would be valuable in case of accidents, particularly in case of bombings and evacuations.[143]

In addition to the Gallup poll, the strength of the public opinion is evident in the letters to the *New York Times* and the *Los Angeles Times*. Some people argued that the good derived from nationwide identification systems more than offset whatever disadvantages might exist in such systems. One *New York Times* reader, who lived in South America for twelve years but was now in Clarksburg, West Virginia, spoke highly of ID cards (with photographs and fingerprints) required of all citizens and aliens in many countries. He argued that no law-abiding American can honestly object to such measures, and "Congress should see the need of identification in the present emergency and pass a measure requiring complete registration while there is less opportunity for politicians to object."[144] It is possible that supporters of national ID cards framing the issue in such opportunistic terms added to the fear, and sometimes the paranoia, exhibited by some of the opponents of ID cards.

One argument in favor of ID cards was that anonymity, or "undisclosed identity," enabled criminals. For instance, in a letter to the *New York Times*, one reader from New York called for a universal federal identification bureau that would issue a "domestic passport identification" that would act as a "crime deterrent" to all Americans over the age of fifteen. He argued that it was difficult to achieve legislation on the subject in the past because of the "timidity of legislators who regarded such a program as an infringement of civil liberties." Allowing citizens to conceal their identity "is untenable for the proper maintenance of law and order." The society that allows that "is only rendering its own structure vulnerable to attack from within." He added that a person who commits an antisocial crime should pay for it by the loss of a passport bestowed on him for his protection by his fellow men.[145]

Another argument in favor of ID cards was that only ID cards and a national central register of all persons living in the United States could help form a full picture of the American work force. Robert Kempner, a

143 George Gallup, "Card of Identity for All Favored," *NYT*, February 4, 1942.

144 J. R. Seckman, "Identity Cards Favored," *NYT*, February 15, 1942.

145 Roger Paul Craig, "Passports for All; Identity Cards Regarded as Necessary Here," *NYT*, February 8, 1942.

New York Times reader from Philadelphia (and later an assistant US chief counsel at the Nuremberg war crimes trials), even went as far as to say that the introduction of ID cards was one of the most important points in the defense of the Western Hemisphere. Kempner pointed out that the government could build relatively easily and rapidly the administrative machinery and procedure of a general residents' registration, as evidenced, for instance, by the effective and quick creation of the system of alien registration. He added that the information gained from general registration, used by experts with scrupulous regard to civil liberties, would also be of use in providing for the general welfare after the war.[146]

Kempner pointed out three objections most frequently raised against general registration. First, there was the psychological argument that someone could abuse general registration for purposes that we could not even visualize at the time of its adoption. Kempner argued that, theoretically, people could raise this objection against every new administrative measure, but it was only valid when there was a lack of general confidence in the executive branch. Second, there was the argument that general registration meant a restriction of civil rights. However, Kempner argued that registration per se did not restrict civil rights at all; only its abuse would mean an infringement of civil liberties. He pointed out that certain forms of registration were already customary in the United States: the census, draft registration, and the registration of taxpayers, workers, voters, car owners, holders of driver's licenses, and many others. General registration "only means the coordination of the too many disintegrated special registrations." Third, there was the argument that general and centralized registration would promote dictatorship because it would help to strengthen the executive branch. Kempner argued that we have to remember that European dictatorships developed in countries with weak administrations and still weaker executives.[147] He implied that this would not be the case in the United States.

Some Americans argued that ID cards and national registration would have a tremendous psychological effect, as they would strengthen national consciousness "by showing everybody that he is a registered member of our democratic community and of our common national effort."[148] Similarly, some argued that ID cards would emphasize the value of citizenship. One person who made this argument was Frank Abbott, a medical doctor in California, who proposed that the State

[146] Robert M. W. Kempner, "Full Registration Favored," *NYT*, February 17, 1942.
[147] Ibid. [148] Ibid.

Bureau of Vital Statistics "should issue for each newborn child an identification card containing the essential facts of birth." These ID cards should be presented when the person enters school and college and when they register to vote. He argued that the "citizen of the United States of America needs to have something like this to impress him with the value of his citizenship."[149] A year later, in May 1943, the California Federation of Women's Clubs campaigned for an ID card marked with photograph, date of birth, and thumbprint, for every minor over the age of twelve.[150]

SUMMARY

Wartime conditions played a key role in the development of identity policing measures. Both WWI and WWII were historical crises of massive proportions and both resulted in new identification measures, albeit temporary, aimed mainly at aliens and enemy aliens. However, policymakers and members of the public also put forward multiple proposals to introduce universal registration and fingerprinting, and national ID cards, for all US citizens. The proposed bills and resulting debates offer fascinating insight into how policymakers and the public perceive identity policing in times of crises and beyond them. Some of those who supported universal registration, fingerprinting, and national ID cards because of specific war-related reasons were open to their potential benefits in providing for the general welfare after the war.

My examination of the legislative histories of the relevant bills reveals a true range of attitudes toward universal registration, fingerprinting, and national ID cards for US citizens. Despite modern-day claims that the American people despise national ID cards, the historical evidence suggests that ID card proposals have generated not only significant opposition, but also significant support. Police professionals, forensic experts, veterans, and members of Congress were not the only ones favoring universal fingerprinting and national ID cards. Many ordinary people did, too. Opinion polls in WWII revealed that 69 percent of Americans believed that everyone in the United States should be required to carry an ID card with a picture and fingerprints.

149 Frank F. Abbott, "How to Prove You Were Born!," *Los Angeles Times,* March 19, 1942.

150 Bess M. Wilson, "Women's Group Urges Minors' Identity Cards," *Los Angeles Times,* May 19, 1943.

Despite the public support, policymakers did not introduce national ID cards. Yet the 1930s and 1940s saw the evolution of two basic forms of identification: driver's licenses and Social Security numbers. Some subsequent proposals have suggested using them as foundations for national ID card schemes. The next chapter looks at those developments.

3

Identification Documents in the United States in the Second Half of the Twentieth Century

INTRODUCTION

As the previous chapter showed, during WWII policymakers and members of the public put forward multiple proposals to introduce national ID cards in the United States. However, despite the public support, policymakers did not introduce national ID cards. Yet the 1930s and 1940s saw the evolution of two basic forms of identification: driver's licenses and Social Security numbers (SSNs). Those two in many ways became functional equivalents of national ID cards in the United States. Some subsequent proposals have suggested using driver's licenses and SSNs as foundations for national ID card schemes.

This chapter briefly looks at the development of driver's licenses and SSNs during the twentieth century. It then looks at the proposals to introduce national ID cards in the United States in the second half of the twentieth century. Public figures put forward these proposals in the 1970s, 1980s, and 1990s; all the proposals were unsuccessful. The chapter also looks at various successful and unsuccessful efforts at immigration reforms, including the 1986 law mandating employers to verify employment eligibility of new workers using identification documents under the threat of employer sanctions.

During WWI and WWII, those policymakers and members of the public who advocated the introduction of national ID cards did so primarily because of concerns about enemy aliens. Later in the century, those who advocated the introduction of national ID cards, or at least making other identification documents more secure, did so primarily because of concerns about fraudsters and illegal immigrants. In the twenty-first century the focus remained, to some extent, on illegal immigrants, but most importantly moved to concern about terrorists.

EVOLUTION OF DRIVER'S LICENSES

The states of Massachusetts and Missouri were the first to establish drivers' licensing laws in 1903, but Massachusetts had no examination laws for commercial chauffeurs until 1907 and for general operators until 1920, and Missouri had no driver examination laws until 1952. South Dakota was both the last state to institute driver's licenses (1954), and the last state to require examinations (1959). The contemporary belief that states instituted driver's licenses to keep incompetent drivers off the road is false.[1]

Sociologist Steven Nock shows that even in the early twentieth century a driver's license "was a form of *identification* as much as it was a certification that the operator knew anything about how to operate the vehicle" and that, if anything, the identification function of driver's license has increased over the years. By 1989, 79 percent of females and 91 percent of males (aged sixteen and older) in the United States held driver's licenses. The overall percentage of driving-age individuals licensed to drive increased from 57 percent in 1950 to 86 percent in 1989. The use of driver's licenses as identification documents became so common that all states, since 1979, have also issued in their motor vehicle departments, for a fee, state identification cards to nondrivers.[2]

EVOLUTION OF SOCIAL SECURITY NUMBERS

Meanwhile, the SSN, printed on the Social Security card, while not originally intended for identification, over the years became something of a universal identifier. The Social Security Act, which became law in August 1935, did not expressly mention the use of the SSN, but it authorized the creation of some type of record-keeping scheme. In June 1936, the Social Security Board (SSB) approved the number, which contained no significant facts about the employee other than the state where

[1] Carl Watner, "Drivers Licenses and Vehicle Registration in Historical Perspective," in *National Identification Systems*, ed. Watner and McElroy, 103.

[2] Steven L. Nock, *The Costs of Privacy: Surveillance and Reputation in America* (New York: Aldine de Gruyter, 1993), 56–65. Emphasis in original.

the employee applied for a card. In November, the SSB issued the first SSNs (then known as Social Security account numbers).[3]

Critics of FDR attacked the Social Security program for many reasons. One of the criticisms was that the program promoted government snooping and tagging and curtailed individual freedom. During a speech in St. Louis, Alf Landon, the 1936 Republican presidential candidate, talked about the 26 million workers who would be subject to Social Security, and asked, "Imagine the field opened for federal snooping. Are these 26 million going to be fingerprinted? Are their photographs going to be kept on file in a Washington office? Or are they going to have identification tags put around their necks?" John Hamilton, the Chairman of the Republican National Committee, held up dog tags as he spoke in Boston and noted sarcastically that at least Washington was going to make them out of stainless steel so that they would not stain the skin. Radio ads threatened that workers in the future would have only identification numbers, not names, as far as the government was concerned.[4]

In November 1936, on the day before the presidential election, the *New York Journal-American* published a front-page drawing of a man with his identity masked, stripped to the waist, wearing a "dog tag" with an identifying number. The label read "Snooping and Tagging."[5] Importantly, the paper's owner was William Randolph Hearst, a fervent enemy of Roosevelt. Hearst expected all his newspapers to publish unfavorable stories about New Deal programs regularly. On that day, all his papers carried front-page stories with a bold-type question: "Do You Want a Tag and a Number in the Name of False Security?"[6]

Although the SSB never contemplated the use of dog tags, Landon and his supporters might have gotten the idea because the Addressograph Corporation had made a prototype stainless steel tag on a chain and had tried to sell the SSB on the idea of issuing such tags to all registrants.[7] Arthur Altmeyer, who was a member of the SSB from October 1935, and then the head of Social Security from 1937 until 1953, vetoed this idea as soon as he heard about it. However, he kept Addressograph's prototype nametag as a souvenir in his desk drawer throughout his career with the Social Security Administration (SSA), which replaced the SSB in 1946,

[3] SSA, "Social Security Chronology 1930s," www.ssa.gov/history/1930.html.

[4] Nancy J. Altman, *The Battle for Social Security: From FDR's Vision to Bush's Gamble* (Wiley, 2005), 104.

[5] Robert Ellis Smith, *Ben Franklin's Web Site: Privacy and Curiosity from Plymouth Rock to the Internet* (Providence, RI: Privacy Journal, 2000), 286.

[6] Altman, *The Battle*, 104–105. [7] Ibid., 114.

and he donated it to SSA after his retirement. The one and only Social Security "dog-tag" ever issued is now on display in the History Room at the SSA headquarters in Baltimore.[8]

The SSB considered various numbering systems and ways by which an employee could indicate that the SSB had issued them a number.[9] In the end, the SSB decided to issue cards (made of banknote paper) that contained the SSNs of their holders. An artist from Albany, New York, designed the cards, which looked almost identical to those issued today. Meanwhile, management expert Harry Hoff helped devise the numbering system. The SSNs consisted of three digits (area numbers), followed by two digits (group numbers), followed by four digits (serial numbers). The system permitted a billion permutations, enough numbers to take care of the working population well into the future. At the time, SSB officials assigned numbers not from one centralized location, as they do today, but from locations around the country. Still, the way Hoff and the SSB set up the numbering system prevented SSB officials around the country from inadvertently assigning the same number to two people.[10]

On November 5, 1936, the Department of the Treasury authorized the assignment of Social Security identification numbers to employers and account numbers to employees. To help distribute and return the application forms for SSNs, the SSB decided to use the postal system's 45,000 post offices. On November 24, the Post Office Department distributed applications for account numbers (Forms SS-5) to persons who were working or expected to work in jobs covered by old-age insurance.[11] As Social Security expert Nancy Altman points out, letter carriers delivered applications for numbers, helped people fill out the forms, answered questions about the program, returned the forms to typing centers that then produced the cards, delivered the cards to the workers, and transmitted the applications of workers together with their newly assigned SSNs to Baltimore.[12] Most of that happened in just three short weeks in November 1936.

Notwithstanding these successes, there were fears. Privacy advocate Robert Ellis Smith notes that trade unions feared that companies could use SSNs to blacklist pro-union men and women involved in the labor

[8] SSA, "Historical Information, Social Security Numbers," www.ssa.gov/history/ssn/ssncards.html.

[9] SSA, "Social Security Number Chronology," www.ssa.gov/history/ssn/ssnchron.html.

[10] Altman, *The Battle*, 113–115.

[11] SSA, "Social Security Chronology 1930s."

[12] Altman, *The Battle*, 115.

strife at the time. The United Mine Workers and the United Steelworkers apparently persuaded some friendly officials in Roosevelt's administration to include in the Social Security Act of 1935 a provision allowing an individual to replace an existing SSN with a second one when they can show "good reasons for a change," a provision that remains in the law. Smith points out that many religious groups feared national registration because of the biblical threats that plague might follow, and recent immigrants from Europe were concerned with the idea of registering all citizens, given their experiences with Nazi registration schemes. He quotes Altmeyer's recollection that to reassure the public bureaucrats referred to the process in place as an "assignment" of SSNs instead of "registration."[13]

Despite the misgivings of some Americans, most people did not want to miss out on a government pension and they quickly returned their application forms by post. In just the first few months, between November 1936 and June 1937, officials processed 30 million applications for SSNs.[14]

When the government created the SSN, it meant it only as an account number associated with the administration of the Social Security program. But the uses grew over the years. The first step of turning the SSN from a specific program into a general numerical identifier took place in 1943, when the Executive Order 9379 authorized all federal agencies to use the same number. In 1961 the Civil Service Commission adopted the SSN as an official federal employee identifier. In 1962 the Internal Revenue Service (IRS) adopted the SSN as its official taxpayer identification number. In 1966 the Veterans Administration began to use the SSN as the hospital admissions number and for patient record keeping. In 1969 the Department of Defense (DOD) adopted the SSN in lieu of the military service number for identifying Armed Forces personnel. In 1970 the Bank Records and Foreign Transactions Act required all banks, credit unions, and brokers to obtain the SSNs of all their customers.[15]

While Social Security officials did not intend the SSN for identification purposes other than in their program, federal agencies, corporations, and individuals gradually started to use it for such purposes. The first Social Security cards, issued starting in 1936, did not mention anything about allowing or prohibiting their use for identification purposes. It was only beginning with the sixth design version of the card, issued starting in 1946,

[13] Smith, *Ben Franklin's Web Site*, 284–286.
[14] SSA, "Social Security Number Chronology." [15] Ibid.

that the SSA added a legend to the bottom of the card reading "For Social Security Purposes – Not for Identification." The SSA removed this legend as part of the design changes for the eighteenth version of the card, issued starting in 1972. The legend has not been on any cards issued since 1972.[16]

IDENTIFICATION PROPOSALS IN THE AFTERMATH OF WWII

The aftermath of WWII saw the emergence of some proposals to introduce a universal personal identification system. In 1948, the National Office of Vital Statistics and cooperating state and local records agencies proposed a national birth certificate number, to be given to every individual born after January 1, 1949. This would be a unique lifetime identifying number. Government agencies and some private business groups vigorously publicized this proposal as a much needed and desirable measure for health, safety, and statistical purposes. However, in 1949 and 1950 some newspapers denounced the idea as an oppressing "police state" and "Big Brother" measure. Privacy scholar Alan Westin notes that this opposition was sufficiently strong to persuade twenty-four states to reject participation in the plan and to cause Congress to drop legislative proposals that had been put forward to provide for federal participation in the system. In the early 1960s, vital statistics officials and other federal and state agencies continued to favor the creation of a personal identification system. However, they were convinced that a more powerful publicity campaign than could be marshaled at that time would be necessary to overcome public resistance to the invasion-of-privacy aspect of the program.[17]

When the IRS began to automate its data-processing procedures, it needed unique personal identification numbers to feed all the reports on income transactions for each taxpayer into his or her proper account. As Westin points out, rather than devise a new numbering system, with the public and congressional opposition this might have drawn, the IRS sought and obtained legislation to use the SSN. The legislation made it a legal requirement to provide the SSN on income returns. For those people who did not have a SSN, the SSA issued a number for tax identification purposes. By 1964, the SSA issued 160 million numbers, about five million of these for tax identification rather than for Social Security purposes. In 1964, Rep. Arnold Olsen (D-MT), Chairman of the

[16] SSA, "Frequently Asked Questions," www.ssa.gov/history/hfaq.html.
[17] Alan F. Westin, *Privacy and Freedom* (New York: Atheneum, 1967), 304.

Subcommittee on Census and Government Statistics, expressed concern over this numbering system. In a letter to Alan Westin, Rep. Olsen explained that

> a number can never have the dignity and respect of a name, as our jailkeepers well know. It concerns all of us that mass processing techniques applied to an individual's personal data can lend themselves to various kinds of abuses and, in my opinion, it is in these potential abuses that the real danger lies.[18]

The 1960s and 1970s marked the rise of information privacy as a social, political, and legal issue in the age of developing technology. As the country went through civil rights struggles, antiwar movements, and Watergate, the government and the private sector embraced advances made in data surveillance. But privacy scholars such as Westin raised alarms that helped lead the government to initiate commissions and studies that investigated the impacts of technology and explored ways to protect privacy.[19]

PROPOSALS FOR NATIONAL ID CARDS IN THE 1970S: BACKGROUND

Although the uses of the SSN have expanded considerably, it is still not a universal identifier, and policymakers have consistently rejected efforts to make it one. In 1971 the SSA task force published a report that proposed that the SSA should take a "cautious and conservative" position toward SSN use and do nothing to promote the use of SSN as an identifier.[20]

In 1972, Elliott Richardson, the Secretary of Health, Education, and Welfare (HEW), appointed the Advisory Committee on Automated Personal Data Systems to study questions posed by increased use of computers to collect information and keep records on individuals. Among other issues, the committee looked at the increasing uses of SSNs. In June 1973, the committee chairman, Willis Ware, submitted a report to the new HEW Secretary Caspar Weinberger. The report concluded that the adoption of a universal identifier by the United States was not desirable. It also found that the SSN was not suitable for such a purpose as it does not meet the criteria of a universal identifier that distinguishes a person from all others.[21]

[18] Ibid., 309.

[19] Alan F. Westin, "Social and Political Dimensions of Privacy," *Journal of Social Issues* 59, 2 (July 2003): 436.

[20] SSA, "Social Security Number Chronology." [21] Ibid.

The report argued that a permanent standard universal identifier issued at birth "could create an incentive for institutions to pool or link their records, thereby making it possible to bring a lifetime of information to bear on any decision about a given individual." The report noted that "American culture is rich in the belief than an individual can pull up stakes and make a fresh start, but a universally identified man might become a prisoner of his recorded past."[22]

The report also argued that "Congress should be sparing in mandating use of the SSN, and should do so only after full and careful consideration" preceded by well-advertised hearings that elicit substantial public participation.[23] The committee recommended against the adoption of any nationwide, standard, personal identification format, with or without the SSN, "that would enhance the likelihood of arbitrary or uncontrolled linkage of records about people, particularly between government and government-supported automated personal data systems."[24]

A year later, in October 1974, Attorney General William Saxbe appointed a committee to study the use of false identification documents to commit crimes. The Federal Advisory Committee on False Identification (FACFI) was a diverse volunteer task force. The eighty-member committee included representatives of fifty government agencies at the federal, state, and local levels, law enforcement groups, and business organizations, such as the American Bankers Association, the American Express Company, the American Bank Note Company, and the Polaroid Corporation. A $200,000 DOJ grant to the MITRE Corporation provided staff support to FACFI.[25] David Muchow and Douglas Westbrook, both of the Criminal Division at the DOJ, co-chaired FACFI.[26]

In April 1975, FACFI estimated that the US economy was losing billions of dollars annually because of illegal use of easily obtained false identity papers.[27] In June 1976, FACFI gave a more precise figure, saying that a nationwide identification crisis was costing at least $20 billion a year. This included tax burdens caused by illegal immigration, as well as

22 Report of the HEW Secretary's Advisory Committee on Automated Personal Data Systems, "Records, Computers and the Rights of Citizens," July 1973, chapter VII.

23 Ibid., Summary and Recommendations. 24 Ibid., Chapter VII.

25 FACFI, "The Criminal Use of False Identification" (Washington, DC: GPO, November 1976), xi–xii.

26 FACFI, xxxii.

27 David Binder, "False Identities Costly to Nation," *NYT*, April 11, 1975.

credit card fraud, welfare, food stamps and Social Security abuses, and the extra law enforcement expenses necessary to catch fugitives using false identification.[28]

Just as the FACFI was working to uncover the extent of abuse of identification documents, some organizations were trying to make the problem seem insignificant. For instance, the Chairman of the American Committee for Protection of Foreign Born, Dr. Paul Lehmann, argued in a July 1976 letter to FACFI that "false identification is at most a peripheral facet of the problem of aliens not in status."[29]

In November 1976, FACFI published an 800-page report that aimed to unmask false identification crimes and to provide a comprehensive, commonsense plan that federal, state, and local agencies; the private sector; and the public could use to prevent such crimes. The report discussed the three fundamental methods of using an identification document for false purposes: alteration, counterfeiting, and imposture.[30] The report shed light on some important and often shocking information, including the fact that there are over 7,000 vital records offices in the United States authorized to issue certified copies of birth certificates.[31] The report also emphasized that there was no birth/death matching in the United States, since birth and death files were separately stored and rarely coordinated, and therefore it was very easy to obtain another person's birth certificate, especially if that person was dead.[32] The report also noted that fifteen states issued driver's licenses with no photograph[33] and that over 4.2 million people had more than one SSN.[34]

The report stated: "Every American man, woman, and child pays the price in taxes, the cost of goods, and in the human suffering and tragedy caused by the success of false identification crimes." The report argued: "False identification is a criminal's best friend. With it, criminals can appear and disappear at will by creating fictitious 'paper people.' Often victims are not even aware they have been victimized. The exploding use of false identification must be stopped."[35]

The report pointed out that prosecutors usually place a low priority on prosecution of false ID cases. This is largely due to a lack of awareness of the potential seriousness of the crime; altering a document does not look nearly as serious as a murder case – until one

[28] "Identity Study Urges Matching of Birth and Death Certificates," *NYT*, June 15, 1976.
[29] FACFI, F-9. [30] Ibid., 13. [31] Ibid., 17. [32] Ibid., D-69. [33] Ibid., D-129.
[34] Ibid., 24. [35] Ibid., xi.

realizes that the use of false IDs is what keeps many major crimes unsolved and their perpetrators free and "hidden."[36]

FACFI considered several steps to ease the identification crisis, including the establishment of a national ID card for every American. FACFI considered three arguments in favor of a national ID card. First, a national ID card could be more easily recognized, controlled, and protected against abuse than other documents. Second, document systems that include everybody would thereby be "foolproof." Third, the government has an obligation to provide a reliable means of personal identification for public and private transactions among its citizens.[37]

FACFI listed three arguments against a national ID card. The first was the belief that such documentation "is in opposition to American traditions." Unfortunately, FACFI did not provide any evidence to support this assertion. The second was the belief that it would represent an invasion of personal privacy. The third was the belief that data required for citizen identification could be abused by government or private interests.[38] The entire analysis was very short and occupied only about two pages in the 800-page report.

The law enforcement and vital statistics officials on the committee were apparently tempted to recommend the creation of a national ID card and were sure that this would solve all problems related to fraud. But they would not say so publicly because they apparently thought that the public reaction would be negative. So the pro-law enforcement group voted down a proposal to create a national ID card and number.[39] The only official openly in favor of a national ID card was Deane Huxtable, State Registrar and Director of Bureau of Vital Records and Health Statistics in the Commonwealth of Virginia. Only Huxtable argued that the advantages of adopting tamper-resistant identification documents by far outweighed their risks.[40]

Huxtable noted: "The only way that a person can prove who he is, that he is a citizen, that he has rights to certain benefits – or conversely, the only way that it can be proven that a person is not what he claims – is through the record keeping system of this country." Huxtable argued for the strengthening and reorganizing of "our deficient, decentralized, and demoralized record keeping system regarding personal data." Huxtable argued that the federal government should assume responsibility and operational control over the vital statistics registration system in this

[36] Ibid., 55. [37] Ibid., xvi. [38] Ibid., xvii. [39] Smith, *Ben Franklin's Web Site*, 301.
[40] Eaton, *Card-Carrying Americans*, 39, 201.

country and that at the age of eighteen, or some arbitrary age to be established, the system should issue unique, numerically designated identity cards to the American public. In his July 1976 letter, Huxtable warned: "To establish a system for identifying our citizens in a democratic society may cost us a minor degree of personal freedom. Not to do so may cost us all of it."[41]

There is little evidence of corporate views presented to FACFI with respect to national ID cards, except for a statement by the Polaroid Corporation. Polaroid, a major supplier of identification systems, had been directly involved in the sale of equipment designed to make identification cards. Polaroid had developed a policy that reflected the company's concerns with the use of identification cards as they may affect the freedom and privacy of the individual. In December 1975, Peter Wensberg, Polaroid's Senior Vice President of Marketing, issued the following statement as to Polaroid's position on national ID cards:

> We (Polaroid) are neither opposed to nor supportive of the idea of a national identity card. If Congress were to enact legislation for such a program we would support it only if we felt the rights of individuals were fully protected. If there were the possibility of misuse of such a program, such as availability of copies for other purposes, citizen identification files, etc., we would not support it.
>
> A card with a picture and a signature is useful to the individual as a means of positive identification. Our concern is with the possible misuse of information beyond the purposes of identification.[42]

One of Polaroid's representatives on FACFI, Ronald O'Connor, a Government Sales Manager, further outlined his company's position toward national ID cards in an April 1976 report to FACFI, though it was not clear if O'Connor was speaking on Polaroid's or just his own behalf. O'Connor wrote that one solution to the general problem of false identification was to provide an unquestionable base document or group of base documents that were readily available to all citizens. But according to O'Connor this solution would present several drawbacks: "most importantly, this approach would be unacceptable to the citizens of this country." He wrote that a decision to implement a national ID card policy deserved the attention of the entire population and as such would deserve being placed on the ballot for national referendum. He concluded that "it is the author's opinion that the creation of a new mandatory national identification card is unnecessary and unjustifiable when viewed

[41] FACFI, F-5. [42] Ibid., D-167.

from the position of either the civil libertarians, the business and commercial interests, law enforcement, or the taxpayer." Instead, O'Connor proposed to upgrade the security of state-issued driver's licenses.[43]

The final FACFI position was that the case against a national ID system was self-evident.

Although the FACFI report found that easy access to breeder documentation aided broad patterns of crime and abuse, from drug smuggling and money laundering to fraudulent veterans claims, it rejected the idea of a national identifier and did not consider the SSN for such a purpose.[44]

In fact, one of the few comments FACFI had on the SSN was that the use of the SSN as a universal identifier "seems unlikely at this time," because of "the danger of invasion of privacy, the cost to the Federal Government, the time required to institute the system and the effectiveness of such a system for alleviating the problem." Moreover, FACFI did not like the idea of fingerprinting all applicants for SSNs and benefits in order to establish their identity. It dismissed this idea as "probably ... unfeasible and not readily accepted by the public."[45]

The FACFI report opposed any national ID card and any new type of state or local government–issued ID intended to supersede existing documents. The report concluded that "any new system designed to verify and store identity information on over 200 million people would be extremely expensive and require a major national effort." It added that it was highly probable that proposals for such a system would be opposed politically. A national ID system "would be subject to defeat by imposters or counterfeiters taking advantage of careless inspection of documents or through corruption of officials." The report maintained that occasional errors would also occur in such a system that could adversely affect innocent people. In addition, organized crime would take advantage of any national ID system because of the presumption of validity surrounding such a large system. The report stated that under a national ID system criminals could reap benefits far greater than they obtained under the current multifaceted system of identification.[46]

In the end, FACFI rejected proposals for the establishment of a national ID card, or, as the *New York Times* put it, an "internal passport" for every American. Instead, to ease the identification crisis, FACFI favored the matching of birth and death certificates on an interstate basis, so that criminals could not assume dead persons' names. FACFI also

[43] Ibid., D-172, D-174. [44] Eaton, *Card-Carrying Americans*, 39. [45] FACFI, A-30.
[46] Ibid., xvii.

recommended that the state-issued driver's license (or state-issued ID) be recognized as the primary form of personal ID for use in commerce and in transactions between individuals and government. FACFI favored minimum federal standards to tighten the security of the existing state document systems and the documents themselves, particularly breeder documents such as birth certificates and driver's licenses. FACFI recommended increased security both in the document application phase and in the use phase.[47]

FACFI concluded the report: "To the enterprising criminal, a driver's license in a false name is literally a 'license to steal' or to commit numerous other crimes … We *can* limit the abuse of our identification documents without jeopardizing either our liberties or our personal privacy if we discard our present complacency toward this growing national problem and work together towards its solution."[48]

FACFI was keen to emphasize that it attempted to maintain a careful balance in formulating recommendations for dealing with the national false identification problem. In its report, FACFI stated that it "considered both *protection against crime* and *protection of privacy* to be guarantees provided to all in a free society."[49]

It is important to remember that the government convened FACFI under the shadow cast by the Watergate scandal. As Alan Westin notes, the late 1960s and 1970s saw a majority of Americans shift from trusting to distrusting government institutions. FBI and CIA excesses, Watergate, and other Nixon administration intrusions were examples of government abuse of power that made politically possible the enactment of the Federal Privacy Act of 1974.[50] But the 1976 FACFI report, after a flurry of media reports following its publication, soon disappeared from public concern. Policymakers did not even commission a policy study on the social and political costs and benefits of available antifraud strategies, since neither of the major political parties, nor Presidents Ford, Carter, and Reagan placed the prestige of their office behind efforts to fully utilize available technological means to inhibit the use of false documents.[51]

Still, because of the FACFI report, identity fraud became a federal crime through the False Identification Crime Control Act of 1982. The Act amended the federal criminal code and established penalties for knowingly and unlawfully producing or transferring an identification document or false identification document. The Act imposed penalties

[47] Ibid., xvii, xx. [48] Ibid., 136. Emphasis in original. [49] Ibid., xv.
[50] Westin, "Social and Political," 437. [51] Eaton, *Card-Carrying Americans*, 39.

for possessing five or more false identification documents. It also imposed penalties for possessing false identification documents with the intent to defraud the United States, and for possessing an identification document that appeared to be a US document with knowledge that it was stolen or produced without authority. The Act defined the term "identification document" to mean any document issued by any level of US government or foreign government, or by any international governmental or quasi-governmental organization.[52] Despite those important improvements, Congress never enacted many of the FACFI recommendations.

Westin argues that what the 1970s did produce in terms of privacy developments was a sort of political consensus that data banks should not be allowed to consolidate citizen information from separate local or national government agency files, even if this might provide a more complete picture of citizen–government relationships. Though not expressed in law, this consensus governed data bank applications throughout the 1970s and 1980s. It also became clear during this period that views on privacy did not always follow traditional liberal-conservative ideological lines. Liberals and libertarian-oriented conservatives frequently had the same views on privacy issues. Meanwhile, the media, now accustomed to exposing Watergate and other intrusions, began to attack regularly the privacy invasions of different institutions and warn the public about various Big Brothers.[53]

While the law enforcement and vital statistics officials on FACFI were afraid to recommend a national ID card since they presumed a public backlash, two prominent public figures in the 1970s did independently propose national ID cards. The first one was Frances G. Knight, the Director of the Passport Office, who in 1975 recommended national ID cards with fingerprints. The second one was Theodore Hesburgh, who supported national ID cards during his tenure as Chairman of the Select Commission on Immigration and Refugee Policy.

PROPOSALS FOR NATIONAL ID CARDS IN THE 1970S: FRANCES G. KNIGHT

Frances G. Knight was the Director of the Passport Office at the Department of State (DOS) from 1955 until she was forced into retirement in 1977. Many of her contemporaries described her as the "J. Edgar Hoover

[52] The False Identification Crime Control Act of 1982, Public Law 97–398.
[53] Westin, "Social and Political," 437–438.

of the State Department."[54] She was an efficient and expert bureaucrat whom no politician dared to cross. Her February 1975 statement on the benefits of a national ID card caused a political storm, and no major policymaker would openly support her views on this issue.[55]

Knight had always been concerned with the issue of fraud, not only in passports, but also in Social Security cards, birth certificates, and driver's licenses. For years she had been pointing out that the recorded history of passport frauds dates back to the early 1920s and that the Passport Office had been ringing the alarm on passport and identification frauds since the early 1930s. In fact, within the US government, the Passport Office was the leader in the fight against identification fraud, and Knight was instrumental in the creation of FACFI.[56] She argued that the "lack of decisive, expeditious action and effective control by the upper echelons of our Government who have received these warnings is a sad commentary on those areas charged with official responsibility for our national well-being." She added:

> We are all interested in the well-being of our citizenry. We most certainly should be concerned with the integrity of Government records. The Government owes every American citizen a true identification and protection against the criminal using credentials of either living or deceased citizens. At the present time the victims of sophisticated document fraud are fair-game for life-long blackmail as accessories to this national shame.[57]

On February 23, 1975, Knight gave an interview to the *U.S. News and World Report*. The interview appeared in the March 3 edition, but it received significant attention from February 24 onward, and the controversy surrounding Knight's statements would last for months to come.

In the interview, Knight warned that the United States was facing a fraud and illegal immigration crisis. In her opinion, the government "owes every American citizen a true, recorded identity to protect him from criminal impersonations which can and often do result in blackmail, financial loss, and embarrassment." Knight argued that "national registration eventually will come to this country because it will be demanded by citizens who are sick and tired of supporting nontaxpaying criminals

[54] Sanford J. Ungar, "J. Edgar Hoover Leaves the State Department," *Foreign Policy* 28 (Autumn 1977): 110–116.

[55] Papers of Frances G. Knight, The Manuscript Division, Library of Congress, Washington, DC (Knight Papers).

[56] Ibid.

[57] Frances G. Knight, Talk before the Corporate Travel Association of New York, February 13, 1975.

and illegal aliens." This would involve, in due course, the issuance of an ID card – with fingerprints – to every citizen. She acknowledged that any proposal for a nationwide registration of all American citizens is "loaded with political dynamite, and touches on the sensitive issues of personal privacy and a free society." Yet she concluded that only "an insignificant number" of citizens would be opposed to national registration and having a national ID card.[58]

Knight did not provide any details as to who would be responsible for implementing the project. However, in subsequent clarifications of her position, Knight stressed repeatedly that the Passport Office would not be involved in issuing national ID cards.[59]

Knight's interview stirred up a tempest, and the issue of a national ID card "struck a national nerve."[60] The *Wall Street Journal* proclaimed: "A free people does not submit willingly to government control measures, however innocent they may seem. A society lives by its symbols and any government issued passport or ID card is a symbol of authority."[61] Playwright Arthur Miller ironically referred to Knight's proposal as "an awesome idea," and then ridiculed it.[62] Privacy advocate Robert Ellis Smith argued: "Millions of Americans prize this nation because it still maintains the right to be anonymous, to get a new start in life, to be let alone. A national identity card could mean an end to all that."[63] Some stressed that the government owes the citizen many things, but foremost it owes him the right to be left alone. Others pointed out that Knight chose a particularly bad time to endorse the idea, so soon after Watergate.

Newspaper readers reacted to Knight's proposals. In May 1975, the *National Star* reported that hundreds of its readers had written, and, by a narrow margin, most opposed the scheme. One reader, Mrs. Jean Maria Howard of New Brunswick, New Jersey, wrote, "The very idea of fingerprinting makes me see red – American red! That's how it all started in Germany and Russia. Always for the same slimy excuse – it's for your own good." However, another reader, Lillian Rottmann of Brooklyn,

58 "A National Identity Card for Every American? Interview with Frances G. Knight," *U.S. News and World Report*, March 3, 1975.
59 Knight Papers.
60 Frances Spatz Leighton, "The Case for a Federal Identification Card," *Boston Globe*, April 28, 1975.
61 "Political Dynamite," *Wall Street Journal*, March 7, 1975.
62 Arthur Miller, "On True Identity," *NYT Magazine*, April 13, 1975.
63 Robert Ellis Smith, "The ID Game's Double Standard," *Washington Post*, August 10, 1975.

New York, wrote, "Fingerprinting is a good idea – as deterrent to crime and as an aide in identification in the event of an accident. I was fingerprinted during World War II as a civilian working for the Brooklyn Army Base, and it didn't make me feel like a criminal!"[64]

Milton Valera, editor of the *National Notary*, said that when Knight suggested a national ID card in 1975, "explosions erupted throughout the land as though the fireworks for our '76 Bicentennial had made a premature appearance." He was "among the seething," but then he began to question his "adamant opposition," and came to realize that "ID cards for every American are inevitable." He concluded that Knight's idea is not perfect, but added that

> until someone else offers a solution to curtail the billions of dollars lost through fraud ... prevent the pirating of my good name ... protect me from continuing to support – through taxes – criminals and illegal aliens ... and put an end to the giant governmental bureaucracy that is losing the battle to identify its citizens ... then all Americans will have to realize the time has come for government to provide a recorded identity for every citizen if it intends to enjoy another 200 years as a successful democracy.[65]

Meanwhile, Knight's proposal met with opposition from the ACLU, which protested it to the Secretary of State Henry Kissinger.[66] In April, Attorney General Edward Levi said that he did not like the idea of requiring every employee to carry a card before he gets a job, but he conceded that "we may have to come to that" if the flood of illegal aliens is not stemmed.[67] In June, Levi said that requiring ID cards for all citizens "could happen," but he thought "it would be a great shame if it occurred." He also said he was already greatly concerned with Social Security card being "a kind of domestic passport."[68] Finally, speaking at Stanford University in September 1975, President Gerald Ford indicated he would oppose the idea of a national ID card for every American. He warned that bureaucratic expansion coupled with electronic technology threatens "to strip the individual of privacy and reduce him to a faceless set of digits in a monstrous network of computers."[69] This frightening

64 "Take Your Hands Off Our Fingerprints. That's Your Verdict – But It Was a Close Vote," *National Star*, May 10, 1975.
65 Milton G. Valera, "Comment," *National Notary* 17, 3 (May/June 1975).
66 Knight Papers.
67 "'Domestic Passport' Plan Voided by Levi," *The Miami Herald*, April 4, 1975.
68 "The Attorney General Speaks Out," *U.S. News and World Report*, June 30, 1975.
69 "No Room for a National ID Card," *Washington Star*, September 24, 1975.

image must have added to people's concerns about the dehumanizing effects of ID cards, about being reduced to a number.

Interestingly, there was a discrepancy between attitudes of policymakers and parts of the public opinion. In August 1975, Knight reported that 68 percent of those who wrote letters to her after the March interview supported a national ID system by the federal government.[70] A 1977 Roper poll showed that 51 percent of a nationwide sample favored a mandatory ID card for everybody (citizens and aliens). Of those opposed, 29 percent favored issuance of a tamper-resistant Social Security card in place of the current version.[71] A 1980 Gallup poll found an even larger majority, though the poll did not specifically ask about a national ID card. Rather, the poll asked: "Do you believe everyone in the United States should be required to carry an identification card, such as a Social Security card, or not?" Sixty-two percent of those surveyed believed that everyone should be required to carry such a card, 33 percent stated that they should not have to do so, and 5 percent had no opinion.[72] Still, when 62 percent of people respond in favor of an identification card to be carried by everyone, it seems that they do, in fact, support a national ID card.

PROPOSALS FOR NATIONAL ID CARDS IN THE 1970S AND 1980S: THEODORE HESBURGH AND SCIRP

Frances G. Knight was not the only prominent public figure in the 1970s to support national ID cards. The other person to do so, though independently from Knight, was Father Theodore Hesburgh, the president of Notre Dame University and Chairman of the Select Commission on Immigration and Refugee Policy (SCIRP) between 1979 and 1981.

SCIRP dealt with the question of national ID cards, and Hesburgh was very vocal about his support for such documents. In fact, many years later, after 9/11, sociologist Joseph Eaton wrote that, until recently, no major political figure endorsed properly targeted reliance on biometric identifiers other than Hesburgh.[73] This ignored the role of Knight but, putting that aside, Eaton was largely right.

70 Frances G. Knight, "Of Fingerprints and Identity Cards," *Washington Post*, August 27, 1975.

71 Eaton, *Card-Carrying Americans*, 101–102.

72 Nicholas Laham, *Ronald Reagan and the Politics of Immigration Reform* (Westport, CT: Praeger, 2000), 43.

73 Joseph Eaton, *The Privacy Card: A Low Cost Strategy to Combat Terrorism* (Lanham, MD: Rowman & Littlefield, 2003), xvi.

To understand where Hesburgh's passion for reliable identification documents came from, one has to understand that in the 1970s the United States was beginning to face an illegal immigration crisis. In 1975, the INS estimated the number of illegal aliens living in the United States at about 8 million. The number of illegal aliens was increasing at the rate of more than 250,000 per year.[74]

Hesburgh was one of the people to realize that such crisis could not be resolved without introducing identification documents and employer sanctions. In fact, in the 1970s, 1980s, and 1990s almost all proposals for identification documents tightly overlapped with proposals to fight fraud, address illegal immigration, and introduce employer sanctions.

Many of the illegal immigration problems stemmed from the existence of the so-called Texas Proviso in the Immigration and Nationality Act of 1952. The Proviso had favored farmers and other employers of illegal aliens by exempting them from criminal action for hiring illegal aliens, and in fact permitting it, although it was still illegal for workers to immigrate without documents.[75] In the early 1970s, congressional liberals attempted to make it a crime to employ illegal aliens – an idea first put forward in the 1950s by liberal Senator Paul Douglas (D-IL), an economist of the Cobb–Douglas production function fame. But congressional liberals were blocked by the conservative Senator James Eastland (D-MS), a large-scale farmer interested in cheap agricultural labor, who helped insert the Proviso in 1952, and whose long tenure in the Senate (1943–1978) made him a powerful force. The drive to repeal the Texas Proviso did not succeed until 1986, when the Immigration Reform and Control Act became law.

President Ford felt the popular alarm at illegal aliens, and turned to Attorney General Edward Levi.[76] There are reports that Levi, as a Jew, was "particularly troubled by the prospect of identity cards, roundups, and deportations."[77] Sensing what might come, Levi appointed a committee and stalled. The election of 1976 took Levi and Ford out of the

[74] FACFI, 33.

[75] Michael C. LeMay, *Guarding the Gates: Immigration and National Security* (Westport, CT: Praeger, 2006), 173.

[76] Otis L. Graham, Jr., *Unguarded Gates: A History of America's Immigration Crisis* (Lanham, MD: Rowman & Littlefield, 2004), 106–107.

[77] Roberto Suro, *Watching America's Door: The Immigration Backlash and the New Policy Debate* (New York: Twentieth Century Fund Press, 1996), 33.

picture, and the problem was passed to Jimmy Carter. President Carter made some reform suggestions that received little support on the Hill.[78]

In April 1977, Rep. Peter Rodino (D-NJ), Chairman of the House Judiciary Committee, announced that he would be working with the Carter administration to address the issue of illegal immigration. Rodino stressed that there was a rising cry of protest from unemployed Americans that illegal aliens, accepting pay well below legal minimums, had taken their jobs. He suggested fines and criminal penalties for unscrupulous employers who employed illegal aliens, forgiveness for the bulk of illegal aliens already in the country, a "brown-skin provision" intended to eliminate discrimination, and the development of some kind of "fraudulent-proof" card – in addition to the Social Security card – to be carried by all people in the labor force. Rodino said that the use of Social Security cards had not worked as an identifying device to protect against illegal aliens because criminals could easily counterfeit the cards. Yet, as the *New York Times* noted, Americans are very touchy about being required to carry the type of national ID card used in most foreign countries. The *New York Times* saw Rodino's proposal for an ID card, presumably with a photograph, for people in the labor force as a possible "middle way." Rodino summarized the situation: "A lot of us are reluctant to talk of requiring identity cards, but unless we have some kind of document, we're not going to be able to solve the problem of millions of illegal aliens."[79]

In August 1977, the Carter administration proposed that the Social Security card be one of the authorized documents by which an employer could be assured that a job applicant could work in this country, but also stated that the SSN card should not become a national ID card.[80] President Carter's cabinet witnessed an important split between the Secretary of Labor, Ray Marshall (an economist close to organized labor) and the INS Commissioner, Leonel Castillo (the Carter administration's ranking Latino). Marshall sought only a limited legalization program coupled with the establishment of mandatory worker-eligibility cards, whereas Castillo advocated a large-scale legalization program and opposed worker-eligibility cards on civil liberties grounds.[81] However, the issue that proved particularly divisive was the issue of employer sanctions, that

[78] Graham, *Unguarded Gates*, 106–107.

[79] Edward C. Burks, "ID Cards Suggested to Uncover Aliens," *NYT*, April 25, 1977.

[80] SSA, "Social Security Number Chronology"; Daniel Tichenor, *Dividing Lines: The Politics of Immigration Control in America* (Princeton and Oxford: Princeton University Press, 2002), 234.

[81] Zolberg, *A Nation by Design*, 344.

is, penalties against employers who knowingly hire aliens who are unauthorized to work in the United States.[82]

Wary of intraparty conflicts and with a tough primary and possibly also a presidential campaign on the horizon, Senator Ted Kennedy (D-MA), together with Rep. Rodino and Rep. Joshua Eilberg (D-PA), engineered a postponement of the immigration debate by entrusting the issue to SCIRP, scheduled to report in late 1980.[83] They had the power to make this happen: Rodino was the Chairman of the House Judiciary Committee; Eilberg until January 1979 was the Chairman of the Subcommittee on Immigration, Citizenship, and International Law, of the House Judiciary Committee; and Kennedy would become the Chairman of the Senate Judiciary Committee in January 1979.

President Carter and Congress created SCIRP in October 1978. It became operational in July 1979 and completed its work in the spring of 1981. A joint undertaking of the legislative and executive branches, SCIRP was composed of sixteen commissioners. Four of the commissioners were members of the House of Representatives (two from each party), four were Senators (two from each party), and eight were presidential appointees: four cabinet secretaries (all Democrats) and four public members who represented major Democratic constituencies. SCIRP was a blue-ribbon commission, an independent commission of nonpartisan officials and experts formed to investigate an important governmental issue.

The representatives came from the House Judiciary Committee and included its Chairman Peter Rodino and Representatives Elizabeth Holtzman (D-NY), Robert McClory (R-IL), and Hamilton Fish (R-NY). The senators came from the Senate Judiciary Committee and included its Chairman Ted Kennedy and Senators Alan Simpson (R-WY), Dennis DeConcini (D-AZ), and Charles Mathias (R-MD).

The four cabinet secretaries were Attorney General Benjamin Civiletti, Secretary of Health and Human Services Patricia Roberts Harris, Secretary of Labor Ray Marshall, and Secretary of State Cyrus Vance (replaced in May 1980 by Edmund Muskie).

The four public members were Joaquin Otero, a Cuban-American official at the American Federation of Labor and Congress of Industrial Organizations (AFL-CIO); Rose Ochi, a Japanese-American attorney and

82 Alan K. Simpson, "U.S. Immigration Reform: Employer Sanctions and Antidiscrimination Provisions," *University of Arkansas at Little Rock Law Journal* 9, 4 (1986–1987): 564.

83 Zolberg, *A Nation by Design*, 344.

executive assistant to Los Angeles mayor Tom Bradley; Cruz Reynoso, a Mexican-American judge; and, initially, Reuben Askew, a former governor of Florida.[84] Askew served as SCIRP's chair until his appointment as US trade representative. Hesburgh replaced him on the commission and agreed to chair SCIRP after a personal plea from Vice President Walter Mondale.[85]

Hesburgh, who had already chaired the Civil Rights Commission (1969–1972), chaired SCIRP from 1979 until 1981. SCIRP's staff director was Professor Lawrence Fuchs of Brandeis University, a political scientist known for his research on ethnic interest groups. Fuchs also served on the executive board of the Mexican-American Legal Defense and Education Fund (MALDEF).[86] According to Fuchs, Hesburgh "was just a wonderful boss," had a clear sense of priorities, delegated effectively, supported the staff, and spoke clearly and forcefully.[87]

The issue in front of SCIRP was pressing. A rising influx of illegal aliens from Mexico and increasing refugee pressure from Southeast Asia had made immigration and refugee policy reform imperative, and, as Hesburgh's biographer Michael O'Brien wrote, the issues were exceptionally complex and politically sensitive. Organized labor pushed for employer sanctions against hiring illegal aliens, but civil libertarians, Mexican-American advocacy groups, agri-business, and the Chamber of Commerce opposed the move. Agri-business and the *Wall Street Journal* endorsed a guest worker program, but labor unions, Mexican-American groups, and many liberals opposed it. According to O'Brien, Hesburgh "tried to rise above all the bickering and sought to make the country's policy fair, racist-free, intelligent, open, and systematic."[88]

In his autobiography, Hesburgh recalled how formidable the assignment of SCIRP was:

> to devise a national policy that would with fairness control the millions of illegal aliens who were crossing our borders every year and playing havoc with the labor supply and economics of the country. What made this task doubly difficult, if not near impossible, was that the various economic and political segments in our own pluralistic society had diametrically divergent views on the subject.[89]

[84] "SCIRP Appointment of the Four Public Members," March 22, 1979, www.presidency.ucsb.edu/ws/?pid=32078.

[85] Michael O'Brien, *Hesburgh: A Biography* (Washington, DC: Catholic University of America Press, 1998), 157.

[86] Zolberg, *A Nation by Design*, 354. [87] O'Brien, *Hesburgh*, 157–158. [88] Ibid.

[89] Theodore Martin Hesburgh, *God, Country, Notre Dame*, 2nd ed. (Notre Dame, IN: University of Notre Dame Press, 1999), 257–258.

During its tenure, SCIRP organized seven task forces, examined fifty briefing papers, and held a dozen regional hearings with nearly 700 witnesses and twenty-four seminars with specialized scholars.[90] In the end, SCIRP produced thirteen thick volumes of testimony, findings, and recommendations. The one-volume summary of findings and recommendations was as thick as the New York telephone directory.[91]

Constituted to examine the immigration and refugee laws of the United States, SCIRP was the first joint presidential/congressional commission on the issue. The first major immigration commission in the United States was a congressional commission appointed by President Theodore Roosevelt in 1907. The Dillingham Commission reported in 1911; its race-based recommendations became law in 1921. In 1965, Congress passed the Immigration and Nationality Act, and the country got its first immigration law that attempted to administer immigration without regard to race, color, or national origin. The 1965 law also put limits on immigration, by allowing in only 230,000 immigrants per year, with no more than 20,000 per country.[92]

Hesburgh was frustrated that while the Act allowed for a total of 230,000 immigrants each year, "somewhere between 800,000 and 900,000 were being allowed in as political refugees and anywhere up to 2 million more were coming in illegally each year," though not all were staying. Hesburgh argued that by 1979 "we had between 6 and 12 million illegal aliens living in the United States. All of which meant, in short, that immigration into the United States, legal or not, was massively out of control."[93] Interestingly, a 1980 Census Bureau study for SCIRP argued that the number of illegal aliens residing in the United States was "almost certainly below 6 million and may be substantially less, possibly only 3.5 to 5 million."[94]

Hesburgh believed that the best way of discouraging excess immigration was to make it difficult, if not impossible, for illegal aliens to get jobs without legal entry papers. SCIRP eventually recommended widening the front door to immigration and closing the back door to illegal aliens. Hesburgh argued that "the price for opening the front door to more people was to close the back door by prohibiting companies from hiring people without proper working or immigration papers." SCIRP also recommended an increase in the overall number of aliens permitted to

[90] Zolberg, *A Nation by Design*, 591–592. [91] Hesburgh, *God*, 259. [92] Ibid., 258.
[93] Ibid., 259.
[94] Robert Pear, "Identity Cards Weighed for All Workers in U.S.," *NYT*, July 8, 1980.

enter the United States and work legally, and an amnesty to all illegal aliens who had lived here for five years or more. If they had not been convicted of a felony, they would receive permanent residence and in another five years could apply for citizenship. No longer would they have to fear deportation, and they could begin to pay taxes without fear of discovery. SCIRP members spent much time debating those issues and reaching various compromises. In the end, they believed their recommendations were moderate, doable, and effective.[95]

In closing the back door, SCIRP recommended a law that would require employers to check the identification documents of each of their workers to see if they have a permission to work in the United States (if they have "working papers"). The law would also make the employer legally responsible with penalties of fines and jail (i.e., employer sanctions) if the employer received conviction for knowingly hiring illegal aliens. As Hesburgh put it, people might be able to slip into our wide-open borders, but if they could not get jobs without legal papers, it would do them little good to sneak in. The catch, however, was that millions of illegal aliens were working with forged papers, either a phony Social Security card or a false driver's license. These cards were made of paper and easily duplicated and sold on the black market.[96]

In May 1980, the *New York Times* pointed out that if the government implemented employer sanctions, there would have to be some way of distinguishing citizens and legal aliens from illegal aliens, lest all Mexican-Americans become suspect. Presumably, a worker's ID card would be such a way. At its executive council meeting in February 1980, the AFL-CIO endorsed the idea of an amnesty for illegal aliens, combined with a worker-identification system using counterfeit-resistant Social Security cards. This idea, according to the *New York Times*, was finding growing support on the commission. While some SCIRP members feared that such cards could be used to violate privacy and civil liberties, Hesburgh and others maintained that the potential for abuse could be minimized with a well-written law.[97]

Fuchs argued that the introduction of identification cards could become "the occasion for strengthening the fabric of civil liberties" rather than threatening them. To penalize employers for hiring illegal aliens without providing workers with a means of identification, he believed,

[95] Hesburgh, *God*, 259–260. [96] Ibid.

[97] "U.S. Immigration Panel Near an Agreement on New Policy Goals," *NYT*, May 28, 1980.

would threaten rights of Hispanic Americans and other minorities who might be suspected of being illegal aliens. Fuchs maintained that SCIRP was very conscious of the need to protect civil liberties, but that continued illegal immigration carried risks of its own, including an increased potential for social and political tension. The tension, he warned, could lead to a "xenophobic, racist reaction."[98] The *New York Times* stressed that many experts have concluded that "the problem is serious enough to justify the inconvenience of identification cards. Otherwise, they say, there could be a backlash against minorities and aliens that would pose more danger to civil liberties than the cards would pose."[99]

Hesburgh's solution to the problem, which he could not persuade the commission to adopt, was to pass a law requiring all American citizens and legal residents to carry an upgraded Social Security card in the form of a plastic credit card with embedded microchip carrying essential information. "The card could be made so that it could not be counterfeited – not easily at least – and that would put an end to most of the illegal hiring of aliens."[100] The card would have the owner's photograph and some personal data, probably not including home address. The authorities would phase in the system by issuing work authorization cards to everyone who changed jobs or entered the labor force. The AFL-CIO backed Hesburgh.[101]

Meanwhile, as SCIRP was debating identification documents for workers in the United States, a separate federal commission was hard at work directly opposing what SCIRP was considering. The Civil Rights Commission (formerly chaired by Hesburgh and at the time chaired by former HEW Secretary Arthur Flemming), issued a report in September 1980 titled "The Tarnished Golden Door: Civil Rights Issues in Immigration." It warned of discriminatory practices in the enforcement of immigration law. Three of the five commissioners who participated in the development of the Civil Rights Commission report said they opposed proposals that SCIRP was considering, including a compulsory national ID card, compulsory work permits, and a statute to penalize employers who hired illegal aliens. The commission argued that a national ID card would provide a tool that some could use to violate the right to privacy of individuals. However, two members of the commission issued separate

98 Robert Pear, "Alien Identification Cards Called Civil Rights Threat," *NYT*, June 17, 1980.

99 Pear, "Identity Cards."

100 Hesburgh, *God*, 260–261.

101 Pear, "Identity Cards."

dissenting statements. In support of an employer sanctions law, one commissioner, Frankie Freeman, a civil rights attorney, said that the federal government should make it "more difficult for persons entering illegally to secure employment" by developing an identification system "which will minimize or effectively prevent discrimination against persons legally here." Another commissioner, Stephen Horn, president of California State University at Long Beach, said that he supported an employer sanctions law if it went hand-in-hand with the creation of a "secure and counterfeit-proof Social Security card" that would be used by employers to prevent the inadvertent employment of illegal aliens.[102] Horn, a Republican, would go on to serve in the US House of Representatives (1993–2003) and would become the Chairman of the House Subcommittee that would look into national identifiers in 2001.

The divisions within the Civil Rights Commission and within SCIRP showed just how contentious the issue of identification documents was. In his autobiography, Hesburgh recalled that his proposal for a secure national identification document or just an upgraded Social Security card also raised the hackles of the ACLU and libertarians who argued vociferously that ID cards were an invasion of privacy and the first step toward a totalitarian state. He could not convince these opponents that "all hope of citizen privacy had gone out the window with the advent of computers, computer data banks, and credit-checking organizations." He claimed that American workers already carried Social Security cards, which were registered in Washington, DC, and presented them for identification for a whole host of reasons. An up-to-date, plastic, microchip card would serve the same purpose yet would have the advantage of being difficult and expensive to counterfeit. But he lost that argument.

> The feeling was that our citizens would resent even the idea of carrying identity cards, which are common in Europe. Our position was that the cards need not be carried, would only be used to obtain employment, and could not be demanded or used in any way by the police. We still lost.[103]

At a meeting in December 1980, Hesburgh asked for a vote on tightening current identification requirements. A majority of SCIRP members was in favor.[104] At a news conference that month, Hesburgh said a preliminary vote of seven to five indicated that the panel might recommend the use of identification cards. Hesburgh said that SCIRP's

[102] "Panel Finds Flaws in Immigration Law," *NYT*, September 14, 1980.
[103] Hesburgh, *God*, 261. [104] Smith, *Ben Franklin's Web Site*, 301.

recommendation to punish employers for hiring illegal aliens was "meaningless" without identification cards. However, as the *New York Times* reported, the proposal met with vehement opposition from Hispanic Americans, who asserted that the card would be discriminatory, and civil libertarians, who protested the idea as an invasion of privacy by the government.[105]

On January 6, 1981, after months of intense lobbying and internal dissension, SCIRP announced that it had decided against national ID cards for American workers. The final vote on the identification proposal was nine to six against the idea. One commissioner abstained.[106] It seems that while most of the votes the commissioners took were close to unanimous, votes on identification documents were not. One such close vote was a nine to seven vote on behalf of maintaining existing identification documents, such as Social Security cards, driver's licenses, or INS-issued Green Cards.[107]

The final SCIRP position was that employers should use existing means of identification, including birth certificates, driver's licenses, and immigration documents, to establish whether job applicants were legally entitled to work in the United States. This was so even though along the Mexican border there was a brisk trade in bogus documents of every kind, from passports to Social Security cards, driver's licenses, and baptismal certificates. Birth certificates were available for as little as $50. Despite this, SCIRP did not endorse the use of work permits, identification cards, or a computerized data bank to verify the status of citizens and aliens authorized to work in the United States.[108]

SCIRP members such as Senator Simpson and Chairman Hesburgh regretted that the divided SCIRP failed to endorse a national work permit/identification document that would help employers tell whom they could hire. Simpson dismissed fears of civil libertarians on the commission that a government-issued counterfeit-resistant work permit might become a national ID card, and said he hoped that Congress would approve one. "Enforcement can't work without some kind of identification," he said.[109] Hesburgh warned that "employer sanctions don't work very well

105 "Identification Card Idea Shelved by a U.S. Panel," *NYT*, January 7, 1981.

106 Ibid.

107 Thomas R. Maddux, "Ronald Reagan and the Task Force on Immigration, 1981," *Pacific Historical Review* 74, 2 (2005): 208–209.

108 Robert Pear, "Federal Commission Supports Amnesty for Illegal Aliens," *NYT*, December 8, 1980.

109 John W. Crewdson, "New Administration and Congress Face Major Immigration Decisions," *NYT*, December 28, 1980.

without identification." But Secretary of Health Patricia Roberts Harris said that she was "unalterably opposed" to identification cards because of the potential for wrongful use. She said that adopting a nationwide system of identification cards to deal, at most, with six million illegal aliens would be "a historic redirection of government policy."[110]

SCIRP published its 453-page report on March 1, 1981. Senator Kennedy argued that it represented "the most significant and thoughtful study of American immigration law in three decades."[111] The report contained sixty-seven recommendations designed to reassert control over immigration. In keeping with the longtime aspirations of organized labor, SCIRP advocated imposing sanctions on employers of illegal aliens, yet the final report did not recommend a national ID card or a mandatory work card. Over twenty years later, Joseph Eaton dedicated his 2003 book to Hesburgh and stated that "September 11, 2001 might never have happened had his advocacy of biometric ID documents been supported."[112]

In his autobiography, Hesburgh recalled that SCIRP members thought their recommendations were moderate, and with the backing of President Carter and the active support of Vice President Mondale, the report would face little trouble in Congress in becoming the law of the land.[113] However, Carter lost the election. Ronald Reagan won the White House and Republicans gained control of the Senate for the first time since 1954.

In the final days of Carter's administration, the SCIRP staff worked virtually around the clock to complete the report to the president and Congress as mandated in the law that created the commission. However, as Hesburgh recalls, once Reagan became president, the new Republican administration decided to reinvent the wheel. President Reagan set up his own fact-finding commission and that commission spent another two years going over the same material, the same issues, the same difficulties as SCIRP did, and in the end adopted the same recommendations as SCIRP had.[114] Despite the change in administration, SCIRP set the agenda for an entire decade, leading to the enactment of major legislation in 1986 and 1990.[115]

110 Pear, "Federal Commission."
111 Robert Pear, "Panel Asks Rise in Immigration, with Tighter Law Enforcement," *NYT*, February 27, 1981.
112 Eaton, *The Privacy Card*, dedication page. 113 Hesburgh, *God*, 261. 114 Ibid.
115 Zolberg, *A Nation by Design*, 354.

IDENTIFICATION PROPOSALS IN THE 1980S

As historian Thomas Maddux demonstrated, immigration was not a major priority for President Reagan and his conservative agenda in 1981. On March 3, 1981, Walter Cronkite of CBS News visited Reagan in the White House for a prime time special focusing on the first two months of his administration. Although most of the questions focused on other issues, Cronkite did bring up immigration at the end of the interview. When he asked the president about illegal immigration and proposals for employer sanctions and national ID cards to help employers verify the status of workers, Reagan redirected the discussion to a proposal by US and Mexican border state governors and commented that it intrigued him.[116] The *Washington Post* later suggested that Reagan had jumped over the recent SCIRP report: "That swarm of loose papers you saw blowing around Lafayette Square the other day" might have been the SCIRP report, as Reagan, in "a truly flabbergasting way ... brushed past its recommendations and pronounced himself 'very intrigued' by a suggestion from elsewhere."[117]

Importantly, just a couple of weeks earlier, in February 1981 Reagan established an interagency Immigration Task Force of his own administration under Attorney General William French Smith. The Task Force consisted of representatives from the Departments of State, Justice, Commerce, Defense, Labor, Treasury, Transportation, and the Office of Man agement and Budget (OMB).[118] According to Maddux, it was a "combination of political, economic, congressional, and diplomatic pressures" that prompted Reagan to establish a task force on immigration and to propose in July significant legislative and administrative changes that ultimately contributed to the Immigration Reform and Control Act of 1986. Between February and August 1981, the Task Force and a White House working group on immigration prepared recommendations that Reagan approved with a significant revision only on illegal immigrants. However, many immigration specialists and historians have dismissed what Reagan submitted to Congress as having little consequence. Others have criticized him as taking the least risky political path and abdicating leadership on the issue to Congress.[119]

[116] Maddux, "Ronald Reagan," 195.

[117] "A President 'Intrigued,'" *Washington Post*, March 6, 1981.

[118] William French Smith, *Law and Justice in the Reagan Administration: The Memoirs of an Attorney General* (Stanford, CA: Hoover Institution Press, 1991), 193–195.

[119] Maddux, "Ronald Reagan," 198.

The relative lack of treatment of the Task Force in the scholarly literature means even leading immigration scholars such as Aristide Zolberg and Daniel Tichenor differ on what the Task Force recommended. According to Zolberg, the Task Force substantially agreed with SCIRP on the legalization of unauthorized residents currently in the United States, though it differed from SCIRP on employer sanctions. According to Zolberg, the Task Force members suggested the establishment of a national ID card. According to Tichenor, however, most Task Force members agreed that national ID cards "would invade the privacy of individuals and threaten civil liberties." When polls revealed sharply negative reactions to a national ID card, Task Force members quickly dropped the idea.[120]

Yet the story is more nuanced. As Maddux shows, during the 1980 campaign and his transition to the White House, Reagan gave immigration little attention. However, the expected arrival of the SCIRP report and the political and public concerns about the Cuban and Haitian refugees prompted a White House working group to review the immigration and refugee issues on February 9. The working group noted a series of "action forcing events," such as the publication of the SCIRP report on March 1. White House officials recognized that congressional leaders would hold hearings and propose legislation on immigration as soon as possible after the SCIRP report arrived. White House officials Frank Hodsoll and Edwin Gray warned that the SCIRP report, "plus political (including Congressional) reaction to the immigration/refugee problem make 1981 a year in which we must make progress."[121]

Reagan agreed to Attorney General Smith's request to set up an interagency Immigration Task Force. The initial timeline for the Task Force set aside little more than a month to review the SCIRP report, consult other governmental reviews and specialist studies, and submit recommendations to the White House after Reagan's scheduled meeting with Mexican President Lopez Portillo in April. The attempted assassination of Reagan on March 30 pushed the meeting with Portillo back to June, and the task force submitted its recommendation to Reagan on July 1.[122]

As Maddux shows, it was Frank Hodsoll, who had no prior experience with immigration, who became the main White House liaison with the Task Force and the coordinator of the White House working group on immigration. Hodsoll anticipated that immigration could divide the

[120] Zolberg, *A Nation by Design*, 357; Tichenor, *Dividing Lines*, 256.
[121] Maddux, "Ronald Reagan," 204–205. [122] Ibid., 205.

conservatives since some conservatives favored a law-and-order approach against illegal immigrants; libertarians resisted any expansion of the federal government's control over individuals; and congressional Republicans remained responsive to agricultural and other business supporters and wanted a reliable, semi-skilled workforce. What Hodsoll may not have recognized then was that he would face strong opposition from within the White House. The opposition would be led by Martin Anderson, the Assistant to the President for Policy Development. Anderson worried from the start about not having policy control over the issue and the Task Force, even as his wife, Annelise Anderson, represented the OMB on the Task Force and the working group.[123]

The Task Force and White House officials viewed continued illegal immigration as the most serious issue. By the end of April, the Task Force recommended a package of options to deal with the illegal immigration problem. It talked about creating a small-scale amnesty program for long-time illegal aliens and a short-term foreign worker program for the much larger number of illegal aliens in the United States. The Task Force hoped that legalization would lessen Mexico's concern about employer sanctions. The Task Force mentioned an option for a call-in data bank that would help employers verify employee eligibility. It also mentioned an option to create a more secure, tamper-proof Social Security card, which the government would phase in for 20 million hires a year, at an estimated cost of $89.4 million per year.[124]

Maddux shows that the Task Force's preliminary recommendations on employer sanctions and verification initiated divisions between the Task Force and the White House senior staff, including Counselor Edwin Meese and Martin Anderson. Anderson even attended the Task Force meeting on April 30, and used "Reagan's record" as his authority to express reservations about employer sanctions and a new worker identification card and to push for a large temporary worker program. Meanwhile, Hodsoll tried to reassure Meese, Anderson, and Chief of Staff James Baker about the Task Force recommendations, and he pointed out the strong support in polls and among Republican and Democratic congressmen for both employer sanctions and a way to verify the status of workers. Hodsoll told Baker: "The additional infringements on American liberties (we already require a Social Security card number) are minimal."[125]

[123] Ibid., 205–206. [124] Ibid., 219–221. [125] Ibid., 221.

On June 3, Meese and Baker presented Reagan with two approaches to the immigration problem, both of which would increase legal immigration. The first involved a major temporary worker program of up to 600,000, split between illegal aliens in the United States and Mexican workers, and conversion to permanent resident status only after ten years. Meese and Baker favored this solution since it avoided a direct amnesty, would not introduce employer sanctions, and would minimize the expansion of governmental regulation and reduce the pressure for a national ID card. But most of the departments on the Task Force favored a second approach, which involved a large legalization program, employer sanctions, and reliance on a more secure Social Security card.[126]

The Task Force submitted its report on July 1, but, according to Maddux, the White House conflict over employer sanctions and worker verification only intensified. Reagan's advisers lacked a clear direction from the president, so they maneuvered and competed to get approval for what they considered to be his views based on his conservative philosophy and past record. Anderson led the opposition to the Task Force report, and Hodsoll mounted a defense. Anderson emphasized the escalating costs of employer sanctions and ID cards and libertarian hostility to ID cards. He also skillfully used the results of an opinion poll, conducted by pollster Richard Wirthlin, which appeared to show the public's opposition to national ID cards.[127]

The poll, conducted by Wirthlin in early June 1981, found that only 29 percent of respondents supported the creation of a national ID card, while 68 percent opposed it. This, Wirthlin claimed, was so even though the poll raised the issue in the context of a way to deal with the problem of illegal aliens. Political scientist Nicholas Laham rightly noted that Wirthlin's poll was in direct conflict with the Gallup poll released in November 1980, which showed that an overwhelming majority of the public supported the creation of a national ID card. However, while Gallup asked its respondents a straightforward question ("Do you believe that every individual should be required to carry an identity card?"), Wirthlin's poll was biased as he framed his poll questions with arguments against ID cards. Such arguments must have contributed to a strong negative reaction, which Wirthlin then described as a consensus across political affiliation and ethnic background. Wirthlin claimed that liberals opposed the plan as an abridgement of civil liberties, while conservatives opposed

[126] Ibid., 222. [127] Ibid., 222–223.

the plan because it was yet another intrusion by Big Brother government into the lives of its citizens. Wirthlin also warned that no one believed very strongly the notion that any system could in fact be forge-proof. Laham noted that rather than acting as an objective pollster, who was attempting to provide the White House with the accurate information it needed to decide whether to recommend the creation of a national ID card, Wirthlin turned out to be an advocate for those opposed to such a proposal. The biased results of Wirthlin's poll "essentially eliminated whatever chance existed that the Reagan administration would include the creation of a national identity card among the recommendations on immigration reform which it planned to make to Congress."[128]

This does ignore, however, the role of a cabinet meeting that took place in July 1981, either on July 13 (according to Maddux) or on July 16 (according to Anderson). Anderson's fascinating account shows how close Reagan and his cabinet were that day to agreeing to Attorney General Smith's proposal for an improved Social Security card, or perhaps even a national ID card. Anderson recalled that Smith presented a logical review of the immigration issue: since INS could not stop illegal immigrants at the border, the United States had to discourage them from coming by keeping them from getting jobs and by making it illegal to hire them. An improved Social Security card would accomplish this objective. Smith emphasized broad support for action from Congress and a Gallup opinion poll and stressed that we "need to move now."[129] Smith, who was Reagan's former personal lawyer and held his trust and confidence, outlined his plan to the president and the cabinet and seemed to win them over. Then, according to Anderson, just a short intervention by Anderson himself, followed by an equally brief one by James Watt, the Secretary of the Interior, was all it took to convince Reagan to end the proposal. After Smith finished outlining his proposal and cabinet members did not voice any comments or express any objections, Anderson broke the unwritten rule that senior staff members may sit in on cabinet meetings but are not to speak unless spoken to. He raised his hand, and when Reagan called on him to speak, Anderson stated, "Mr. President, one of my concerns about the national identity card is that the [OMB] has estimated that it could cost several billions of dollars to produce a counterfeit-proof Social Security card for everyone." Anderson recalls that this statement did not seem to make much of an impact, and he knew that this was not the time

[128] Laham, *Ronald Reagan*, 91–97. [129] Maddux, "Ronald Reagan," 224.

for a long-winded, theoretical critique of ID cards, so he decided to try humor and a little shock. Anderson proclaimed:

> I would like to suggest another way that I think is a lot better. It's a lot cheaper. It can't be counterfeited. It's very lightweight, and impossible to lose. It's even waterproof. All we have to do is tattoo an identification number on the inside of everybody's arm.

This silenced the room and eventually James Watt commented that to him it sounded like talking about "the mark of the Beast," a reference to the Book of Revelation in the Bible. When the Attorney General wanted to defend his position, Reagan cut him off and joked: "Maybe we should just brand all the babies." Anderson recalls that for about ten seconds "everybody laughed and smiled, and that was the end of the national identification card for 1981."[130]

Later in July, Hodsoll attempted to rescue part of the plan. On the ID card issue, Hodsoll dropped the Task Force's call for an improved Social Security card and instead proposed to use the existing card and other supporting identifiers. With Baker's support, Hodsoll received Reagan's approval for all of the Task Force's recommendations, with the exception of an improved Social Security card for employee verification. Reagan also opposed the creation of a national ID card. His recommendations included a requirement for employers to request from the prospective employees either an INS-issued document such as a Green Card or any two of the following: birth certificate, driver's license, Social Security card, Select Service registration certificate, sworn statement of lawful US residence, or other evidence of lawful US residence or citizenship.[131]

The president approved a continuation of legal immigration as an affirmation of "America's tradition as a land that welcomes peoples from other countries, a shining city upon the hill, a beacon of freedom." He endorsed the Task Force's recommendation of an increase in yearly admissions. Most of Reagan's proposals focused on illegal immigration. First, Reagan recommended temporary legal status for all illegal immigrants in the country before January 1980, which could be changed to permanent-resident status after ten years if they demonstrated proficiency in English. Second, Reagan proposed measures to prevent the influx of more illegal immigrants by requesting increased funding for INS for

[130] Martin Anderson, *Revolution: The Reagan Legacy* (Stanford, CA: Hoover Institution Press, Stanford University, 1990), 272–277.

[131] Maddux, "Ronald Reagan," 225–226, 234.

improved enforcement. Third, Reagan asked Congress to enact the Task Force's system of employer sanctions and worker verification procedures, including a specified list of valid employee identification documents, but no national ID card and no new, improved Social Security card.[132]

While the administrative initiatives represented a new and important beginning, equally important were legislative reforms. According to Attorney General Smith, "the nation owes a debt of gratitude" to Senator Alan Simpson, Rep. Romano Mazzoli (D-KY), and Rep. Dan Lungren (R-CA) for the persistence and hard work required to bring immigration legislation to passage. "It would never have happened without them. This was legislation in the long-term public interest but which cut against a host of short-term special interests. There was no political benefit, only travail for the sponsors."[133]

Indeed, Alan Simpson, one of the two Republican senators on SCIRP and the Chairman of the Immigration Subcommittee of the Senate Judiciary Committee, emerged as a key player on immigration issues. Simpson's counterpart in the still-Democratic House was Rep. Mazzoli, a Notre Dame graduate who earlier helped persuade Hesburgh to become the chair of SCIRP.[134] After SCIRP published its report in March 1981, the House and Senate Subcommittees on Immigration, chaired respectively by Mazzoli and Simpson, began a series of hearings on SCIRP's findings. In March 1982, Simpson and Mazzoli introduced in each body a joint bill, which followed closely the recommendations of SCIRP. It was clear that both Simpson and Mazzoli held Hesburgh and his work in high regard. The bill included provisions for penalties against employers who knowingly hire illegal aliens and procedures for an employer verification system, including provisions to make that system more secure. The bill required employers to check the documents of all new employees – even if they were US citizens and regardless of their immigration status – and to keep a record of this check. The bill also required a presidential study of the existing documents that would be used to establish employment eligibility. The bill directed the president to, within three years, make improvements to make the system more secure against fraudulent use. While the bill did not specify what changes could be made, it prohibited any new ID document that might be developed from being a national ID card. It also prohibited it from being required to be carried on one's

132 Ibid., 226–227. 133 Smith, *Law and Justice*, 199–200.
134 Zolberg, *A Nation by Design*, 357–358.

person, being used for other law enforcement purposes, and being withheld for any reason other than lack of employment eligibility.[135]

Simpson and Mazzoli believed – as did many SCIRP members – that, without secure identification documents, employers would be less likely to accept without question certain current documents that were easily counterfeited. Not only would such a situation dilute the effectiveness of employer sanctions, but it could lead to increased incentive for employers to scrutinize the documents of those employees who appeared foreign. While increased document scrutiny is not a form of discrimination that is as objectionable as actual denial of employment, Simpson and Mazzoli nonetheless wished to avoid it.[136]

The Simpson–Mazzoli bill died with the expiration of the 97th Congress (1981–1983), but Simpson and Mazzoli reintroduced it in the 98th Congress (1983–1985). Senator Mark Hatfield (R-OR), who wanted to avoid the development of a national ID card, sponsored an amendment that required the president to send any proposal for a new card or other document to Congress, which could reject the proposal if within thirty days it passed a concurrent resolution objecting to the new card. *Immigration and Naturalization Service v. Chadha* has since invalidated such amendment mechanism, legislative veto. As Simpson would later reflect, the amendment was an omen of things to come in the House, where there was much less support for a secure worker verification system. Just as in the 97th Congress the Senate passed the bill by a vote of seventy-six to eighteen, in the 98th Congress, in May 1983, the Senate passed the bill once again by a vote of seventy-six to eighteen.[137]

The bill in the House was subject to significant changes. Lungren successfully reinserted a requirement that employers must record the document numbers of all new employees, whether or not the employer had previously violated the section. The House approved an amendment by Rep. Sam Hall (D-TX) that required establishment of a nationwide "telephone call-in" system that would verify the SSNs of all applicants and act as the sole step an employer would be required to take in verifying an employee's eligibility. Rep. Edward Roybal (D-CA) successfully proposed an amendment that deleted the requirement that the president study the security of existing documents and report back to Congress in three years. The House bill now contained no provisions – other than the Hall telephone system, which relied on existing Social Security cards – that

[135] Simpson, "U.S. Immigration Reform," 571–573. [136] Ibid., 573.
[137] Simpson, "U.S. Immigration Reform," 574–575.

would provide for a secure worker verification system. In June 1984, Roybal claimed this approach was necessary to avoid a "national identification system." The House narrowly passed the bill, by a vote of 216 to 211, and a conference committee convened to resolve the differences between the House and Senate bills. Eventually, Senate conferees reluctantly agreed to delete all of the secure verification provisions in the conference bill with the exception of the telephone system. However, there were other irresolvable differences, and in October 1984 the bill died in the conference committee.[138]

Policymakers introduced immigration reform legislation again in the 99th Congress (1985–1987). The Senate bill, S.1200, continued to encourage employers to verify employment eligibility and to retain employment records, but avoided creating a civil penalty structure for mere paperwork violations. In addition, the bill altered the proposal for the secure worker verification system to respond to concerns that Congress would not have sufficient opportunity to review any new verification system that the president might decide to implement. While the bill still directed the president to implement a more secure system if current documents did not prove adequate, it added two new restrictions. First, the president could not implement a nonmajor change in the system (such as an improvement or change in the existing Social Security card) without sixty days' notice to Congress. Second, the president could not implement a major change to the system (such as a new document or identifier, or a telephone verification system) without two years' notice to Congress and without Congress specifically appropriating funds for it.[139]

In a 1985 congressional testimony, Hesburgh expanded on the need for a secure employment verification system. During Senate hearings, Simpson asked Hesburgh: "How do you respond to those persons who claim that discrimination is only going to increase due to employer sanctions?" Hesburgh replied:

> I find that the most flimsy argument that I have heard in this whole area, because if you take seriously what I have said as a kind of tripartite approach to this problem; namely, employer sanctions, a good ID card of some kind, and legalization, then if you go to get employment, and someone says I am not interested because you look un-American, or some such things, you just flash a card that says you are eligible for employment, and [if] someone does not employ you, there is a very serious law about that kind of behavior. The ID is what saves you from discrimination.[140]

[138] Ibid., 575–579. [139] Ibid., 580–581. [140] Quoted in ibid., 569–570.

The bill passed the Senate by a vote of by eighty to nineteen. Smith, who was Attorney General until February 1985, recalled that, "as always," "the problem was in the House."[141] Yet during the conference committee consideration of the legislation, House conferees agreed to adopt the Senate provisions regarding a future method of establishing a secure worker verification system. This provision had been very controversial in the House during the 98th Congress, but the added safeguards of the Senate bill removed much of the opposition in the House during the 99th Congress. Both the House and the Senate passed the conference reports. Reagan signed the bill on November 6 and the Immigration Reform and Control Act of 1986 (IRCA) became law.[142]

Time would reveal that IRCA's most important legacy was an amnesty program that enabled some 2.7 million illegal immigrants to gain legal permanent resident (LPR) status in the United States (i.e., receive a Green Card) and put them on the road to citizenship. The amnesty applied to illegal immigrants who entered the United States before January 1, 1982, and to certain illegal seasonal agricultural workers. Nearly 1.6 million people received the LPR status under general legalization and nearly 1.1 million people received it under the Special Agricultural Workers program.[143] Because of the cut-off date, IRCA excluded about half of the illegal population, thereby "leaving the goal of wiping the illegal immigration slate clean well short of reality," according to the Migration Policy Institute (MPI) report on the consequences of IRCA. Some 2.5 million people remained illegal: 2 million people excluded by the cut-off date and 500,000 who were eligible but did not legalize. Many of the people who were not eligible for legalization under IRCA had immediate family members who were eligible and legalized. The government eventually granted such noneligible people "indefinite voluntary departure," a semi-legal status allowing them to stay and work in the United States. The Immigration Act of 1990 helped such people by creating a "family unity" program, which extended the semi-legal status of these family members until they could receive Green Cards through the normal family preference categories.[144]

IRCA made it illegal to hire an illegal alien but imposed sanctions only if the employer knew the worker was in the country illegally. IRCA,

141 Smith, *Law and Justice*, 199.

142 Simpson, "U.S. Immigration Reform," 589.

143 Muzaffar Chishti and Charles Kamasaki, "IRCA in Retrospect: Guideposts for Today's Immigration Reform," MPI, January 2014, 13.

144 Ibid., 6.

which is still the law, requires that employers determine the legal status of any new worker hired after November 6, 1986, by examining documents that establish the worker's identity and employment authorization. In some cases, two documents may be required. For instance, a new worker may show a driver's license (or just a school ID card with a photograph) to prove identity, and a US birth certificate or a Social Security card to prove employment authorization. In other cases, one document alone may achieve both purposes, as passports issued to US citizens and Green Cards issued to LPRs show both. The government presents a list of acceptable documents at the end of the Employment Eligibility Verification Form I-9. The law requires every employer to sign a Form I-9, attesting under penalty of perjury that he or she examined the required documents. The law also requires every employee to sign the same form, attesting under penalty of perjury that the employee is either a US citizen, a lawfully admitted permanent resident, or an alien authorized to work. Employers must retain completed I-9 forms and make them available for inspection by US government officials.

One important loophole in the law is the provision that employers are not required to verify the immigration status of contractors. Therefore, following IRCA's implementation, there has been a major increase in the purposeful misclassification of workers as independent contractors.[145]

An even greater problem with the law is that IRCA contained no requirement that employers verify the authenticity of the documents presented. While IRCA makes employers attest that they have examined documents that establish their workers' identity and eligibility to work lawfully, the law does not require employers to receive training or to have expertise in detecting fraudulent documents.[146] The MPI report on the consequences of IRCA explains the reasoning behind this rather counter-intuitive decision:

> There is a strong, rational basis for not requiring employers to determine that the documents presented by job applicants are genuine. Since the vast majority of employers lack the expertise to distinguish legitimate papers from false ones, IRCA's drafters feared that some employers would decline to hire legal residents and U.S. citizens based on inaccurate perceptions of the authenticity of documents presented by "foreign-looking" job applicants.[147]

Thirty years since IRCA became law, IRCA's employer requirements are still in place. Since IRCA requires employers to examine documents,

[145] Ibid., 5. [146] Ibid., 3. [147] Ibid., 12.

yet does not give them training in detecting fraudulent documents, the main guidance for employers comes from the "Handbook for Employers," currently issued by the U.S. Citizenship and Immigration Services (USCIS).[148] As employers fill out Form I-9, the instructions on the form refer them to the Handbook, where they can view illustrations of many of the documents acceptable for the purposes of Form I-9. The Handbook reminds employers that immigration authorities do not expect employers to be document experts.[149] The law deems employers in compliance if the document(s) they examined "reasonably appear on their face to be genuine and to relate to the person presenting them."[150]

The Handbook, revised in 2013, tells employers:

> If you are presented with documentation that does not reasonably appear to be genuine or to relate to the employee, you cannot accept that documentation. While you are not legally required to inform DHS of such situations, you may do so if you choose. However, DHS is unable to provide employment eligibility verification services other than through its E-Verify program.[151]

Thus, IRCA left an important but confusing legacy. The law for the first time mandated employer sanctions, but legislative wrangling watered down IRCA's employer sanctions provisions and Congress did not establish any secure identification system for employee eligibility. As Tichenor points out, almost from the start, the odds were stacked against employer sanctions working effectively to curb illegal immigration. The absence of a reliable identification system for verifying employee eligibility made it relatively easy for illegal aliens to evade detection at the workplace. Soon after IRCA's enactment, an underground industry of fraudulent documents flourished in the United States and Mexico, enabling illegal aliens to obtain work with ease. As Tichenor notes, the Reagan and Bush administrations were not zealous in their enforcement of employer sanctions. Few Reagan officials favored rigorous enforcement of employer sanctions at a time when "deregulation" was the watchword of the executive branch.[152]

In 2006, Simpson and Mazzoli wrote an op-ed in the *Washington Post* that reflected on IRCA. They stressed their pride of authorship, but also noted that the shortcomings of the act are due not to design failure but rather to the failure of both Democratic and Republican administrations

[148] USCIS, "Handbook for Employers. Guidance for Completing Form I-9," M-274 (revised April 30, 2013).
[149] Ibid., 53. [150] Ibid., 42. [151] Ibid., 50.
[152] Tichenor, *Dividing Lines*, 261–262.

since 1986 to execute the law properly. They also showed a palpable regret that IRCA did not include a more secure identifier:

> We saw the need for funding to develop a simple, reliable and tamper-proof system, a "more secure identifier," using cards or biometrics. Opponents from the right and the left savaged it as "a National ID," although it was not something that had to be carried on one's person but was to be presented only at the time of "new hire" employment or when applying for government benefits.
>
> After two decades, the system is still not in place. Unfortunately, what is in place is the use of several different identifiers, which were meant to be temporary, and a flourishing underground economy engaged in creating fraudulent documents for illegal immigrants.[153]

Hesburgh expressed similar sentiments. During the five years it took for the Simpson–Mazzoli bill to become IRCA, Hesburgh had set up and operated a small watchdog shadow commission to lobby for the SCIRP recommendations. Hesburgh tried to keep the pressure on Congress so that the Simpson–Mazzoli bill would not slip through the cracks and be lost. By and large, IRCA did incorporate most, if not all, of SCIRP's original recommendations. Writing in 1999, Hesburgh acknowledged that although for the first three years after IRCA illegal entry into the United States slowed perceptibly, in 1990 there was resurgence in illegal entry. In addition, illegal immigrants still use forged documents in great numbers and employers continue to hire them, often knowingly. Hesburgh concluded: "I still like my microchip identity card as a way of curbing illegal working papers."[154]

Interestingly, while many from the right and the left criticized any increases in the security of identification documents and claimed they were inevitably leading to a national ID card, public opinion in the 1980s was significantly more inclined toward both employment sanctions and identification documents. As historian Otis Graham reports, in 1983, 79 percent of Gallup respondents favored the concept of employer sanctions, central to the Simpson–Mazzoli bill. More than six in ten people said that everyone in the United States should be required "to carry an identification card such as a Social Security card." It was not until 1983 that the polls addressed whether all racial and ethnic groups shared such sentiments. Some Hispanic organizations, such as MALDEF, opposed national ID cards and asserted that Hispanics opposed employer

[153] Romano L. Mazzoli and Alan K. Simpson, "Enacting Immigration Reform, Again," *Washington Post*, September 15, 2006.

[154] Hesburgh, *God*, 262.

sanctions and were not supporters of reforms that limited either legal or illegal immigration. Surveys, however, showed a different picture. Surveys taken in 1983 and 1984 revealed that substantial majorities of Hispanics favored penalties on employers hiring illegal aliens and favored increased funding for the Border Patrol, while believing that illegal aliens take jobs from American workers. An October 1984 Gallup poll confirmed these results, reporting that 75 percent of Hispanics supported employer sanctions, even if ID cards would be required. Whether it was representative of the Hispanic public opinion or not, a letter to House Speaker Tip O'Neill (D-MA) sent in October 1983 by Henry Lacayo and Joaquin Otero (who was a SCIRP member) on behalf of the Labor Council for Latin American Advancement stated, "There is indeed more than strong support for immigration law reform. Hispanics support not only a generous amnesty, but strong employer sanctions ... and identification for employment purposes as well."[155] At the same time, the Federation for American Immigration Reform (FAIR) also supported employer sanctions and even national ID cards. FAIR, which emerged as the major restrictionist voice on immigration issues, also backed tighter control of the border and stronger enforcement of immigration laws and opposed amnesty.[156]

IDENTIFICATION PROPOSALS IN THE 1990S

The 1990s generated another set of debates on identification documents and immigration. The start of the decade brought the Immigration Act of 1990, which increased the number of legal immigrants allowed into the United States each year and created a diversity visa lottery program. IRCA and the Immigration Act of 1990 effectively implemented the full set of SCIRP recommendations.

However, the passage of the Immigration Act of 1990 was not smooth. The House and Senate bills looked very different from one another, and a conference agreement was even more difficult to reach than in 1986. Simpson emerged as a major conference player, despite his now minority status. At one point, Simpson won approval for a pilot program officials would carry out in three states to produce fraud-proof driver's licenses, which employers would then check to help verify employment eligibility.

[155] Otis L. Graham, Jr., "Uses and Misuses of History in the Debate over Immigration Reform," *The Public Historian* 8, 2 (spring 1986): 49–50.

[156] Zolberg, *A Nation by Design*, 359–360.

This was not in the original Senate bill, but a General Accounting Office (GAO) report released earlier in the year found that the fear of employer sanctions enacted in 1986 was causing employers to discriminate against foreign-looking workers. Simpson insisted therefore that employers needed a more certain means for determining whether a worker was legal. On October 26, 1990, the Senate agreed to the bill's conference report by a vote of eighty-nine to eight, but the conference agreement ran into unexpected opposition in the House, where the Hispanic caucus challenged Simpson's pilot program for secure driver's licenses. Rep. Roybal once again became a significant obstacle. This time, Roybal pointed out that since the provision regarding Simpson's pilot program had not been included in either the House or Senate versions of the legislation when the two chambers passed them, it was outside the scope of the conference committee to insert the pilot program this late in the process.[157] Roybal was the person who, back in 1984, successfully campaigned against the requirement that the president study the security of existing identification documents and claimed this approach was necessary to avoid a "national identification system."

The Hispanic legislators saw the pilot program as leading to a new identification card linked to employer sanctions. Rep. Esteban Torres (D-CA) drew analogies to passbooks in South Africa and slave certificates in the United States. He argued that "the government of South Africa, after years of struggle, just abolished identifier pass books that were used to discriminate against its black citizens. Ironically, at the same time, the United States considers taking the idea up."[158] Torres argued that a new identification card invited civil rights abuses. Apparently alarmed by this development, Rep. Barney Frank (D-MA) met with Senator Simpson late in the evening to request that he drop his pilot program; Simpson gave in; and the House passed the bill on October 27, by a vote of 264 to 118.[159] President George H. W. Bush signed the Act into law on November 29, 1990.

The Immigration Act of 1990 authorized the creation of a bipartisan Commission on Immigration Reform. Barbara Jordan chaired the commission from 1993 until her death in 1996. Jordan was a former Democratic Congresswoman from Texas (1973–1979). The commission issued

[157] James G. Gimpel and James R. Edwards, Jr., *The Congressional Politics of Immigration Reform* (Boston: Allyn and Bacon, 1999), 193.
[158] Congressional Record, October 26, 1990, H129850.
[159] Tichenor, *Dividing Lines*, 274.

two interim reports (in 1994 and 1995) and two final reports (in 1997), and President Bill Clinton supported many of the commission's recommendations.

The commission's most famous recommendation, which drew fire from both civil libertarians and conservatives, but gathered support from others, called for the creation of a computerized registry of SSNs for verification of work eligibility. A Social Security–based computer system would allow employers and authorities to work together to verify the validity of a SSN and establish that the number tendered had been issued to the person being hired. Commissioners argued that if unauthorized would-be workers could not find work, even with fraudulent documents in hand, the illegal border crossings would drop off.[160]

In July 1994, Jordan appeared to endorse the idea of a mandatory work card with photograph, possibly a plastic national ID card, or at least a tamper-proof Social Security card.[161] But when Jordan testified before a Senate committee in August, she did not propose a national ID card, endorsing instead the idea of a more secure ID document for workers and a better database for employers to verify the identity and citizenship of any job applicant. Jordan also argued for a pilot program in the five states with the highest levels of immigration, which would help determine the respective benefits of a more secure Social Security card, counterfeit-resistant driver's license, and telephone verification system. She added, however, that the pilot and any resulting legislation to establish the system on a permanent basis must provide protection against use of the verification process for purposes other than those specified in law:

> The Commission shares the civil liberties concerns of many in this country that the process for verifying employment authorization [does] not become the basis for a national identity system. We believe the same system could be used, without damage to civil liberties, for verifying eligibility to receive public benefits. However, no one should be required to carry a card, should one be used, or present it for routine identification purposes. There must also be significant penalties for inappropriate demands for the identification.[162]

Meanwhile, Senator Simpson, Chairman of the Immigration Subcommittee and primary advocate of the verification system, emphasized that

160 Gimpel and Edwards, *The Congressional Politics*, 217.

161 Smith, *Ben Franklin's Web Site*, 302.

162 Barbara Jordan, Testimony, Subcommittee on Immigration and Refugee Affairs, Committee on the Judiciary, Senate, 103rd Congress, August 3, 1994.

any proposed card would be required to get a job and to get health care, though he insisted that it would not evolve into an all-purpose card.

Does this mean we are creating a "national ID card"? Not at all. I have always provided in my legislation, as the commission has in its recommendation, that no one would be required to carry a card, should one be used, or to present it to law enforcement officials for routine identification purposes. The card, if there is to be one, would be presented *only* at the time of new-hire employment, or at the time of application for federally funded benefits, including health care.[163]

In May 1995, Simpson reemphasized his position:

[I]n attempting to more reliably verify personal identity, we are not – hear this clearly – we are not attempting to create a national ID card. I have had enough of that accusation. We are not limiting any American's privacy or personal liberties. We are not talking of tattoos or Adolf Hitler. We are trying to address the very, very serious problems our Nation faces today as a result of the widespread availability and use of fraudulent identification.[164]

The 1990s also brought a range of other legislative and executive proposals for identification documents on federal, state, and local levels. Many of these proposals emerged from the public concern about illegal aliens and their impact on public expenditure, and some emerged from the public concern about fraud. During the 1990s, such concern intensified significantly. This was evident in the approval in 1994 in California of Proposition 187, which sought to cut off public education, health care, and other benefits to illegal aliens and their children, and in the 1996 welfare reform legislation, passed by Republicans and signed by President Clinton, that denied benefits to legal and illegal immigrants.[165]

In 1990, Senator Daniel Patrick Moynihan (D-NY), proposed a "plastic, counterfeit-proof Social Security card" that job applicants could use to prove that they are citizens or legal residents entitled to work in the United States. He said that such a card would reduce discrimination against foreign-looking job applicants, and although the card would not eliminate fraud, it could cut it substantially. However, INS Commissioner Gene McNary rejected the idea as intrusive when he appeared before the Subcommittee on Social Security, Pensions, and Family Policy of the Senate Finance Committee, which Moynihan chaired from 1993 to 1995. Although

163 Quoted in Smith, *Ben Franklin's Web Site*, 303.

164 Alan K. Simpson, "Verification of Applicant Identity for Purposes of Employment and Public Assistance," Hearing, Subcommittee on Immigration, Committee on the Judiciary, Senate, 104th Congress, May 10, 1995.

165 Maddux, "Ronald Reagan," 229–230.

Moynihan was not suggesting a national ID card, McNary argued: "It's important . . . we don't come up with a national card [that] is going to have to be carried, that is going to cause people to feel they live under Big Brother." Moynihan's idea did not survive the legislative process.[166]

In 1993, the Clinton administration, as part of an effort to guarantee access to health care for all Americans, advocated the introduction of the "health security card." Such a card would certify that a person has the right to medical care, and would help cut down on waste, fraud, and abuse in the health care system. The administration assured the public that with such a card, issued to every American, they would enjoy full privacy and confidentiality protection. Ira Magaziner, coordinator of President Clinton's health care task force, described the proposed health care identification card, bearing one's SSN, as a tool that doctors and hospitals could use to track medical history and insurance records, and instantly bill a patient's insurer, thereby cutting health industry's $35 billion annual bill for paperwork.[167] However, many critics warned that the health security card would become "a *de facto* national identification card." Some even urged fellow critics to display their disapproval en masse by calling Magaziner's direct phone line.[168] In the end, concerns about the nature of the proposed card and general opposition to the national health care plan led the president to drop the idea.[169]

In February 1993, Rep. Anthony Beilenson (D-CA) introduced bill H.R.1031, which called for the development of a counterfeit-resistant Social Security card containing fingerprint identification, barcode validation, a photograph, or some other identification feature.[170] While nothing came out of this or subsequent bills he introduced throughout the 1990s to improve the security of the Social Security card, in some circles Beilenson gained a reputation for being "at the forefront of the movement to develop a tamper-proof national identification card." One *Los Angeles Times* reader described Beilenson "as the point man for making our American documents secure and credible again."[171]

[166] Spencer Rich, "Tamperproof Card Plan Raises an Old Specter," *Washington Post*, April 19, 1990.

[167] "Health-Care Reform May Take a Number – Social Security," *Seattle Times*, April 6, 1993.

[168] Email exchanges, April 1993, http://cd.textfiles.com/hackchronii/CUD5/CUD528B.TXT.

[169] Amitai Etzioni, *The Limits of Privacy* (New York: Basic Books, 1999), 119.

[170] www.govtrack.us/congress/bills/103/hr1031/text.

[171] Allan Nutkiewicz, "Immigration Reforms," *Los Angeles Times*, September 29, 1993.

In March 1995, Senator Dianne Feinstein (D-CA) introduced bill S.580, which called for increased border controls, enhanced penalties for alien smuggling, a border-crossing fee, expedited deportation for illegal and criminal aliens, and limitations on public assistance for aliens. The bill also called for enhanced penalties for document fraud. Section 401 would subject those who make or present false immigration documents to first-time mandatory penalties of at least two and a half years for a first offense, and up to fifteen years for those with prior felony convictions. Moreover, the bill called for a secure system for work authorization verification. Section 225 mandated the Attorney General, together with the Secretary of Health and Human Services, to "develop and implement a counterfeit-resistant system to verify work eligibility and federally-funded public assistance benefits eligibility for all persons within the United States." The bill continued:

> If the system developed includes a document (designed specifically for use for this purpose), that document shall not be used as a national identification card, and the document shall not be required to be carried or presented by any person except at the time of application for federally funded public assistance benefits or to comply with employment eligibility verification requirements.[172]

Feinstein was clear that she did not want a national ID card. Still, Congress did not enact the bill. Two months later, in May 1995, Senator Feinstein published an article in *Roll Call* in which she continued to advocate for a counterfeit-resistant system to verify work eligibility and public assistance eligibility for all persons within the United States. She argued that such a system would have to include work and benefits eligibility ID cards for everyone. Such cards would be counterfeit-resistant and would be phone- or machine-readable (the phone-readability referred to the ability to verify the data from the card with the data at a data bank, accessible via computer or phone). In addition, cards would incorporate biometric data, for instance, by carrying a magnetic strip on which the bearer's unique voice, retina pattern, or fingerprint is digitally encoded, or by incorporating a digitized photo and signature integrated into the plastic card itself. Feinstein wrote that establishing "a reliable, fraud-resistant, inexpensive, and non-discriminatory means of permitting all employers and all government benefit providers to identify illegal aliens" was the real key to finding a solution to the problem of illegal immigration.[173]

[172] www.congress.gov/bill/104th-congress/senate-bill/580/text.
[173] Dianne Feinstein, "Feinstein: State-of-the-Art ID System Is Necessary to Help Identify Illegal Aliens," *Roll Call*, May 22, 1995.

Feinstein wrote that providing employers and benefit providers with a reliable way of checking all applicants' eligibility was a vital but not the only part of the solution. New laws would also have to enhance border control, weaken the economic incentives for aliens to come to the United States illegally, hold the sponsors of legal aliens liable for their promises of support, and crack down on alien criminals, document forgers, and alien smugglers.

Feinstein did not refer to the proposed work and benefits eligibility ID cards as national ID cards, and she did not say that people would have to carry such documents at all times. Rather, employers and benefit providers would ask for such cards only when they needed to verify work or benefits eligibility of applicants. Feinstein's logic was similar to that expressed in the bill she proposed in March. However, by the time Feinstein wrote her article in May she was much more certain that an identification card would have to be part of the new system. She argued that it is clear that "state-of-the-art work and benefits eligibility IDs can and must replace the Dinosaur Age documents now being used."[174]

Senator Feinstein understood the urgency of the problem, and that made her question the need for pilot programs; there simply was no time to waste. Although the legislation introduced by Senator Simpson called for several pilot programs to study how best to meet this pressing documentation need, Feinstein argued that we "know enough now to rapidly develop and deploy this kind of card and the databases necessary to support it." She asked:

> Is it really necessary to take three to four years to study the issue and, as Attorney General Janet Reno testified recently, even longer to phase in the new documentation? Shouldn't we simply press forward with a single integrated system now, require everyone (not just immigrants) to obtain the new document within a reasonable phase-in period, and subject that document to annual renewals to minimize the effect of any residual fraud or change in eligibility status?[175]

Feinstein argued that her proposal for work and benefits eligibility ID cards for everyone "deserved careful consideration." However, her congressional colleagues did not oblige. In addition, some in the press sharply criticized her proposal. One *Los Angeles Times* op-ed said that Feinstein wanted "a national identity card for every man, woman, and child in America." The same op-ed warned, "A national ID database represents the slipperiest of all civil liberty slopes." While such rhetoric was

[174] Ibid. [175] Ibid.

common, the author of this particular op-ed, Ron K. Unz, a Republican activist and an entrepreneur, made an interesting point:

> Requiring the law-abiding 98% of American's population to carry a national ID card or undergo retinal scanning is un-American in the strongest sense of the word, and the only long-term beneficiaries of such federal policies would be the recruiting sergeants of the Michigan Militia. Our fractured society already contains large numbers of violent and paranoid individuals terrified of imaginary government plots against their freedom. Politicians who would give true substance to such fears by affixing microchips to every American's identity must be held accountable for the likely consequences. One Oklahoma City bombing is enough.[176]

Opposition to Feinstein's proposal for an identification card containing a person's photograph and fingerprints also came from opposite political poles represented by the ACLU and the National Rifle Association (NRA). While the ACLU feared a general misuse of data and threat to civil liberties, the NRA feared that registration of people would lead to registration of guns.[177]

The Cato Institute, a libertarian think tank, also criticized Feinstein's proposal. Cato also warned that congressional Republicans were quickly moving forward with "Orwellian legislation that would create a national computerized registration system for all American workers." It added that the "computer registry and national ID card, which would confer on the federal government vast new police-state powers, is highly incompatible with the Republican theme of expanding freedom and reducing government."[178]

Indeed, the Republicans were the ones pushing for the establishment of a national registry to check workers' legality, though, interestingly, House Majority Leader Dick Armey (R-TX) opposed it. In a 1995 speech to Cato, Armey said that "a national computer registry" was just a euphemism for a national ID card, and any system in which Americans would be forced to possess such a card, for any reason, "is an abomination and wholly at odds with the American tradition of individual freedom." Other opponents of a national registry included small-business owners

176 Ron K. Unz, "Big Brother, Meet Big Sister: Immigration: Sen. Feinstein Wants Everyone to Carry an Encrypted, Database Linked National Identity Card," *Los Angeles Times*, June 12, 1995.

177 Steven A. Holmes, "The Strange Politics of Immigration," *NYT*, December 31, 1995.

178 John J. Miller and Stephen Moore, "Cato Institute Policy Analysis No. 237: A National ID System: Big Brother's Solution to Illegal Immigration," Cato Institute, September 7, 1995, 1.

concerned about the hassle of phoning Uncle Sam every time they hire someone and civil libertarians who feared that a government database might be misused.[179]

Proponents argued that a computer verification of immigration status was "a virtually foolproof method of determining who can and cannot legally work in the United States, one offering far more reliability than the easily forged work-authorization documents now reviewed by employers." Proponents believed that every time a business makes a hire, the employer should first dial a toll-free telephone number to verify the immigration status of the new worker. As the *Los Angeles Times* explained, just like the process that occurs at the cash register when a customer hands over a credit card, a central computer would instantly relay back a thumbs-up or thumbs-down.[180]

As the *Los Angeles Times* noted, the conflicting views were evident in slogans offered by different Republican members of Congress to describe the hot line. Rep. Elton Gallegly (R-CA) called it "1-800-END FRAUD," arguing that the verification system is so essential to immigration reform that any legislation adopted by Congress will be largely toothless without it. Meanwhile, Rep. Steve Chabot (R-OH), dubbed the hotline "1-800-BIG BROTHER." Chabot called it "an undue expansion of federal powers" and said that it is "inappropriate to require every employer to get the federal government's approval to hire someone."[181]

The Cato Institute, opposed to legislation to create a computer registry, aimed its criticism specifically at moderate Republicans such as Senator Simpson and Rep. Lamar Smith (R-TX), who chaired the Immigration Subcommittees of their respective chambers.[182] Cato criticized Simpson for introducing, in January 1995, S.269, a bill that would, among other things, mandate the development of counterfeit-resistant driver's licenses and Social Security cards and increase penalties for document fraud. The bill would also require the Attorney General, together with the Secretary of Health and Human Services, to develop and implement a system to verify eligibility for employment in the United States, and eligibility for benefits under government-funded programs of public assistance. The bill clearly stated that it was not creating a national ID card. People would not have to carry or present any new or existing identification document

[179] Marc Lacey, "Legislation Proposes Verification of Workers' Immigration Status," *Los Angeles Times*, February 20, 1996.
[180] Ibid. [181] Ibid. [182] Miller and Moore, "Cato Institute," 2.

except to verify eligibility for employment or benefits. The president would be required to institute an improved verification system within eight years.[183]

Cato also criticized Rep. Smith for introducing H.R.1915 in June 1995. The bill aimed to improve the verification system for employment eligibility, make improvements to border crossing identification cards, and increase criminal penalties for fraudulent use of government-issued documents. The bill did not say anything about national ID cards.[184] Still, in the eyes of the Cato Institute, the bill "would have a national identification system running in 1999."[185]

In June 1995, Stephen Moore, an economist at the Cato Institute, together with several prominent people and organizations, wrote to members of Congress to express concern that both Congress and the administration were moving toward the implementation of a national worker registry/verification system. The signatories of the letter included the ACLU, the American Fathers Association, the National Federation of Independent Business, the United States Hispanic Chamber of Commerce, and the Massachusetts Immigrant and Refugee Advocacy Coalition. The signatories also included Republican strategist Bill Kristol, David Koch of Koch Industries, Grover Norquist of Americans for Tax Reform, Phyllis Schlafly of the Eagle Forum, and Martin Anderson of the Hoover Institution.[186] Anderson, in particular, has been a major force opposing national ID cards throughout the years. He was the person who helped stop the 1981 proposal during a cabinet meeting with President Reagan, and he has subsequently published numerous articles opposing national ID cards.[187]

In March 1996, as part of a debate over a larger immigration bill, the House voted on an amendment that would require the government to develop a more counterfeit-resistant Social Security card. The House rejected the amendment by a vote of 221 to 191. A bipartisan group of congressmen, as well as interest groups on the left and right, opposed the GOP-sponsored amendment, claiming it could lead to the imposition of a national ID card that would compile personal information on every US citizen and infringe on individual liberty. Rep. Jim Bunning (R-KY) argued: "While I strongly support appropriate measures to curb illegal

[183] www.congress.gov/bill/104th-congress/senate-bill/269/text.
[184] www.congress.gov/bill/104th-congress/house-bill/1915.
[185] Miller and Moore, "Cato Institute," 2. [186] Ibid., 12–15.
[187] For a list of the articles, see ibid., 16–17.

immigration in employment, I must oppose any proposals that would change the issuance or purpose of the current Social Security card without thorough examination."[188]

In the end, Senator Simpson and others had to settle for a law enacted by the new Republican Congress in the form of the Illegal Immigration Reform and Immigrant Responsibility Act of 1996 (IIRIRA). On September 28, 1996, IIRIRA overwhelmingly passed the House in a 370 to 37 vote, and President Clinton signed it into law on September 30. IIRIRA stiffened penalties for illegal aliens by creating three-year, ten-year, and permanent bars to reentry for those who were unlawfully present in the United States. It also reduced the number of documents acceptable for verifying work eligibility and increased criminal penalties for fraudulent use of government-issued documents.

Congress did not agree to the Jordan Commission's call for a computerized national registry that employers would have to call to verify that new workers had an authorized Social Security card. In IIRIRA, Congress agreed only to set up a pilot program with an electronic government database to check worker eligibility in five of the seven states with most illegal aliens: California, New York, Texas, Florida, and Illinois. However, the government never implemented IIRIRA's provision for a pilot program testing electronic systems for employment eligibility verification/confirmation.[189]

IIRIRA's section 404, dealing with the employment eligibility confirmation system, stated that "nothing in this subtitle shall be construed to authorize, directly or indirectly, the issuance or use of national identification cards or the establishment of a national identification card."[190] However, since national ID cards and Social Security cards are not the same, this clause did not stand in the way of IIRIRA's section 657, which called on the Commissioner of Social Security, with the help from the Attorney General, to develop a "prototype of a counterfeit-resistant Social Security card." IIRIRA stated that such prototype card shall be made of a durable, tamper-resistant material such as plastic or polyester; shall employ technologies that provide security features, such as magnetic stripes, holograms, and integrated circuits; and shall be developed so as to provide individuals with reliable proof of citizenship or legal resident alien status. IIRIRA also stated that the Comptroller General and the Commissioner of Social Security should each conduct a study that

188 "House Votes Down New Social Security Card," *Time Magazine*, March 20, 1996.

189 Graham, *Unguarded Gates*, 157–158.

190 IIRIRA of 1996, Public Law 104–208.

examined different methods of improving the Social Security card application process. The studies should include evaluations of the cost and workload implications of issuing a counterfeit-resistant Social Security card for all individuals over a three-, five-, and ten-year period. The studies should also evaluate the feasibility and cost implications of imposing a user fee for replacement cards. IIRIRA mandated the Comptroller and the Commissioner to each submit copies of their reports, along with facsimiles of the prototype cards, to the House Committees on Ways and Means and Judiciary, and the Senate Committees on Finance and Judiciary. They were to submit the reports no later than one year after the date of the enactment of IIRIRA.[191]

In September 1997, the SSA issued its report, which looked at alternatives to the current Social Security card. The SSA stressed that the current card, made of banknote paper, served only as an official verification of the SSN assigned by the SSA to the person whose name is on the card; the card is neither proof of the bearer's identity nor citizenship/noncitizenship status and has no data storage capability. The SSA developed seven options in response to the legislative mandate: plastic card, card with picture, secure barcode stripe, optical memory stripe, magnetic stripe, magnetic stripe/picture, and microprocessor/magnetic stripe/picture.[192]

The SSA estimated that the cost of issuing an enhanced card to 277 million number holders would range from $3.9 billion to $9.2 billion, depending on the card option selected. The SSA also studied the feasibility of imposing a user fee for enhanced cards. Even though the SSA historically opposed charging a fee in connection with the card issuance, the report stated that such a plan was feasible. The full-cost fee, including card issuance and fee remittance processes, would range from $19 to $38 per card, depending on the option selected. SSA's Inspector General studied Canada's Social Insurance Number fee-charging operation and concluded that SSA should charge a fee of $13 for each card. The cost of collecting fees in conjunction with the issuance of 277 million Social Security cards would be $1.3 billion, so the total cost for issuing an enhanced card and collecting a user fee would range from $5.2 billion to $10.5 billion.[193]

[191] Ibid.

[192] SSA, "Report to Congress on Options for Enhancing the Social Security Card," September 1997, www.ssa.gov/history/reports/ssnreportsum.html.

[193] Ibid.

The 1997 SSA report concluded that while a plan for issuing enhanced cards, either prospectively or as a mass reissuance, was feasible, "the issuance of an enhanced card raises policy issues about privacy and the potential for the card to be used as a national identification card."[194] Yet again, the mere mention of a national ID card contributed to another pause in the planning of improvements to identification documents. The SSA never implemented any of the seven options it developed in response to the IIRIRA's mandate.

IIRIRA also provided federal standards for state driver's licenses and birth certificates when used as identification for federal purposes. It did so through a provision that gave authorization to include SSNs on driver's licenses effective October 2000. Under this provision, a state had two choices. The state could require that each of its licenses include the licensee's SSN in machine-readable or visually readable form. Alternatively, a state could require that each applicant submit his or her SSN, and the state would verify the legitimacy of that number with the SSA. In 1996, not many people noticed the new requirement, but when the Department of Transportation (DOT) proposed regulations in 1998 to implement the congressional mandate, many individuals, groups, and politicians registered their objections.[195] The coalition against the provision included many conservative members of Congress, those who objected to enumeration on religious grounds, the conservative Eagle Forum, and the ACLU. They were alleging that the provision could be a step toward a national ID card system. In response, Congress prohibited funding to implement the requirement and in 2000 repealed the requirement.[196]

In the interim, in January 1997, Rep. Bill McCollum (R-FL) introduced H.R.231, a bill to "improve the integrity of the Social Security card and to provide for criminal penalties for fraud and related activity involving work authorization documents for purposes of the Immigration and Nationality Act." One of the subsections of the bill was entitled "Not a National Identification Card." It argued that "cards issued pursuant to this section shall not be required to be carried upon one's person, and nothing in this section shall be construed as authorizing the establishment of a national identification card."[197] Cato nevertheless accused him of

[194] Ibid. [195] Smith, *Ben Franklin's Web Site*, 306–307.

[196] Todd B. Tatelman, "The REAL ID Act of 2005: Legal, Regulatory, and Implementation Issues," CRS, April 1, 2008, 1.

[197] www.gpo.gov/fdsys/pkg/BILLS-105hr231ih/content-detail.html.

advocating a national ID card. In a congressional testimony in May 1997, Cato's Stephen Moore said that while supporters of this idea argue vehemently that making the Social Security card fraud-proof is not the same as establishing a national ID card, it was, in fact, the same thing, and "H.R.231 would do exactly that." Moore congratulated Rep. Mel Watt (D-NC) for his "courageous opposition to this bad idea." He also added that it is noteworthy that the leaders of virtually every libertarian, conservative, and civil liberties organization in America – from Bill Bennett (Empower America) to Grover Norquist (Americans for Tax Reform) to the Nobel economist Milton Friedman – denounced both the national ID card and the computer registry as "misguided and dangerous."[198] Nothing came out of McCollum's bill.

Meanwhile, states and localities across the United States were considering their own proposals for identification documents and increased identity policing. California, in particular, played a central role in many proposals, as it was the principal receiving state for both legal and illegal immigrants. Especially during 1993 and 1994, Californians expressed strong support for cutting off public benefits to illegal aliens, the deportation of convicted illegal alien criminals, the use of the National Guard along the border, and a charge of one dollar as a border-crossing fee to assist the Border Patrol. Some Californians even proposed to deny citizenship to children born in the United States to mothers who were illegal aliens.

California's Proposition 187, approved in November 1994, though subsequently found unconstitutional, aimed to deny most public services and education to illegal aliens and their children. In addition, it underscored that manufacturing, distribution, sale, or use of false citizenship or residency documents is a state felony punishable by imprisonment or fine, and it outlined changes to the penal code regarding the size of those penalties.

In fact, one aspect to the concerns about illegal aliens and their impact on jobs, schools, and social and medical services involved attitudes regarding mandatory ID cards. One might assume that those worried about illegal aliens taking jobs from Americans would embrace such a measure. However, Elliott Barkan's study of public opinion on immigration in California between 1982 and 1998 shows that the attitudes

198 Stephen Moore, Testimony, "National Identification System," Subcommittee on Immigration and Claims, Committee on the Judiciary, House of Representatives, 105th Congress, May 13, 1997.

toward ID cards varied considerably with how the question was phrased and whether an ID would be required of all persons or just noncitizens.[199]

In January 1982, 30 percent of Californians viewed ID cards as a good idea; in August 1993 the figure was 72 percent; in April 1994 it was 42 percent, in October 1994 it was 31 percent; and in August 1998 it was 36 percent. Importantly, the 1993 question was limited to ID cards for legal aliens only, while all the other polls asked about ID cards for all people. This largely explains why in 1993 there were significantly higher percentages in favor of ID cards. Importantly, the August 1993 poll was taken shortly after the ship smuggling episodes involving the Chinese had dominated the media, which also contributed to the higher percentages in favor of ID cards. Five years later, in 1998, just 36 percent of Californians approved of ID cards as a "good idea." In fact, only among those with low incomes and less education – persons more likely to be competing with illegal aliens – was there a majority favoring ID cards. People who supported ID cards were often those more pessimistic about their financial prospects and about the direction in which California was moving, although here, too, a majority still rejected the idea. Even a majority of those regarding illegal aliens as a very serious problem nonetheless saw mandatory ID cards as a "bad idea." Those most likely to think it was a bad idea were those with college degrees, and those most likely to consider it a good idea were Catholics, conservatives, and those earning less than $20,000 a year. Latinos, fearing widespread discrimination by employers, supported ID cards at a higher rate than did non-Latinos: 38 percent of Latinos supported ID cards in 1998, versus 32 percent of non-Latinos. However, the percentage of Latinos favoring ID cards did fall sharply after mid-1993 (in August 1993 it was 75 percent; in April 1994 it was 63 percent; in October 1994 it was 40 percent).[200]

SUMMARY

Nationwide polls taken throughout the twentieth century show that Americans have supported proposals for identification documents (even though, as Barkan showed, most Californians were wary). In polls where demographic subcategories are indicated, immigrants favor the card at a

[199] Elliott R. Barkan, "Return of the Nativists? California Public Opinion and Immigration in the 1980s and 1990s," *Social Science History* 27 (2003): 258.

[200] Ibid., 259–261.

higher rate than native-born Americans.[201] It may be that immigrants prefer tougher identification themselves since they see it as "a symbolic reward of citizenship."

A Gallup poll in 1942 revealed that 69 percent of Americans believed that "everyone in the United States should be required to carry an identification card containing, among other things, his picture and his fingerprints."[202] Gallup polls in 1949 and 1950 showed that more than 80 percent of Americans supported the idea of an identification card that could aid in the event of accident or bomb attack.[203] A 1977 Roper poll showed that 51 percent of Americans favored a mandatory ID card for everybody.[204] A 1980 Gallup poll found that 62 percent of Americans believed that everyone should be required to carry an identification card, such as a Social Security card.[205] In 1983, more than 60 percent said that everyone in the United States should be required "to carry an identification card such as a Social Security card." A 1984 Gallup poll reported that 75 percent of Hispanics supported employer sanctions, even if ID cards would be required.[206] The 1990 and 1992 Roper polls and a 1993 Gallup poll found nationwide majorities supporting ID cards for all citizens (62 percent, 60 percent, and 57 percent, respectively).[207] The 1995 Gallup poll showed 62 percent of Americans favored a requirement "that all citizens and legal residents have a national ID card to distinguish them from illegal immigrants."

Despite such public opinion data, the conventional wisdom is that Americans are, and have always been, deeply against national ID cards. Moreover, any identification document resembling a national ID card "within the American context ... would be perceived to alter profoundly the established balance between freedom and control."[208]

Writing in 1986 Joseph Eaton argued:

> If politicians were the guardians of conventional wisdom, the question of a national ID card would still be in the closet. No major national figure is in favor of the wide loophole through which it is easy to acquire and use multiple identities. But not even top FBI officials wish to be quoted that they favor combating crimes by resorting to a national identity card.[209]

[201] Marti Dinerstein, "America's Identity Crisis. Document Fraud Is Pervasive and Pernicious. Backgrounder," Center for Immigration Studies, April 2002; David Simcox, "Public Opinion Supports National I.D.," *The Social Contract* 9, 2 (winter 1998–1999).

[202] Gallup, "Gallup Poll Reveals." [203] Barkan, "Return of the Nativists?," 259.

[204] Eaton, *Card-Carrying Americans*, 101–102. [205] Laham, *Ronald Reagan*, 43.

[206] Graham, "Uses and Misuses," 49–50. [207] Barkan, "Return of the Nativists?," 259.

[208] Zolberg, "Guarding the Gates," 297. [209] Eaton, *Card-Carrying Americans*, 66.

Writing in 2003 about biometric identifiers, Eaton stated that "even idealistic elected officials and their senior staff are understandably cautious about expending their political capitals on a seemingly marginal controversy ... Why risk losing their votes in the next election?"[210]

Yet throughout the twentieth century, there were public figures arguing for more secure identification documents and even national ID cards. Between the 1970s and 1990s alone, figures such as Deane Huxtable, Frances G. Knight, Milton Valera, Father Hesburgh, Lawrence Fuchs, Ray Marshall, Rep. Peter Rodino, Senator Alan Simpson, Rep. Romano Mazzoli, Rep. Dan Lungren, Frankie Freeman, Rep. Stephen Horn, Frank Hodsoll, William French Smith, Henry Lacayo, Joaquin Otero, Rep. Barbara Jordan, Senator Daniel Patrick Moynihan, Ira Magaziner, Rep. Anthony Beilenson, Senator Dianne Feinstein, Rep. Elton Gallegly, Rep. Lamar Smith, Rep. Bill McCollum, and Joseph Eaton, among others, all embraced and even promoted proposals for more secure identification documents, though only some of them wanted those documents to be national ID cards. Passionate opposition to national ID cards has been, and remains, present in the United States, but many policymakers and members of the public see national ID cards more positively than conventional wisdom would let us believe.

The post-WWII saga of debates over identification documents in the United States largely overlaps with the story of immigration reforms and employer sanctions. One scholar argues that one of the biggest failures of immigration reform efforts occurred in 1981, when the Task Force and the White House working group lost the internal White House battle over developing an employee verification system with a more reliable Social Security card. Historian Thomas Maddux concludes that the fact that the United States has still failed to solve this issue, decades later, "suggests not only a failure of leadership in the White House and Congress but also the seriousness of concerns about individual rights and privacy and the enduring political strength of domestic interests that resist an effective solution to illegal immigration."[211]

Nicholas Laham, highly critical of President Reagan's handling of immigration policy, describes the fear of some of Reagan's advisers that if any one form of identification is preferred over others, then this preferred form, especially if it is a Social Security card, could evolve into a national ID card. Accordingly, the White House recommended that a

[210] Eaton, *The Privacy Card*, xvi. [211] Maddux, "Ronald Reagan," 231.

variety of different documents be used to verify the eligibility of individuals to work in the United States. The argument that the use of a single document, like a tamper-proof Social Security card, for worker verification purposes would represent an invasion of individual privacy is, according to Laham, groundless. Laham argues that the fact that the White House would accept such a groundless argument in determining the design of a worker verification system under IRCA represents a severe indictment of Reagan's conduct of immigration policy.[212]

Immigration remains a divisive issue and immigration reform efforts receive criticism from all sides of the political spectrum. Some observers describe IRCA as "a public policy failure of major proportions." Otis Graham, historian and member of FAIR National Board of Advisors, notes that sanctions on employers of illegal aliens entered American law, where they should have been all along, but opponents defeated a proposed system of worker verification based on computer registry of SSNs because of objections to a national ID card, which was never proposed. This allowed employers to accept as proof of legal residence any two of a wide range of documents, most easily counterfeited.[213] Economist Philip Martin concludes that one of the most dramatic changes, at least in the farm labor market, due to IRCA was "the switch from 'undocumented workers' to 'falsely documented' workers."[214]

In 1981, Senator Simpson stated, "[T]his nation of ours has been historically and consistently ambivalent about enforcing its immigration laws."[215] One could add that the United States has been equally ambivalent about legislating on immigration and identity policing. It is also possible to add that proposals for a national identification card are likely to be part of the "perennial debate over U.S. immigration policy."[216] This view may be difficult to reconcile with Eaton's view that public figures in the United States rarely, if ever, propose national identification documents. The truth is that public figures and members of the public have proposed national ID cards in the United States over the past 100 years, but such proposals have not gotten very far, even as similar

[212] Laham, *Ronald Reagan*, 147–148, 157. [213] Graham, *Unguarded Gates*, 108.

[214] Philip L. Martin, "Good Intentions Gone Awry: IRCA and U.S. Agriculture," *The Annals of the American Academy of Political and Social Science* 534 (July 1994).

[215] Alan K. Simpson, "On a New Temporary Worker Program with Mexico," Hearing, Subcommittee on Immigration and Refugee Policy, Committee on the Judiciary, Senate, 97th Congress, October 22, 1981.

[216] DeLaet, *U.S. Immigration Policy*, 116.

proposals have been adopted almost everywhere else in the world. While many Americans support the use of identification documents and identity policing to control immigration and improve security, others very much oppose it – and are very vocal about it. Consequently, and as the following chapters show, the United States is experiencing incremental, rather than comprehensive, changes to identity policing.

4

Identity Policing in the Post-9/11 United States

The Changing Patchwork

INTRODUCTION

Even though supporters of better identity policing do not seem to be gaining much ground, and the United States still has easily counterfeited identification documents, no national ID card, and no plans to implement one, the United States is implementing a variety of schemes aimed at improving identity policing. These include REAL ID–compliant driver's licenses and ID cards, and Western Hemisphere Travel Initiative–compliant enhanced driver's licenses (EDLs) and ID cards. In addition, the United States has been a forerunner in recording face and fingerprint biometrics from foreign nationals entering the country.

This chapter analyzes the post-9/11 political developments regarding identification documents and identity policing in the United States. It first outlines the political history of the 2005 REAL ID Act. It then outlines other post-9/11 identity policing schemes, emphasizing the notion of patchwork in identity policing in the United States.

Legislation quoted in this chapter talks about driver's licenses and state ID cards, where the latter refers to state-issued identification cards for nondrivers (known as state identification cards, state-issued ID cards, and nondriver IDs). For conciseness, all references to driver's licenses in the context of the REAL ID Act and other legislation also apply to state ID cards, unless noted otherwise.

POLITICAL HISTORY OF THE 2005 REAL ID ACT

The Immediate Aftermath of 9/11

Of the nineteen terrorists who committed the attacks on September 11, 2001, seventeen entered on tourist visas, one on a business visa, and one on a student visa. Two of the hijackers were on a government watch list of suspects, two had overstayed their visas, and another violated the terms of his student visa by not showing up for classes, yet they were able to operate freely while in the United States. They had SSNs, opened bank accounts, used ATM cards, and were able to rent cars. Two enrolled in flight schools. Many flew all over the country on commercial airlines, and some of them flew several times in and out of the United States. Although they would have been able to conduct many of these activities using their foreign (primarily Saudi) passports, the National Commission on Terrorist Attacks upon the United States (the 9/11 Commission) established that the hijackers had methodically obtained US identification documents to make their travels and transactions as inconspicuous as possible.

All but one of the 9/11 hijackers acquired some form of US identification, some by fraud.[1] The 9/11 Commission established that the nineteen hijackers obtained at least thirty driver's licenses and identification cards between them. On September 9, 2001 – two days before hijacking United Airlines flight 93 – one of the group's leaders was stopped for speeding in Maryland as he headed north on I-95; the state trooper checked his records, found that his Virginia driver's license and rental car registration were valid, issued him a ticket, and released him.

Because some of the terrorists were known to be security risks or had visa violations and still were able to spend months undetected in the United States while traveling, attending flight schools, and renting apartments, proposals for creating a national identification card system have gained new attention in the aftermath of 9/11. Tova Andrea Wang, a program officer at the Century Foundation, wrote in 2002 that some people have argued that a national ID card could have helped prevent the tragedy. If the United States required citizens and residents to have an ID card with a unique identifier, such as a fingerprint or retinal image, the way to confirm a person's identity – during a traffic stop or at an airport – would be to match this person to their card and to the information in the

[1] *The 9/11 Commission Report: Final Report of the National Commission on Terrorist Attacks on the United States* (New York: W. W. Norton, 2004), 390.

database. In addition, the system would retrieve information about the cardholder from databases of law enforcement and immigration agencies and would notify the operator if the cardholder turned out to be on any government watch list.[2]

Following reports that the 9/11 terrorists acquired numerous driver's licenses and other credentials, primarily from Florida, which did not require any proof of permanent residency, Senator Dick Durbin (D-IL) was among the first to emphasize the need to standardize identification credentials and link identification-related databases. On December 20, 2001, Durbin told Congress:

> I am certainly not asserting that the September 11 attacks would have been avoided had the terrorists not had these driver's licenses. Clearly, there is little direct connection between the cards these evil men carried and the ungodly deeds that they carried out.
>
> But what these driver's licenses – which have now become the most widely used form of personal ID in the country – gave these terrorists was the cover of legitimacy that allowed them to walk around and mingle into American society without being detected.
>
> A driver's license is a key that opens many doors. In America, anyone who can produce a valid driver's license can access just about anything ... If you can produce a driver's license, we just assume that you are legitimate, and you have a right to be here.[3]

Durbin was clear that his aim was not to create a national ID card or develop one centralized mega database that houses everyone's personal data. Instead, he wanted to make "the driver's license – which many consider a *de facto* national ID card – more reliable and verifiable as a form of personal identification than it is today."[4]

On October 10, 2002, Durbin introduced a bill, S.3107, which, if passed, would have become the Driver's License Fraud Prevention Act. The aim was to improve the security of state-issued driver's licenses, enhance highway safety, and verify personal identity.[5] Durbin noted that the fifty states follow fifty different methods for verifying a person's identification when they process driver's license applications, and they apply different standards for defining what the acceptable documents are that they require from applicants. The level of security in the driver's licenses and state identification cards varies widely, from those states that

[2] Tova Andrea Wang, "The Debate over a National Identification Card," The Century Foundation, May 9, 2002, 1.

[3] Congressional Record, December 20, 2001, S27634. [4] Ibid., S27635.

[5] www.gpo.gov/fdsys/pkg/BILLS-107s3107is/pdf/BILLS-107s3107is.pdf.

incorporate high-tech biometric identifiers to ones that simply laminate their cards. Durbin noted that law enforcement officials estimate that there are more than 240 different formats of valid driver's licenses in circulation. Durbin concluded that because of the disparity in the state issuance processes and the varying degrees of security of the cards themselves, it is extremely easy for individuals to abuse the system by shopping around for licenses in those states with the weakest practices.[6]

Durbin noted the existence of two federal programs that deal with driver's licenses: the National Driver Register and the Commercial Driver's License Information System. However, he said that the current limited scope of these programs leaves a gaping loophole: one deals only with records of problem drivers, while the other deals only with records of commercial drivers. Durbin's bill would close this loophole by consolidating the appropriate functionalities of these two programs and by adding new security measures that would allow every state to check all other states' records of all drivers before issuing commercial or regular driver's licenses. "This new process will help prevent states from issuing more than one license to any one individual, which will end forum shopping, abuse, and fraud."[7]

S.3107 would require states to make their driver's licenses and identification cards more resistant to tampering, altering, or counterfeiting. Durbin said his bill would crack down on internal fraud and bribery that occurs behind the counters of the Departments of Motor Vehicles (DMVs). The bill would also enhance privacy protection for license holders. It would prohibit state motor vehicle agencies from displaying SSNs on any driver's license, motor vehicle registration, or any identification document.[8] Durbin's bill was read twice (no objection was heard), and referred to the Senate Committee on Commerce, Science, and Transportation, where it died.

In addition to S.3107, other bills in the 107th Congress (2001–2003) also focused on the security of driver's licenses. In May 2002, Rep. James Moran (D-VA) and Rep. Tom Davis (R-VA) introduced a bill, H.R.4633, which, if passed, would have become the Driver's License Modernization Act. As the bill explains, "the terrorist attacks of September 11, 2001, illuminated many flaws in the Nation's domestic security, especially in its identification system." The bill aimed to remedy those flaws by establishing standards for state programs for the issuance of driver's licenses and

6 Congressional Record, October 10, 2002, S10386.
7 Ibid., S10387.
8 Ibid., S10388.

identification cards. Within five years the licenses would have to contain computer chips with encoded biometric data and multiple tamper-resistant security features. The bill went to several committees before dying in the House Science Committee's Subcommittee on Research.[9] One of the bill's opponents was the Home School Legal Defense Association. It claimed that the bill creates what could become a de facto national ID, and that "H.R.4633 is one of the most ambitious efforts by Congress in recent years to implement national identification requirements and to link state ID databases for government background checks."[10] A left-right coalition of the ACLU and the Eagle Forum also opposed the bill.[11]

Even though opposition to H.R.4633 included people both on the left and on the right, 9/11 made many Democrats and Republicans less afraid to talk about their support for stricter identification standards. This was in contrast to the period before 9/11 when legislation that aimed at improving identification documents might have enjoyed support from individual lawmakers in both parties, but – fearing backlash from vocal opponents – few lawmakers dared to support it openly. However, even in the aftermath of 9/11, lawmakers did not introduce any bills that proposed a national identification card. Rather, they focused on border security, documents for aliens, and the use of biometrics at consulates abroad and at US ports of entry (POEs). Still, even just in those areas, not all the proposals became law. Even legislating in the aftermath of 9/11 did not make Congress act on all the measures its members proposed.

However, some relevant bills did result in legislation in the 107th Congress. Senators Ted Kennedy (D-MA), Dianne Feinstein (D-CA), Sam Brownback (R-KS), and Jon Kyl (R-AZ), as well as Representatives Jim Sensenbrenner (R-WI) and George Gekas (R-PA), drafted and sponsored bills supportive of the adoption of biometric techniques to enhance the border security of the United States. Their bills – S.1749, H.R.1885, and, most importantly, H.R.3525 – ultimately became law as the Enhanced Border Security and Visa Entry Reform Act of 2002. The Act required the INS to make interoperable all its internal databases, so that authorities may access all information about a particular alien with a

9 www.congress.gov/bill/107th-congress/house-bill/4633.

10 "Congressmen Introduce National Standardized Driver's License Legislation," May 6, 2002, www.hslda.org/docs/news/hslda/200205062.asp.

11 ACLU, "Right-Left Furor over National ID Cards Heats Again in House," June 28, 2002, www.aclu.org/technology-and-liberty/right-left-furor-over-national-id-cards-heats-again-house.

single search. It also required federal law enforcement and intelligence agencies to share data on aliens with the INS and the DOS. In addition, it required that all travel and entry documents, including visas, issued to aliens by the United States be machine-readable and tamper-resistant and include a biometric identifier.[12]

The aftermath of 9/11 saw not only new legislation, but also a new organizational structure of the US government. On October 8, 2001, President George W. Bush established the Office of Homeland Security (OHS) within the White House. The Office became the Department of Homeland Security in November 2002. In July 2002, OHS produced the first "National Strategy for Homeland Security." The report stated:

> While the issuance of driver's licenses falls squarely with the powers of the states, the federal government can assist the states in crafting solutions to curtail the future abuse of driver's licenses by terrorist organizations. Therefore, the federal government, in consultation with state government agencies and non-governmental organizations, should support state-led efforts to develop minimum standards for driver's licenses, recognizing that many states should and will exceed these standards.[13]

The 9/11 Commission had as one of its tasks a mandate to provide recommendations designed to guard against future attacks. In July 2004, it issued a report containing forty-one recommendations. While some of the 9/11 Commission recommendations remain unfulfilled, many of the recommendations became part of the Intelligence Reform and Terrorism Prevention Act of 2004 (IRTPA), signed into law in December 2004. The Act addressed multiple issues relating to the intelligence community, information sharing, and transportation security.

A former counsel to the 9/11 Commission told me:

> It was in the course of our investigation into the 9/11 hijackers ... we had a team put together on determining how the terrorists got into the country and stayed in the country ... the issue of IDs was not something we ever knew was going to come up. It just was discovered in the course of our investigation that the hijackers had acquired these IDs. So it became very clear that there was another vulnerability there that nobody else on the Commission was going to look at. And if we didn't do it, it was going to be lost forever to America, this issue of access to the IDs.[14]

12 CIS, "The Enhanced Border Security and Visa Reform Act of 2002," June 2002, http://cis.org/EnhancedBorderSecurityVisaReformAct2002-HR3525.

13 NCSL, "The History of Federal Requirements for State Issued Driver's Licenses and Identification Cards," www.ncsl.org/research/transportation/history-behind-the-real-id-act.aspx.

14 Interview with a former counsel to the 9/11 Commission, Washington, DC, June 2013.

One of the 9/11 Commission recommendations concerned identification documents. The commission argued, "Secure identification should begin in the United States." The commission recommended that the federal government should set standards for the issuance of birth certificates and driver's licenses. The commission stated:

> Fraud in identification documents is no longer just a problem of theft. At many entry points to vulnerable facilities, including gates for boarding aircraft, sources of identification are the last opportunity to ensure that people are who they say they are and to check whether they are terrorists.[15]

On the issue of identification documents, IRTPA delegated authority to the Secretary of Transportation, in consultation with the DHS Secretary, empowering them to issue regulations with respect to minimum standards for federal acceptance of driver's licenses. Prior to IRTPA, there were no national standards with respect to driver's licenses and identification cards; standards were determined on a state-by-state basis. Even though IIRIRA provided federal standards for state driver's licenses and birth certificates when used as identification-related documents for federal purposes, in 1998 many individuals, groups, and politicians registered their objections, and in 2000 Congress repealed an IIRIRA provision that gave authorization to include SSNs on driver's licenses.[16]

IRTPA mandated the DHS Secretary to issue regulations within eighteen months of enactment requiring all driver's licenses and state ID cards to possess certain features if federal agencies were to accept them for official purposes. Section 7212 of IRTPA stated that no federal agency was to accept state-issued cards unless they conformed to the minimum standards.

Specifically, cards had to include the individual's full legal name, date of birth, gender, driver's license or identification card number, digital photograph, address, and signature. The cards had to contain physical security features that would make them "resistant to tampering, alteration, and counterfeiting," and a common machine-readable technology with defined minimum elements. States were required to confiscate a card if they discovered that anyone compromised any of the security components.[17]

IRTPA also required that the DHS regulations address how states issue driver's licenses. The regulations were to include minimum standards for the documentation provided by the applicant and for the procedures

[15] *The 9/11 Commission Report*, 390. [16] Tatelman, "REAL ID," 1.
[17] IRTPA of 2004, Public Law 108–458.

utilized for verifying the documents and processing the applications. Importantly, IRTPA prohibited the DHS regulations from infringing upon the state's power to set criteria concerning which categories of individuals were eligible to obtain a driver's license from that state. Therefore, if a state granted illegal aliens permission to obtain a license, nothing in the implementing regulations was to infringe upon that. In addition, the regulations were not to require a single uniform design and were required to include procedures designed to protect the privacy rights of applicants.[18]

In summary, IRTPA required the Secretaries of Transportation and Homeland Security to issue regulations with respect to minimum standards for federal acceptance of driver's licenses and identification cards, but states were to retain their own criteria concerning the categories of individuals that were eligible to obtain the documents.

Importantly, IRTPA called for a negotiated rulemaking among DOT and DHS representatives, state officials, state DMV representatives, and other interested parties. Such a rulemaking process would allow for cooperation among various stakeholders and would let states keep much of their authority when it came to driver's licenses. However, the negotiated rulemaking committee had met only once after IRTPA became law in December 2004. Soon after, the REAL ID Act replaced the negotiated rulemaking provision.

The Introduction of the 2005 REAL ID Act

Congress passed the REAL ID Act in May 2005. The Act repealed Section 7212 of IRTPA and replaced negotiated rulemaking with a stricter set of federal requirements for the issuance of driver's licenses and identification cards. The Act also shifted the responsibility of dealing with the federal standards from the DOT to the DHS. Opponents argue that by repealing IRTPA's negotiated rulemaking to create federal standards for driver's licenses, the REAL ID Act directly imposed prescriptive federal driver's license standards.[19]

The REAL ID Act contains provisions relating to improved security for driver's licenses and state identification cards, and instructions for states that do not comply with its provisions. As DHS describes it, "REAL ID is a coordinated effort by the states and the federal government to improve

[18] Tatelman, "REAL ID," 2–3. [19] NCSL, "The History of Federal Requirements."

the reliability and accuracy of state-issued identification documents, which should inhibit terrorists' ability to evade detection by using fraudulent identification."[20]

The REAL ID Act establishes minimum standards for the production and issuance of state-issued driver's licenses and authorizes grants to assist states in implementing the requirements. The Act also prohibits federal agencies from accepting for official purposes (accessing federal facilities, entering nuclear power plants, and boarding federally regulated commercial aircraft) driver's licenses and identification cards from states unless the DHS determines that the state meets the standards. The Act covers fifty-six jurisdictions: fifty states, the District of Columbia, and five US territories (Puerto Rico, the Virgin Islands, Guam, American Samoa, and North Marianas).[21]

Of the thirty-nine benchmarks, jurisdictions have to meet eighteen most important benchmarks for material compliance so that their licenses comply with REAL ID. The Act does not use the term "benchmarks," but the final rule and subsequent documents use it. The eighteen benchmarks are primarily concerned with security standards. They include a mandatory facial image capture and retention, and requirements for documentation of date of birth, SSN, address, and lawful status. There also need to be improvements in the security of the license-issuing process and DHS-approved security marks on materially compliant licenses.

Rep. Jim Sensenbrenner (R-WI), then Chairman of the House Judiciary Committee, crafted the REAL ID Act and pushed it to enactment. The vote in the House was 261–161. In the Senate, legislators inserted the bill in the military appropriations bills (the Emergency Supplemental Appropriations Act for Defense, the Global War on Terror, and Tsunami Relief, 2005), so there was not a separate vote.

On May 11, 2005, President Bush signed REAL ID Act into law. Since then, REAL ID has been highly contested among state legislatures, governors, and advocacy groups, who criticize it for being an unfunded mandate, where the federal government makes the rules and the states bear the costs. Opponents argue also that the Act will create a national ID. Sensenbrenner claims that this will not happen because states, not the federal government, will issue the standardized driver's licenses, and not all states will participate. He declares that no one could be more opposed to a national ID than he is.[22] While some REAL ID supporters are willing

[20] DHS, "REAL ID FAQs," www.dhs.gov/real-id-public-faqs. [21] Ibid.
[22] Peter Katel, "Real ID," *CQ Researcher*, May 4, 2007, 387.

to recognize similarities with national ID cards, others are not. For example, a policy analyst at the Heritage Foundation, an influential conservative think tank, told me: "REAL ID is a very easy way to enhance our security. It's not a national ID. If it were, Heritage would be against it. Nobody likes a national ID. Very few people do."[23]

Provisions of the 2005 REAL ID Act

REAL ID does not directly impose federal standards with respect to states' issuance of driver's licenses and ID cards. However, states need to adopt such standards and modify any conflicting laws or regulations to continue to have such documents recognized by federal agencies for official purposes, including accessing federal facilities, boarding federally regulated commercial aircraft, entering nuclear power plants, and any other purposes that the Secretary of Homeland Security shall determine.[24]

Before going further, it is important to note that there is a common misconception that the aftermath of 9/11 brought a requirement that all domestic passengers need government-issued identification documents to board planes. That is not the case. The rules of the Transportation Security Administration (TSA) allow for ticketed passengers lacking photo identification to board planes, subject to extra screening measures. The TSA says:

> Adult passengers 18 and over must show valid identification at the airport checkpoint in order to travel. We understand passengers occasionally arrive at the airport without an ID, because of losing it or inadvertently leaving it at home. If this happens to you, it does not necessarily mean you won't be allowed to fly. If you are willing to provide additional information, we have other ways to confirm your identity, like using publicly available databases, so you can reach your flight. If we clear you through this process, we may give you additional screening. If we can't verify your identity, you may not be allowed to enter the screening checkpoint or to board a plane.[25]

Still, even though driver's licenses and ID cards are not required to board an aircraft, the security of such documents is of utmost importance. REAL ID establishes minimum issuance standards for federal recognition of driver's licenses and ID cards. Those standards require that before a

[23] Interview with a policy analyst at the Heritage Foundation, Washington, DC, June 2013.
[24] The REAL ID Act, Public Law 109–13.
[25] TSA, "Acceptable IDs," February 13, 2015, www.tsa.gov/traveler-information/acceptable-ids.

state can issue a driver's license, it must verify several things with the agencies that issued the documents that applicants present in the application process for a license. First, the state will have to verify the issuance, validity, and completeness of a photo identification document or a non-photo document if it contains both the individual's full legal name and date of birth. Second, it will have to verify documentation showing the date of birth. Third, it will have to verify proof of an SSN or the individual's ineligibility for an SSN. Fourth, it will have to verify documentation showing the name and address of the individual's principal residence. To the extent that information verification requirements previously existed, they were a function of state law and varied from state to state. REAL ID preempts state verification standards and replaces them with the new federal standards.

States can issue REAL ID-compliant driver's license only to people who have valid documentary evidence that they have a lawful status in the United States. Previously, the categories of persons eligible for driver's licenses were determined on a state-by-state basis. IRTPA specifically prevented the Secretary of Transportation from enacting regulations that would interfere with this authority.

REAL ID establishes a system of temporary licenses that states can issue to applicants who are not US citizens but who can present evidence that they are "lawfully present" in the United States. Noncitizens are eligible for REAL ID–compliant temporary driver's licenses if they fall into one of the six categories. They must have a valid, unexpired nonimmigrant visa or nonimmigrant visa status for entry into the United States; have a pending or approved application for asylum; have entered the United States in refugee status; have a pending or approved application for temporary protected status in the United States; have approved deferred action status; or have a pending application for adjustment of status to that of an alien lawfully admitted for permanent residence or conditional permanent resident status in the United States.

A driver's license for a lawfully present noncitizen must have an expiration date that is the same as the expiration date of the authorized stay of such a person in the United States. For example, an individual with a four-year visa may only receive a REAL ID-compliant driver's license that is valid for four years. Such a temporary license must clearly state this expiration date both on its face and in its machine-readable zone. Holders of temporary licenses can renew them only upon presentation of valid documentary evidence that DHS has extended the status.

Importantly, states can still issue driver's licenses that are not compliant with REAL ID. The Act requires only that the noncompliant documents clearly state so on the face of the document, and use a unique color identifier or design to alert officials not to accept those documents for federal identification or for any official purpose.

REAL ID requires states to adopt procedures and practices (1) to employ technology to capture digital images of identity source documents, (2) to retain paper copies of source documents for a minimum of seven years or images of source documents for a minimum of ten years, (3) to subject each applicant to a mandatory facial image capture, (4) to establish an effective procedure to confirm a renewing applicant's information, (5) to confirm an SSN presented by an applicant with the SSA (if an SSN is already registered to another person to whom any state has issued a driver's license, the state is required to resolve the discrepancy), (6) to refuse issuance of a driver's license to a person holding a driver's license issued by another state without confirmation that the person is terminating or has terminated the license, (7) to ensure the physical security of locations where cards are produced and the security of document materials and papers from which licenses are produced, (8) to subject all persons authorized to manufacture driver's licenses to appropriate security clearance requirements, (9) to establish fraudulent document recognition training programs for employees engaged in the issuance of driver's licenses, and (10) to limit the length of time for which a driver's license is valid to eight years.

REAL ID requires the states to maintain a motor vehicle database that, at a minimum, contains all data fields printed on the driver's license or ID card and all motor vehicle driver histories, including violations, suspensions, and points. To be eligible to receive any grant or financial assistance made available under REAL ID, states shall provide electronic access to their databases to all other states. Contrary to the assertion of some REAL ID opponents, REAL ID does not create a federal database.

REAL ID requires the DHS Secretary to enter into the appropriate aviation-screening database the relevant information of anyone convicted of using a false driver's license at an airport. REAL ID provides the DHS Secretary with the statutory authority to announce regulations, set standards, and issue grants to the states to assist them in conforming to the standards. REAL ID requires the DHS Secretary to consult with both the Secretary of Transportation and the states when acting pursuant to this authority.

Draft and Final Regulations of the 2005 REAL ID Act

In March 2007, nearly two years after Congress passed the law, DHS issued draft regulations on REAL ID Act implementation. Officials acknowledged that they took a long time writing the regulations because they reached out to all sides at the beginning of the process, rather than at the end. DHS Secretary Michael Chertoff said that writing the regulations took the same amount of time that an alternative procedure, negotiated rulemaking (in which the federal government and states agree on a system in lieu of federal legislation), would have taken. Chertoff said, "We did an awful lot of discussion with the very people who would have been in the negotiated rulemaking," so "at the end of the day, we've achieved the same result."[26]

The published notice of proposed rulemaking (NPRM) for REAL ID included the following proposed requirements to meet the minimum standards required under the Act: the information and security features that states must incorporate into each driver's license, the physical security standards for state facilities that produce licenses and cards, and the information applicants must present to establish their identity and immigration status. In response, DHS received over 21,000 comments during the sixty-day public comment period. In January 2008, DHS issued a final rule establishing benchmarks (minimum standards) for state-issued driver's licenses that federal agencies will accept for official purposes.[27]

The new regulations require that REAL ID–compliant driver's licenses contain the name that appears on the source documents that the applicant presents to establish identity. The name that appears on a REAL ID–compliant license must be the same as the name that is on the identification document (passport, birth certificate, Social Security card, etc.) that the applicant presents at the time of application. The regulations provide for an exception for persons whose names appear differently on identification documents due to "marriage, adoption, court order, or other mechanism permitted by state law or regulation." Critics have pointed out that given the lack of a uniform convention with respect to the listing of names on federal documents, this requirement is burdensome to state

[26] DHS, Remarks by Secretary Chertoff at a Press Conference on REAL ID, March 1, 2007, www.dhs.gov/xnews/releases/pr_1172834392961.shtm.

[27] DHS, "Minimum Standards for Driver's Licenses and Identification Cards Acceptable by Federal Agencies for Official Purposes; Final Rule," January 29, 2008.

officials, since applicants may present them with numerous documents, each with variations of the same name. In one commonly cited example, a person named James Joseph Johnson Jr. may have had identification documents issued with the name "Jim Johnson," "J. J. Johnson," or "Jim Johnson Jr." In addition to the myriad of federal documents that utilize different naming conventions, there are foreign documents (each with their own naming rules and conventions) that applicants may present as well. DHS has responded by permitting any and all variations to the applicant's name that are accepted by the issuing state's laws or regulations. It also asserts that it has modified the language in the final rule so that it more closely adheres to the naming conventions utilized by the SSA, DOS, and other document-issuing agencies.[28]

The final REAL ID regulations contain two provisions relevant to the applicant's "principal address," namely, the "location where the person is currently domiciled (i.e., presently resides even if at a temporary address)." One states that a person applying for a REAL ID–compliant document must present at least two documents of the state's choice that include the individual's name and principal residence. The other states that the principal residence must appear both on the face of the REAL ID–compliant document and in the machine-readable portion, although the regulations permit exceptions for individuals enrolled in a state address confidentiality program that allows victims of domestic violence or stalking to use alternative addresses. Critics fear the impact on homeless and low-income individuals who may not have permanent residences. DHS has indicated that its final rule grants the states "wide latitude to address issues concerning an individual's address of principal residence within their state-specific exceptions process." The states will retain sufficient authority to issue REAL ID–compliant documents to individuals, including the homeless, so long as the states properly document the exceptions in their issuing systems. Nevertheless, critics also fear the effect of the "principal address" provision on those who, because of personal safety, may have a legitimate need to keep their address off identifying documents but reside in a state that does not have a law permitting them to do so. In turn, DHS has indicated that under the final rule the states have "broad authority to protect the confidentiality of the address of principal residence for certain classes of individuals."[29]

[28] Tatelman, "REAL ID," 20–21. [29] Ibid., 21–22.

REAL ID requires states to verify the validity of the supporting documents presented by the applicant with the documents' issuing agencies. The final regulations require the states to "make reasonable efforts" to ensure that applicants do not have multiple REAL ID–compliant documents issued under different identities, and require the states to verify documents presented via electronic validation systems "as they become available or use alternative methods approved by DHS." The regulations provide verification requirements for five different types of documents.[30]

First, regarding documents issued by DHS, such as documents establishing lawful presence, the regulations require verification through the Systemic Alien Verification System for Entitlements.

Second, regarding SSNs, the regulations require verification through the SSA. The American Association of Motor Vehicle Administrators (AAMVA) has created the Social Security Online Verification (SSOLV) application in conjunction with SSA. SSOLV permits a jurisdiction's motor vehicle agency to submit a real-time inquiry to SSA to verify a driver's SSN, name, and date of birth.[31]

Third, regarding birth certificates, the regulations require verification through either the Electronic Verification of Vital Events (EVVE) system or other electronic systems whenever the records are available. However, in 2008 DHS acknowledged that EVVE was not yet ready for full implementation. Given that birth records are retained by the individual states and not the federal government, it was unclear what other methods of birth-certification verification were available and how the states were going to comply with this requirement.[32] However, by January 2015, the National Association for Public Health Statistics and Information Systems, which operates EVVE, reported that of the fifty-seven vital registry jurisdictions (fifty states, five territories, the District of Columbia, and New York City), fifty-three jurisdictions were online with EVVE, two were in development, and two were not online (the states of Washington and New York).[33]

Fourth, regarding documents issued by the DOS, such as passports, the regulations require verification through the DOS or by means approved by DHS.

30 Ibid., 22–23.

31 AAMVA, "SSOLV FAQs," www.aamva.org/SSOLV-Frequently-Asked-Questions-FAQs/.

32 Tatelman, "REAL ID," 23.

33 National Association for Public Health Statistics and Information Systems, "About EVVE," www.naphsis.org/about-evve.

Finally, regarding REAL ID–compliant documents issued by other states that holders may eventually use as a form of identification, the regulations indicate that the receiving states will need to verify them with the state of issuance.[34]

The final regulations require that all REAL ID–compliant documents use compatible machine-readable technology. The barcode needs to include the cardholder's full legal name, though some states permit an applicant to establish a name other than the name that appears on a source document. The barcode also needs to include the cardholder's date of birth, gender, and address. It also needs to include date of transaction, expiration date, the number of the driver's license or ID card, card design revision date (indicating the most recent change to the visible format of the card), inventory control number of the physical document, and state or territory of issuance. The regulations indicated that forty-six jurisdictions already utilize barcodes that comply with the standard.[35]

Contrary to the assertion of REAL ID opponents, REAL ID does not require or even suggest the use of RFID chips. In fact, REAL ID also does not require sophisticated biometric technology; it requires only that all applicants for REAL ID–compliant documents be subject to digital facial image capture. A digital facial image can be used in biometric matching only when it is subjected to facial recognition analysis.

However, the machine-readable requirement does raise security and personal privacy concerns that DHS tried to address in the final rule. With respect to security of the information contained on the barcode, commentators suggested that DHS prohibit the collection and storage of the data on the barcodes by third parties, specifically businesses. DHS responded by noting that although the underlying statute does not provide them with the legal authority to prohibit such data collection, at least four states – California, Nebraska, New Hampshire, and Texas – currently have such provisions in place, and DHS is supportive of additional state efforts in this regard.[36]

In response to comments concerning the sensitive nature of storing a potentially vast amount of personal data, DHS has indicated that there can be some modifications to the requirement that states retain paper or digital copies of source documents presented by applicants. Specifically, if an applicant requests it, and state data-retention laws permit it, a state can just "record and retain the applicant's name, [date of birth], certificate

[34] Tatelman, "REAL ID," 23. [35] Ibid., 24. [36] Ibid., 24–25.

numbers, date filed, and issuing agency in lieu of an image or copy of the applicant's birth certificate."[37]

The final REAL ID regulations also govern the background checks required on all state DMV employees, including contract employees, who are involved in the production of REAL ID–compliant licenses and cards. Background checks are to include a name-based and fingerprint-based criminal history record check. Such check should use, at a minimum, the FBI's National Crime Information Center, the Integrated Automated Fingerprint Identification System database, and state repository records. Background checks are also to include a verification of employment eligibility (states are encouraged to use E-Verify, but are not required to do so), and a reference check, unless the employee has been at the job for at least two years since May 2006. A conviction of espionage or terrorism can disqualify an employee.[38]

REAL ID requires states to ensure the physical security of card production locations and the security of materials from which the cards are produced. The states need to submit a single security plan that addresses DMV facilities involved in the enrollment, production, and issuance of cards. Although the regulations provide requirements for the security plans, some commentators noted the lack of standards and defined best practices. DHS indicated that it would be working with the DOT, AAMVA, and the states to develop such practices.[39]

I learned from a senior DHS official that the REAL ID Program Office did indeed work closely with those entities, especially AAMVA and the individual DMVs. "We built a really close relationship [with them]. We would have a working group with DMVs and AAMVA. They helped out with card standards, the security features, any changes to the regulations, [and] implementation."[40]

Implementation

The original deadline after which federal officials were to accept only REAL ID–compliant state driver's licenses and ID cards for official purposes was May 11, 2008. This was to take effect unless a state had received an extension from DHS. As late as March 2008, Secretary Chertoff stated that REAL ID goes into effect that day and that officials will enforce it. He said, "I'm not bluffing about May 11 ... the law

[37] Ibid., 25. [38] Ibid., 26–27. [39] Ibid., 25–26.
[40] Interview with a senior DHS official, Washington, DC, May 2015.

makes it clear ... if you don't get a waiver, then you're going to have ... a driver's license [that] will not be acceptable for federal purposes as an ID."[41]

All fifty-six jurisdictions covered by REAL ID received an initial extension for compliance from DHS. This was so even though several states made it clear that either due to existing state law or other concerns regarding REAL ID, their request for an extension was not to be viewed as an indication that they intended to implement the REAL ID requirements. For instance, a March 2008 letter from the California DMV Director to Secretary Chertoff stated that "California's request for an extension is not a commitment to implement REAL ID."[42] Although such language in the request letter would appear to make the state ineligible for the extension, DHS granted each of these extensions.[43]

The initial extension for compliance was valid until December 31, 2009. Each state then had the option of filing for a second extension valid until May 2011, if it could demonstrate that it was in material compliance with all eighteen benchmarks established by the final rule. The states then had until May 2011 before they would need to begin issuing licenses that meet the department's guidelines. In March 2011, DHS granted all states a third extension, which pushed the deadline for compliance to January 15, 2013. DHS motivated this decision by saying that

> the inability of states to fully comply with the requirements of REAL ID by May 11, 2011 is the result of a number of factors, including diminished state budgets caused by the economic downturn and the uncertainty throughout much of the 111th Congress about congressional action on the PASS ID Act, which would have modified some of the requirements of REAL ID. Implementation of REAL ID involves a significant financial investment, and, despite the receipt of substantial federal grant funds, a number of states are struggling to come up with the resources necessary to meet the full compliance deadline in these times of budget austerity.[44]

In December 2012, just as it announced that thirteen states already met the REAL ID standards, DHS provided a six-month grace period for remaining states to become fully compliant with the Act. DHS stated that enforcement would then begin at the earliest in the autumn of 2013.[45]

[41] DHS, Remarks by Secretary Chertoff at Pen-and-Pad Briefing on the Department's Fifth Anniversary, March 6, 2008, www.dhs.gov/xnews/releases/pr_1204843734531.shtm.

[42] Letter from George Valverde to Michael Chertoff, March 18, 2008, https://epic.org/privacy/id_cards/calif_dhs_031808.pdf.

[43] Tatelman, "REAL ID," 16–17.

[44] Federal Register, 76, 44, March 7, 2011.

[45] DHS, "DHS Determines 13 States Meet REAL ID Standards," December 20, 2012, www.dhs.gov/news/2012/12/20/dhs-determines-13-states-meet-real-id-standards.

In December 2013, DHS announced a phased enforcement plan for the REAL ID Act. DHS made clear that each phase would begin with a three-month period where agencies provide notice to individuals attempting to use driver's licenses from noncompliant states but still allow access.[46]

The enforcement of the first three phases began between April 2014 and October 2015. Phases One, Two, and Three covered restricted areas for DHS headquarters in Washington, DC (Nebraska Avenue Complex), restricted areas for all federal facilities and nuclear power plants, and semi-restricted areas for most federal facilities, respectively.[47]

Phase Four, for boarding federally regulated commercial aircraft, was to begin "no sooner than 2016." In that last phase, a person holding a driver's license from a noncompliant state will be able to use it only in conjunction with a second form of ID.[48] Not having a REAL ID–compliant document will not prevent individuals from flying. Many people thought that the changes would affect air travel as early as spring 2016.

In January 2016, Secretary Jeh Johnson (who became DHS Secretary in December 2013) announced that it would not be until January 22, 2018, that passengers with a driver's license or ID card issued by a state that is still not compliant with the REAL ID Act (unless that state has been granted an extension) would need to show an alternative form of acceptable identification for domestic air travel. Secretary Johnson stated:

> The overall goal of the REAL ID Act passed by Congress is to prevent the fraudulent issuance and use of driver's licenses and identification cards, thereby ensuring the safety and security of the American public. Given today's threat environment, this requirement is as relevant now as it was when the 9/11 Commission recommended it.[49]

Secretary Johnson announced that DHS would conduct outreach to educate the traveling public about the timeline, and continue engagements with states to encourage compliance with REAL ID standards. Johnson stressed that starting October 1, 2020, every air traveler will need a REAL ID–compliant license, or another acceptable form of identification, for domestic air travel. Put differently, the October 2020 deadline represents

[46] DHS, "REAL ID Enforcement in Brief," June 8, 2017, www.dhs.gov/real-id-enforcement-brief.

[47] DHS, "REAL ID FAQs." [48] Ibid.

[49] DHS, Press Release, Statement by Secretary Jeh C. Johnson on the final phase of REAL ID Act implementation, January 8, 2016, www.dhs.gov/news/2016/01/08/statement-secretary-jeh-c-johnson-final-phase-real-id-act-implementation.

the date DHS will switch from enforcement based on state of issuance to enforcement based on individual cards.[50]

DHS stated (already in late 2014) that the October 2020 deadline

> should give residents of compliant states sufficient time to obtain licenses that satisfy the REAL ID standards, which presumably they will do in accordance with their normal renewal schedule. DHS also is establishing a single document enforcement date, as opposed to a bifurcated approach based on a person's age, to accommodate the phased enforcement schedule and to simplify the implementation process for federal agencies' access control personnel. Nothing in this rule affects the prohibition against federal agencies accepting licenses and identification cards issued by noncompliant states, pursuant to the REAL ID Act and in accordance to the phased enforcement schedule. DHS believes this rule balances the security objective of improving the reliability of identification documents presented for official purposes with the operational and cost burdens on compliant states and their residents.[51]

DHS makes clear that phased REAL ID enforcement would not affect "access for activities directly relating to safety and health or life preserving services, to law enforcement, and to constitutionally protected activities, including legal and investigative proceedings. Existing agency policies will still apply." The DHS website emphasizes that the Act does not require individuals to present identification documents where it is not currently required to access a federal facility (such as to enter the Smithsonian Institution). It also stresses that the Act's prohibitions do not affect other uses of driver's licenses – including cards from noncompliant states – unrelated to official purposes as defined in the Act. For example, the Act does not apply to voting, registering to vote, or applying for or receiving federal benefits.[52]

Individuals visiting the facilities subject to enforcement need to present government-issued identification. Federal agencies will accept only state-issued driver's licenses or ID cards issued by states that are REAL ID–compliant. If a visitor has a license from a noncompliant state, they need to bring an alternative form of government-issued photo ID – such as a passport, passport card, or federal employee, military, or veteran ID card.[53]

[50] Ibid. [51] Federal Register, 79, 248, December 29, 2014.

[52] DHS, "REAL ID Enforcement."

[53] Interagency Security Committee, "REAL ID Act of 2005. Implementation: An Interagency Security Committee Guide," August 2015, www.dhs.gov/sites/default/files/publications/isc-real-id-guide-august-2015-508_0.pdf.

Opposition to the 2005 REAL ID Act

Since President Bush signed it into law in 2005, REAL ID has been highly contested among state legislatures, governors, and advocacy groups. Opponents criticize it for being an unfunded mandate, where the federal government makes the rules and the states bear the costs. Some critics also argue that the Act will create a national ID card.

In April 2006, the National Governors Association (NGA), the National Conference of State Legislatures (NCSL), and AAMVA called for a delay in putting the Act into effect due to practical concerns. However, prior to the publication of the NPRM in 2007, there was relatively little activity at the state level, mainly because officials were uncertain as to what the implementation requirements were going to necessitate in terms of cost and changes to state law.

Since the publication of the NPRM in March 2007, there has been a dramatic increase in state responses to REAL ID and its requirements. By the end of April 2007, seven states, including Maine and Montana, enacted legislation opposing the law. Maine's statute specifically prevents the state's participation in a "national identification card" program, and some people believe that REAL ID is a de facto national identification card. It looks like state officials have interpreted this statue as preventing compliance with REAL ID. Montana has adopted one of the strongest noncompliance laws. On April 17, 2007, declaring "Hell, no," Governor Brian Schweitzer (D-MT), signed one of the toughest anti–REAL ID state laws in the nation. The law not only barred state participation in the program but also directed the Montana Department of Justice and the motor vehicle administration to report to the governor any attempts by DHS to secure REAL ID implementation.[54]

On the one hand, such opposition was not risky because at the time the ramifications of having several noncompliant states were not clear. The Act itself is voluntary, binding only on federal agencies, not on the states. It contains no penalty for noncompliance. On the other hand, such opposition was risky because it put the residents of noncompliant states at risk of carrying the burden for their state's noncompliance. When Montana passed a law prohibiting compliance in 2007 and refused to file for an extension, it seemed that after May 11, 2008, Montana residents would not be able to use their state-issued driver's licenses for

[54] Tatelman, "REAL ID," 18; Katel, "Real ID," 388, 395.

official purposes. Therefore, Montana residents would not be able to use their licenses to board an airplane or enter a federal building. Although this did not mean that residents of noncompliant states could not engage in airplane travel – as the TSA accepts other government-issued identification documents, including passports or military IDs – it would impose an additional burden on the citizen because the state chose not to comply.[55]

In addition, noncompliant states would create holes in the scheme of state-to-state data sharing that is an integral part of REAL ID. Presumably, noncompliant states will not participate in the database creation or information-sharing system envisioned by REAL ID. Thus, potential problems may arise if, for example, an applicant in a compliant state presents a document, such as a birth certificate, that requires verification from a noncompliant state. The existence of noncompliant states also presents the potential for conflicts among the states, in addition to those between the noncompliant states and the federal government. For example, will a driver's license issued by Montana that is not REAL ID–compliant continue to be a valid form of identification in Indiana, a state that has a compliance law in place? Will Montana accept forms of identification that comply with REAL ID as valid within its own jurisdiction? As Todd Tatelman, legislative attorney at the Congressional Research Service (CRS), pointed out in 2008, REAL ID did not address such questions that will likely arise as implementation advances.[56]

All the state opposition, uncertainty about the repercussions, and DHS "caving in" to state requests for extensions or granting extensions even without requests has led critics of REAL ID to declare the Act "effectively dead."[57] Interestingly, something opposite has happened and, despite uncertainty, by 2016 many states had changed their opinion on REAL ID.

The Changing REAL ID Landscape

In 2008, Barack Obama made very little comment on the REAL ID Act in the run-up to his election. When Janet Napolitano began to head DHS in January 2009, the uncertainty was particularly pronounced, not least because she was opposed to the REAL ID Act as governor of Arizona.

55 Tatelman, "REAL ID," 19. 56 Ibid., 20.

57 ACLU, "Bill Introduced to Repeal Failed REAL ID Act," July 31, 2009, www.aclu.org/technology-and-liberty/bill-introduced-repeal-failed-real-id-act.

While she was governor she called REAL ID "feel-good" legislation not worth the cost, and in 2008, she signed a state law opting out of it.[58]

In March 2009, as the DHS Secretary, she announced that her office was working with the NGA to propose revisions to the law, and in April, she talked about replacing REAL ID with something that "accomplishes some of the same goals."[59] Reports then emerged that Napolitano would propose to limit the deployment of the Act, though more to consider cost issues rather than on civil liberties grounds.[60]

Policymakers have introduced bills to repeal REAL ID multiple times; all of the bills failed. There was the Akaka–Sununu Senate bill of 2007 and the Allen House bill of 2007, among others. However, it was not until the 111th Congress (2009–2011) that a bill to repeal REAL ID had the support of the Secretary of Homeland Security. In the 111th Congress, two bills addressed REAL ID: Providing for Additional Security in States' Identification Act of 2009 (PASS ID), introduced by Senators Daniel Akaka (D-HI), George Voinovich (R-OH), and Joseph Lieberman (I-CT); and REAL ID Repeal and Identification Security Enhancement Act of 2009, introduced by Rep. Steve Cohen (D-TN). Both bills failed, but PASS ID was of particular importance.

PASS ID would have kept elements of REAL ID, such as requiring a digital photograph and machine-readable features such as a barcode. States would still need to verify applicants' identities and legal status by checking federal immigration, SSA, and DOS databases. However, it would have eliminated demands for new databases that would allow all states to store and cross-check such information, and the requirement that DMVs verify birth certificates with originating agencies, a bid to fight identity theft. Rep. Sensenbrenner said the new plan would still let people get licenses with fake documents: "We go right back to where we were on September 10, 2001. Maybe governors should have been in the Capitol when we knew a plane was on its way to Washington wanting to kill a few thousand more people."[61]

Janet Napolitano had an interesting role in the push for PASS ID. As a former NGA Chairwoman, she wished to soothe strained relations with the states without appearing to retreat on a recommendation of the 9/11 Commission.[62] In supporting PASS ID, she favored legislation drafted by

[58] Spencer S. Hsu, "Administration Plans to Scale Back Real ID Law," *Washington Post*, June 14, 2009.
[59] Ibid. [60] Whitley and Hosein, *Global Challenges*, 56.
[61] Hsu, "Administration Plans." [62] Ibid.

the NGA and partially negated the commission recommendation. Although PASS ID failed, some states delayed implementation of REAL ID based on promises of PASS ID passage.

In an interview I conducted with a senior DHS official, I learned that Secretary Chertoff was directly involved with REAL ID, while Secretary Napolitano was not. I was able to find out that Darrell Williams, who, between December 2006 and April 2011, was the Director of the REAL ID Program Office (renamed, during that time, the Office of State-Issued ID Support) very regularly briefed Secretary Chertoff on REAL ID, approximately once every month between December 2006 and January 2009. In contrast, Secretary Napolitano attended briefings with him just twice between January 2009 and April 2011. As a senior official told me, "The emphasis flows down from the secretary. If the interest is not exerted at the top level, it will not flow down." The official added, "AAMVA became an advocate of the [REAL ID Program] Office for DMVs. [AAMVA] became more of an advocate for the Office than DHS was."[63]

REAL ID has remained in place as federal law. As Janice Kephart, a former counsel to the 9/11 Commission, noted: "Considering the political tenor of REAL ID, and the assault it suffered for years, it is unexpected that most states are quietly implementing the law. Pace and commitment still differ among the states, but . . . states are finding out implementation, on the whole, is not as expensive as they thought and is achievable." States such as Delaware and Maryland, once committed, have completed implementation of the eighteen benchmarks needed to fulfill material compliance with the law within a year "for only twice the grant monies provided by the federal government."[64]

Despite delays, by January 2011 there were eleven states in full compliance with all eighteen REAL ID material compliance benchmarks.[65]

By November 1, 2016, forty-six of the fifty-six jurisdictions covered by REAL ID either became compliant (twenty-four) or received extensions (twenty-two). Two jurisdictions were under review and eight were noncompliant. According to DHS, approximately 90 percent of all US drivers at the time held licenses from jurisdictions that met the Act's standards or that have received extensions.[66] Most likely, that figure was about

[63] Interview with a senior DHS official, May 2015.

[64] Janice L. Kephart, "REAL ID Implementation. Less Expensive, Doable, and Helpful in Reducing Fraud," Center for Immigration Studies, January 2011, 2.

[65] Ibid., 6. [66] DHS, "REAL ID Enforcement."

86 percent, since the eight noncompliant jurisdictions at the time accounted for about 14 percent of licensed drivers (29.7 million out of 214 million).[67]

Spring of 2017 saw a flurry of legislative and gubernatorial activity in favor of moving toward REAL ID Act compliance in various states, including Washington State, Oklahoma, and Pennsylvania. Secretary John Kelly (who became DHS Secretary in January 2017) has made clear throughout the spring of 2017 that he is committed to enforcement of the REAL ID rules and the January 2018 deadline set by Secretary Jeh Johnson.

By June 8, 2017, fifty-two of the fifty-six jurisdictions covered by REAL ID either became compliant or received extensions. Specifically, twenty-six jurisdictions were compliant, including Arizona, the District of Columbia, Florida, Georgia, Indiana, and Maryland. Twenty-six jurisdictions received extensions into later in 2017, including California, Massachusetts, New York, North Carolina, and Texas. The extensions allow federal agencies to accept driver's licenses from these jurisdictions for official purposes during this time.[68]

Only four (Maine, Minnesota, Missouri, and Montana) were noncompliant and subject to enforcement. However, Maine and Missouri made moves toward compliance and for Minnesota federal officials may continue to accept the EDLs.[69]

This shows that the goal of securing identification documents and increasing identity policing in the United States is being achieved through multiple means and on multiple levels, not always along a single path. The notion of patchwork is even more evident when one considers other identity policing schemes that sprang up in the United States during the post-9/11 decade.

OTHER IDENTITY POLICING SCHEMES

In addition to REAL ID, other identity policing schemes have also emerged in the United States since 9/11, affecting US citizens and noncitizens. Some schemes focus specifically on people entering the United States. Other schemes focus on people already inside the United States as they travel, access secure areas of maritime facilities, interact with law

[67] My own calculations, based on DOT, Federal Highway Administration, "Highway Statistics 2014," Washington, DC, 2015, table DL1-C, www.fhwa.dot.gov/policyinformation/statistics/2014/dl1c.cfm.

[68] DHS, "REAL ID Enforcement." [69] Ibid.

enforcement or local authorities, or vote. The new identity policing schemes tend to result in one or more of the following: the introduction of new documentary requirements, the introduction of new identification documents, and/or the improvements to existing identification documents. Importantly, with regard to schemes focused on travel, while most post-9/11 identity policing schemes are concerned with increasing security, even if it means making travel more burdensome, other schemes aim to increase security while specifically trying to make travel easier for the low-risk travelers.

The Western Hemisphere Travel Initiative

Almost all travelers, US citizens and foreign nationals alike, must now present a passport to enter the United States. In addition, foreign nationals entering the United States are generally required to present a valid visa issued by a US consular official. Visas are not required for those traveling under a Visa Waiver Program and for LPRs (Green Card holders). In addition, citizens of Canada and Bermuda do not require visas to enter the United States for tourism or business. Citizens and permanent residents of Mexico generally must have a visa or a Border Crossing Card (BCC).

In the past, US citizens and citizens of neighboring countries could enter the United States without a passport when coming from neighboring countries. A verbal claim of citizenship and identity was sufficient for entry into the United States. Since January 2007, this is no longer the case for air travel, and since June 2009, this is no longer the case for any kind of travel.

The Western Hemisphere Travel Initiative (WHTI), which originated in IRTPA, requires all travelers, US citizens and foreign nationals alike, entering the United States from Canada, Mexico, and the Caribbean to present a passport, other document, or combination of documents, "deemed by the Secretary of Homeland Security to be sufficient to *denote identity and citizenship*."[70] The document or combination of documents a traveler needs to present depends on the traveler's mode of entry into the United States (by air vs. by sea or land) and the traveler's citizenship and residency status. RFID chips are now part of all WHTI-compliant identification documents: passports, passport cards, enhanced tribal cards, EDLs, trusted traveler cards, Green Cards, and BCCs.

[70] IRTPA, §7209(c)(2) (emphasis added).

WHTI for air travel went into effect in January 2007. It requires US citizens and residents and citizens of Canada, Mexico, and Bermuda traveling by air between the United States and Canada, Mexico, and Bermuda to present a valid passport to enter or depart the United States. Only two documents are acceptable for air travel instead of a passport. The first is the Merchant Mariner Document issued by the US Coast Guard for US citizen merchant mariners traveling on official business. The second is the NEXUS card, for which enrollment is limited to US and Canadian citizens and permanent residents. Mexican citizens need to present a passport and a visa, or a passport and a BCC, to enter the United States by air.[71]

WHTI for sea and land travel went into effect in June 2009. It requires US citizens and residents as well as Canadian and Mexican citizens who enter the United States at land and sea POEs from within the Western Hemisphere to present a WHTI-compliant travel document. This can be a passport (in case of Mexican citizens it must include a visa, but Mexican citizens may use the BCC in lieu of a passport and visa for land border crossings within the border region) or a US passport card. It can also be an EDL from the United States or Canada or a trusted traveler program card (NEXUS, SENTRI, or FAST). LPRs need to present a Green Card. Verbal claims of citizenship and identity alone are no longer sufficient to establish identity and citizenship for entry into the United States.[72]

Although the REAL ID Act contains increased security requirements for state-issued driver's licenses and ID cards, these requirements are focused on ensuring that the documents accurately reflect identity. REAL ID does not require that the documents denote US citizenship. In fact, REAL ID contains specific provisions that permit the issuance of licenses to noncitizens who, by producing the required documentation and having it verified as authentic by the issuing agency, can demonstrate lawful presence in the country. In addition, given the absence of requirements relating to citizenship, a regular (non–REAL ID–compliant) driver's license does not satisfy the statutory standard established by IRTPA for acceptable documents to be shown upon entrance to the United States.

Enhanced Driver's Licenses

At the time WHTI was enacted, a US passport was the only document that satisfied the requirement of denoting both identity and US

[71] CBP, "WHTI FAQs," www.cbp.gov/travel/us-citizens/whti-air-faq. [72] Ibid.

citizenship. To implement WHTI, the DOS and DHS have developed alternative identification documents that satisfy the standards required by Congress. An enhanced driver's license is a driver's license that can also be used as a cross-border travel document to enter the United States by land and sea (but is not valid for international air travel). It denotes both identity and citizenship. Five states – Michigan, Minnesota, New York, Vermont, and Washington – are issuing EDLs and enhanced ID cards for nondrivers. They are available to residents of those states who choose an enhanced document over a standard one.[73]

Although DHS oversees both EDL and REAL ID programs, there are two major differences between the programs. First, unlike REAL IDs, EDLs require that the cardholder be a US citizen. Second, EDLs implement RFID technology, whereas REAL IDs are required only to use two-dimensional barcodes. Thus, although the two programs are related, they are not interchangeable. It is possible for an EDL to qualify as a REAL ID if the document satisfies the requirements of both programs. On the other hand, just because an individual has a REAL ID, it does not automatically follow that they qualify for an EDL or can use their REAL ID as part of the WHTI program. Put differently, some EDLs comply with REAL ID, but not all REAL IDs qualify as WHTI-compliant EDLs. Only after a review of the issuing requirements and document contents can the authorities determine whether a specific driver's license qualifies under both, neither, or only one of the programs.[74]

Passports and Passport Cards

In August 2006, the United States began issuing biometric passports with RFID chips holding a digital photo and personal data. Since August 2007, the United States has been issuing only electronic passports (e-passports), which are the same as regular passports with the addition of a small contactless computer chip embedded in the back cover. The chip stores the same data visually displayed on the photo page of the passport, and includes a digital photograph (which enables biometric comparison using facial recognition technology). The DOS provides a metallic mesh to protect a passport from improper access, skimming, and tracking.

[73] DHS, "Enhanced Driver's Licenses," www.dhs.gov/enhanced-drivers-licenses-what-are-they.

[74] Tatelman, "REAL ID," 31–32.

"Basic Access Control" is supposed to lock the data on the chip. The system requires authentication by an optical scan before the data can be read.[75]

Passport cards are limited-use international travel documents valid for entry into the United States by land or sea from Canada, Mexico, the Caribbean, and Bermuda, per the WHTI. They are not valid for international air travel. They contain RFID chips. The DOS began production of the passport cards in July 2008.[76]

The DOS issues both passports and passport cards. By the end of 2016 there were almost 132 million valid US passports in circulation. In addition, the DOS has issued 12.4 million passport cards between 2008 and the end of 2016.[77]

Trusted Traveler Programs

The 9/11 Commission knew that increased security checks could have a negative impact on legitimate trade and travel. Its report stated that the border screening system "should check people efficiently and welcome friends" and that DHS, supported by Congress, "should complete, as quickly as possible, a biometric entry-exit system, including a single system for speeding qualified travelers."[78]

While a biometric entry-exit system still does not exist, there are now five programs aimed at speeding the travel of qualified, or trusted, travelers. Two DHS agencies run the five trusted traveler programs. The US Customs and Border Protection Agency (CBP) runs four programs and the TSA runs one. The CBP programs, NEXUS, SENTRI, FAST, and Global Entry, aim to expedite international border crossings for frequent travelers. The TSA program, Pre-Check, aims to expedite security screening at US airport checkpoints for domestic and international travel.

The CBP programs provide expedited travel for preapproved, low-risk travelers through dedicated lanes and kiosks. Though intended for frequent international travelers, there is no minimum number of trips necessary to qualify. Members in these voluntary programs must meet eligibility requirements and pay a five-year membership fee. The Global

[75] Lyon, *Identifying Citizens*, 103.

[76] DOS, "Passport Card," http://travel.state.gov/content/passports/english/passports/information/card.html.

[77] DOS, "Passports Statistics," http://travel.state.gov/content/passports/english/passports/statistics.html.

[78] *The 9/11 Commission Report*, 389.

Enrollment System handles the enrollment and vetting process for the four programs. Each program requires a similar application process, featuring background checks, an in-person interview with a CBP officer, and a ten-fingerprint law enforcement check. Every twenty-four hours, CBP conducts vetting checks against FBI databases and revokes the membership of anyone whose eligibility has changed.[79] While these are trusted traveler programs, CBP "trusts but verifies" the travelers through random and targeted inspections.

NEXUS, SENTRI, and FAST programs issue photo identification cards with RFID chips. The Global Entry program initially did not issue identification cards, but in 2011 CBP began issuing Global Entry cards to new members who are US citizens, LPRs, or Mexican nationals (but not to other nationalities).

There were 2.5 million people enrolled in CBP's four trusted traveler programs in January 2014. About 43 percent of trusted travelers were enrolled in Global Entry, and 38 percent were enrolled in NEXUS.[80]

NEXUS is a joint United States–Canada trusted traveler program. Individuals may qualify to participate in NEXUS if they are a citizen or permanent resident of either country. They must pass criminal history and law enforcement checks by both countries. NEXUS cards are WHTI-compliant and approved as an alternative to the passport for air, land, and sea travel into the United States. Program members use dedicated processing lanes at designated northern border POEs, NEXUS kiosks when entering Canada by air, and Global Entry kiosks when entering the United States via Canadian preclearance airports.[81]

SENTRI (Secure Electronic Network for Travelers Rapid Inspection) is a trusted traveler program that expedites crossing between the United States and Mexico. SENTRI, initiated in 1995, allows preapproved, low-risk travelers access to dedicated commuter lanes. Prospective program members must present evidence of citizenship. If they are not US citizens, they must present evidence of immigration admissibility. They must also pass criminal history and law enforcement checks. SENTRI cards are WHTI-compliant for entry into the United States by land or sea.[82]

[79] BPC, "Entry-Exit System: Progress, Challenges, and Outlook," Staff Report, May 6, 2014, 9, http://bipartisanpolicy.org/library/immigration-entry-exit-system/.

[80] GAO, "Trusted Travelers: Programs Provide Benefits, but Enrollment Processes Could Be Strengthened," May 30, 2014, 14–15.

[81] CBP, "Trusted Traveler Programs," www.cbp.gov/travel/trusted-traveler-programs.

[82] Ibid.

FAST (Free and Secure Trade) is a commercial clearance program for known low-risk shipments entering the United States from Canada and Mexico. Initiated after 9/11, this program allows expedited processing for commercial carriers who have completed background checks and fulfill eligibility requirements. FAST enrollment is open to truck drivers who are citizens or LPRs of the United States, Canada, and Mexico. If they are not US citizens, truck drivers must be admissible to the United States under applicable immigration laws.[83]

Global Entry allows expedited clearance for preapproved, low-risk travelers upon arrival in the United States. Global Entry is open to US citizens, LPRs, and citizens of several countries including Germany and the United Kingdom. Applicants pay an application fee, undergo a background investigation with fingerprint check, and complete an interview with a CBP officer. When they arrive in the United States from abroad, Global Entry members bypass the traditional CBP inspection lines and use an automated kiosk to complete their admission. Each traveler scans his or her fingerprints and passport and answers customs declaration questions using the kiosk's touchscreen. The kiosk issues a transaction receipt and directs the traveler to baggage claim and the exit.[84]

In July 2011, CBP began issuing Global Entry cards to new Global Entry members who are US citizens, LPRs, or Mexican nationals. Other members are not eligible for the cards. It is not necessary to have a card to continue using Global Entry. The sole purpose of the cards, which have RFID chips, is to enable Global Entry members to use the SENTRI and NEXUS expedited entry travel lanes coming into the United States.[85]

In October 2011, TSA introduced its own trusted traveler program. Pre-Check, also known as TSA Pre✓™, allows select low-risk travelers to experience expedited, more efficient security screening at participating US airport checkpoints for domestic and international travel. Initially, TSA allowed only frequent flyers who were US citizens into the program, but now applicants no longer have to be frequent flyers and LPRs can apply. Applicants must pass a background check and have their fingerprints taken. There is no card provided by the Pre-Check program. Instead, the traveler receives a Known Traveler Number and uses it when booking travel.[86]

TSA processes some 1.8 million passengers each day at security checkpoints. Most passengers present a low risk to aviation security, but until

[83] Ibid.
[84] CBP, "Global Entry," www.cbp.gov/travel/trusted-traveler-programs/global-entry.
[85] Ibid. [86] TSA, "Pre-Check FAQ," www.tsa.gov/precheck/faq.

the establishment of Pre-Check, TSA used the same security screening procedures for passengers without regard for the risk passengers posed. The only exception to that were the passengers matched to watch lists through the Secure Flight system.

After TSA piloted Pre-Check with certain passengers who were frequent flyers, TSA established separate Pre-Check lists for additional low-risk passenger populations, including members of Congress. In April 2014, about 5.6 million individuals were eligible for expedited screening through the separate TSA Pre-Check lists. That number included 2.5 million people enrolled in CBP's trusted traveler programs, 2.2 million DOD military personnel, 700,000 DOD and Coast Guard civilian personnel, 180,000 individuals who applied and were accepted into the Pre-Check program (an option available since December 2013), and 70,000 individuals employed by the national intelligence agencies.[87]

Green Cards

The US government issues permanent resident cards (Green Cards) to LPRs as evidence of their authorization to live and work in the United States. Since May 2010, the Green Cards feature RFID chips for WHTI compliance.

Transportation Worker Identification Credential

Transportation Worker Identification Credential (TWIC), established in 2002, is a biometric identification credential for all eligible personnel requiring unescorted access to secure areas of maritime facilities and vessels. The US Coast Guard oversees the program, but the TSA runs it. An applicant must undergo a security threat assessment and submit fingerprints and a digital photograph. Non-US citizens can apply for TWIC if they fall into an eligible immigration category. A TWIC card is an acceptable form of identification at airport screening checkpoints.[88]

US-VISIT and a Biometric Entry-Exit System

An essential function of an entry-exit system is to match foreign visitors' arrival records to subsequent departure records. As a 2014 report from

[87] GAO, "Aviation Security: Rapid Growth in Expedited Passenger Screening Highlights Need to Plan Effective Security Assessments," December 12, 2014, 10–12, 24.

[88] TSA, "TWIC," www.tsa.gov/for-industry/twic.

the Bipartisan Policy Center (BPC) makes clear, if the system included all arrivals and all departures, DHS could determine whether and when individuals depart the country and identify those who overstay their period of admission. To establish a high level of confidence in the entry-exit data, the system would have to cover all land, air, and sea POEs.[89] An entry-exit system can include just biographic data (e.g., name, date of birth, and travel history) or it can also include biometric data (e.g., fingerprints and digital photographs).

Proposals to create an entry-exit system, which could be a tool for immigration control and enforcement, date back to at least the 1980s. In 1981, SCIRP recommended a fully automated system of nonimmigrant document control to allow prompt tracking of aliens and to verify their departure. IIRIRA was the first to mandate an automated entry-exit system. The 9/11 Commission recommended a biometric entry-exit solution, and the Enhanced Border Security and Visa Entry Reform Act of 2002 required all POEs to be equipped for biometric authentication of all entry documents issued to foreigners. The INS named that immigration and border management system US-VISIT, or the United States Visitor and Immigrant Status Indicator Technology. Following the creation of the DHS and abolishment of the INS, US-VISIT became part of DHS. IRTPA of 2004 required biometric exit data collection from all individuals who provided biometric entry data under US-VISIT. IRTPA, through the WHTI, also required DHS to inspect passports or other secure travel documents for all travelers, including US citizens.[90]

Congress subsequently reorganized DHS's entry-exit–related functions. In 2006 and 2007, the US-VISIT program was a stand-alone office within DHS, and from 2008 to 2012, the program was coordinated out of the National Protection and Programs Directorate (NPPD). For 2013, Congress realigned the functions of US-VISIT. The overall mission of managing and coordinating the collection of biographic and biometric entry and exit data was transferred to a new Entry/Exit Transformation Office within CBP, the agency charged with securing the nation's borders. Responsibility for identifying overstays was transferred to Immigration and Customs Enforcement (ICE), the agency that conducts interior immigration enforcement. The remaining US-VISIT operations were moved to the new Office of Biometric Identity Management (OBIM). These functions include maintaining the biometric database, conducting

[89] BPC, "Entry-Exit," 1. [90] Ibid., 1, 3, 4.

biometric matching operations for DHS and other agencies, and managing biometric watch lists.[91] OBIM was created in March 2013 and is part of the NPPD.[92]

Authorities have still not put in place a biometric entry-exit system in the United States. However, with US-VISIT they have instituted a system that collects biometrics (ten digital fingerprints and a photograph) from international travelers at US visa–issuing posts and when they arrive at the POEs. US-VISIT has been using these biometric identifiers to screen persons against watch lists and to verify that a visitor is the person who was issued a visa or other travel document. DHS regularly runs the entire biometric database against law enforcement and counterterrorism systems to check for matches. When the traveler arrives with a visa issued at a US embassy or consulate abroad, the system compares the collected biometric data with that taken at the time of visa issuance. For returning travelers, the system compares the collected biometric data with that on file to make a match.[93]

More than a dozen interconnected DOS, DHS, and other databases play a role in screening foreigners at consular offices abroad and at POEs and in recording entry-exit data. As part of the visa application process, DOS consular officers use the Consular Consolidated Database to screen visa applicants. It is a database of over 100 million visa and passport case records and 75 million photographs from twenty-five different DOS systems. It links automatically to the Consular Lookout and Support System database, which consular officers use to identify visa applicants on security watch lists or with other derogatory information. It also links to the Arrival and Departure Information System (ADIS) and the Automated Biometric Identification System (IDENT), which CBP officers use to screen arriving travelers at POEs.[94]

As the BPC report shows, central to entry-exit is ADIS, the main database DHS uses to identify overstays. ADIS contains records on more than 280 million unique foreign travelers, which include biographic arrival and departure information and fingerprint identification numbers (FINs). Based on FINs, ADIS interfaces with IDENT, which contains fingerprint and photograph data. In turn, ADIS and IDENT interface with several other databases that provide travel and criminal history data to CBP officers at POEs, to consular officers abroad, and to law

[91] Ibid., 5. [92] DHS, "OBIM," www.dhs.gov/obim. [93] BPC, "Entry-Exit," 22.
[94] Lisa Seghetti, "Border Security: Immigration Inspections at Ports of Entry," CRS, January 26, 2015, 7.

enforcement agencies. Efforts to make databases interoperable have been critical to DHS efforts to enhance entry and exit screening. Recent improvements in ADIS–IDENT interoperability also allow more complete matching of individual entry records with changes of status.[95]

DHS operates a biographic entry-exit system, which covers nearly all non-US citizens, at air and sea POEs. It does so using the I-94 admission record (i.e., DHS alien arrival/departure record). Traditionally, DHS issued a paper I-94 to all foreigners entering the country. In 2013, DHS discontinued the use of paper I-94s at airports and seaports, switching to electronic records.[96] CBP still issues paper I-94s at land POEs, but for air and sea arrivals, CBP creates and maintains the I-94 admission record electronically. For air and sea POEs, paper I-94s are now provided only in limited circumstances (e.g., for refugees). For most travelers, a CBP officer provides the traveler with a CBP admission stamp on their travel document and the traveler must exit the United States on or before the departure date approved by the officer. At land POEs, a CBP officer generally attaches a portion of the paper I-94 to the nonimmigrant visitor's passport upon entry to the United States. The visitor must exit the United States on or before the departure date stamped on the I-94.[97]

CBP gathers air and sea travelers' arrival/departure information automatically from their electronic travel records.[98] Before the aircraft or vessel departs for the United States, CBP uses the Advance Passenger Information System (APIS) to collect from the carrier biographic manifest data on both passengers and crews. CBP collects the same data for departing international flights and vessels and matches it to entry records. Manifest data collection became mandatory in 2008 and compliance is near 100 percent. All travelers, including US citizens, are included in the APIS data, but filters eliminate data that pertains to US citizens. In addition, based on information travelers provide when purchasing a ticket, air carriers submit Passenger Name Record data to DHS up to seventy-two hours before departure. Although DHS does not import this data into ADIS, it uses it to confirm possible matches in APIS data.[99]

The situation is more puzzling at land POEs. At the northern land POEs, the United States deployed a biographic exit capability in

[95] BPC, "Entry-Exit," 7. [96] Ibid., 14.

[97] CBP, "I-94 Automation," www.cbp.gov/sites/default/files/documents/i94_factsheet_2.pdf.

[98] CBP, "Arrival/Departure Forms," www.cbp.gov/travel/international-visitors/i-94-instructions.

[99] BPC, "Entry-Exit," 21–22.

July 2013. Shockingly, US authorities do not collect biographic exit data at the southern land POEs. Any exit data collection there is limited to individuals who return the exit portion of form I-94 at their own initiative. Compliance is low.[100]

As far as biometric entry-exit system is concerned, US-VISIT (the system whose aim has been to collect, maintain, and share information, including biometric identifiers, on selected foreign nationals who enter and exit the United States) became operational in 2004, though only for the entry part, and only for some travelers. In January 2004, DHS deployed US-VISIT fingerprint scanners at select POEs to facilitate biometric data collection. Since December 2006, workstations have been operational at almost all of the 329 POEs in the United States.[101]

Upon arrival at a US air or sea POE, nearly all non-US citizens are required to undergo biometric screening during primary inspection. During primary inspection upon first entry, DHS screens each individual's fingerprints and photograph and stores them in DHS data systems. Exceptions exist for LPRs on cruises that begin and end in the United States, Canadians arriving for business or pleasure, individuals younger than fourteen or older than seventy-nine, and some other travelers.[102]

Importantly, while CBP collects biometric data from nearly all non-US citizens at air and sea POEs, at land POEs it collects biometrics only from foreign nationals who are not from Canada or Mexico. Overall, only 14 percent of incoming travelers are currently subject to biometric collection, with almost all of the remaining 86 percent being Americans, Canadians, or Mexicans. For these 86 percent of travelers, CBP officers compare the travel document photo with the person presenting the document, but no automated biometric check occurs.[103]

Hence, while a relatively small number of categories of travelers are exempt from the biometric requirement, these exemptions cover most foreign visitors to the United States. There are roughly 362 million travelers (citizens and noncitizens) entering the United States every year (most at land POEs). This includes some 165 million nonimmigrant admissions. Of those, 54 million are I-94 admissions, generally required to provide biometric data, and 106 million are tourists and business travelers from Canada and Mexicans with BCCs, generally exempt from the biometric requirement.[104] Therefore, only 54 million out of 362 million

[100] Ibid., 11, 13–14. [101] Seghetti, "Border Security," 1, 24.
[102] BPC, "Entry-Exit," 22. [103] Ibid., 20. [104] Seghetti, "Border Security," 1, 24.

(or 14 percent) of incoming travelers entering the United States every year are subject to the biometric requirement.

There is no biometric collection at any point of departure from the United States.

Secure Flight

Secure Flight is a TSA-run program, which assumed from air carriers the function of matching passengers against watch lists maintained by the federal government. It fulfilled a 9/11 Commission recommendation, codified into law by IRTPA. TSA phased in the program in 2009, and from November 2010 all passengers need to provide Secure Flight passenger data (SFPD) when booking tickets so the TSA can conduct watch-list matching and approve airlines to issue a boarding pass. TSA collects the following SFPD for flights into, out of, within, and over the United States: full name (first/middle/last), date of birth, gender, and, if applicable, the Known Traveler Number (which allows travelers to be eligible for expedited screening through Pre-Check) or the redress number.[105]

A 2014 GAO report shows that the TSA, through the Secure Flight system, utilizes watch lists derived primarily from the Terrorist Screening Database (TSDB) to identify potentially high-risk passengers. The TSDB is the US government's consolidated watch list of known or suspected terrorists, and it is maintained by the Terrorist Screening Center, a multi-agency organization administered by the FBI. The TSDB is used to develop specialized watch lists, such as the No Fly List (which contains information on individuals who are prohibited from boarding an aircraft) and the Selectee List (which contains information on individuals who must undergo additional security screening before being permitted to board an aircraft). In April 2011, TSA began conducting watch-list matching against an Expanded Selectee List that includes all records in the TSDB with a full name and date of birth that meet the Terrorist Screening Center's reasonable suspicion standard to be considered a known or suspected terrorist, but that are not already included on the No Fly or Selectee List.[106]

[105] TSA, "Secure Flight Program," www.tsa.gov/news/testimony/2014/09/18/tsa-secure-flight-program.

[106] GAO, "Secure Flight: TSA Should Take Additional Steps to Determine Program Effectiveness," September 9, 2014, 1, 2, 8, 14.

Since the program began in January 2009, Secure Flight has expanded from a system that matches airline passengers against watch lists of known or suspected terrorists to a system that uses additional high-risk lists and conducts risk-based screening assessments of passengers. Using new high-risk screening lists, the program now identifies a broader range of high-risk travelers – including ones who may not be on lists of known and suspected terrorists but who nevertheless correspond with known threat criteria. The TSA has also begun using Secure Flight to identify low-risk passengers eligible for expedited screening through Pre-Check.[107]

Airlines must transmit available SFPD to Secure Flight approximately seventy-two hours prior to scheduled flight departure. For reservations created within seventy-two hours of departure, airlines must submit passenger data as soon as it becomes available.[108] Secure Flight then provides TSA officials in the airports with advance notice of upcoming selectees and those prohibited from flying.[109]

Airlines are not to issue boarding passes to passengers prohibited from boarding an aircraft. For everyone else, Secure Flight assigns a risk category and directs the airline to encode each passenger's boarding pass for a certain type of screening. At airport checkpoints, those passengers identified as high-risk receive enhanced screening, passengers identified as low-risk are eligible for expedited screening, and passengers identified as unknown risk generally receive standard screening.[110]

Fraudulent identification or boarding passes could enable individuals to evade Secure Flight vetting, creating a potential vulnerability at the screening checkpoint. Travel Document Checkers (employed by TSA or private contractors) are responsible for verifying the validity of identification documents and boarding passes presented by passengers.[111] In 2012, Kelly Hoggan, TSA Assistant Administrator for Security Capabilities, testified that the wide variety of identifications and boarding passes presented at checkpoints poses challenges to effective manual verification of passenger identity, ticketing, and vetting status. He said that there are approximately 600 different permeations of identification documents that travelers from the fifty states and the territories can present at checkpoints. If one takes into consideration passports, TWIC cards, and Common Access Cards (identification cards for active duty uniformed service personnel, Selected Reserve, DOD civilian employees, and eligible contractor personnel), there are upwards of 2,470 different variations of

[107] Ibid., 36. [108] Ibid., 8. [109] Ibid., 21. [110] Ibid., 11–12. [111] Ibid., 23, 41.

identification documents that travelers can present. Hoggan stated that it is very difficult for a Transportation Security Officer to have a high level of proficiency in verifying all of those documents and that technology allows TSA to have good authentication of the different travel documents that travelers present.[112]

Between May 2012 and July 2013, TSA denied 1,384 individuals access to the sterile area (the portion of an airport beyond the security-screening checkpoint that provides passengers access to boarding aircraft) because of identity checking procedures. These denials include travelers who did not appear to match the photo on their identification, who presented identification that appeared fraudulent or showed signs of tampering, or who were unwilling or unable to provide identifying information. However, TSA would not know how many travelers successfully flew with fraudulent documents unless those individuals came to TSA's attention for another reason.[113]

Voter ID Laws

In most countries around the world, identification documents are required for voting. In the United States, where elections are run at state and local levels, people in many states can vote without showing any identification documents. This makes the United States an outlier. Only relatively recently have some American states started to require voters to present identification documents to establish and confirm their eligibility to vote.

The Department of Justice is challenging the voter ID laws, rather than supporting them. This may seem baffling to outside observers, if they do not know about the American history of racial voting suppression. African-Americans were largely shut out of the electoral process until the Fifteenth Amendment in 1870 outlawed racial discrimination at the polls. But while the amendment effectively granted African-American men the right to vote, many southern states used literacy tests and poll taxes to keep African-Americans from registering or voting. Many of these laws persisted into the 1960s. The Voting Rights Act of 1965 (VRA) struck down literacy tests and poll taxes and required states with a history of

112 "Is TSA's Planned Purchase of CAT/BPSS a Wise Use of Taxpayer Dollars?" Hearing, Subcommittee on Transportation Security, Committee on Homeland Security, House of Representatives, 112th Congress, June 19, 2012.

113 GAO, "Secure Flight," 2, 23.

racial discrimination at the polls to obtain federal approval before changing their election laws. Knowing this history is crucial to understanding US policy and politics in this field. Today, supporters of voter ID laws argue that the laws are aimed at stopping voter fraud, while opponents argue that the laws are aimed at intimidating racial minorities, who vote mainly for the Democratic Party, and suppressing their votes.

In addition to different identification requirements for voters in the United States and for voters in other countries, the voter registration process itself is different. In many countries around the world, the government automatically registers all citizens to vote as soon as they turn eighteen. In the United States, the responsibility for voter registration lies with every citizen. The National Voter Registration Act (NVRA) of 1993, known as the Motor Voter Act, made it easier for Americans to register to vote and to maintain their registration, by allowing citizens to register at DMVs and government offices that provide public assistance. It also allowed citizens to register to vote by mail. The Act did, however, come under criticism from those who claimed that it was "fraud-friendly" and enabled noncitizens to register, too, as examiners at government offices "were under orders not to ask anyone for identification or proof of citizenship."[114] Defendants of NVRA, such as election expert Lorraine C. Minnite, claim that NVRA does not prohibit states from checking individuals' identification prior to registration, as some critics, such as John Fund or Hans von Spakovsky, have alleged. Minnite says that NVRA requires the states to clean their voter registration rolls by deleting voters who have moved out of the jurisdiction or died and requires voters to sign their names attesting to their eligibility to vote under penalty of perjury, and deportation for noncitizens.[115] The Act became effective in most states in January 1995. However, twenty years later, one in eight voter registration records in the United States contains a serious error, according to the Pew Charitable Trusts. In addition, more than 51 million citizens, or 25 percent of the eligible population, remain unregistered to vote.[116]

In 2015, Oregon became the first state in the country to introduce automatic voter registration. While NVRA already requires states to

[114] John Fund, *Stealing Elections. How Voter Fraud Threatens Our Democracy*, 2nd ed. (New York: Encounter Books, 2008), 6, 28–29.

[115] Lorraine C. Minnite, *The Myth of Voter Fraud* (Ithaca, NY: Cornell University Press, 2010), 139.

[116] The Electronic Registration Information Center, www.ericstates.org/.

allow people to register to vote while filling out paperwork for a driver's license, Oregon's law makes the process automatic.[117]

Following the Florida recount troubles in 2000, Congress passed the Help America Vote Act (HAVA) of 2002, which provided federal money and authorized federal standards to help states upgrade voting machines and improve vote-counting procedures. HAVA required each state to create a single statewide voter registration database (still in the making). HAVA also mandated that all states require first-time voters to show identification if they registered to vote by mail and had not provided verification of their identification at the time of registration. HAVA lists a "current and valid photo identification" or "a copy of a current utility bill, bank statement, government check, paycheck, or other government document that shows the name and address of the voter" as acceptable forms of ID.[118] Such first-time voters have to show identification in person when voting at the polling station or send in a photocopy when voting by mail.

Proponents of stricter registration process and voter ID requirements argue that the HAVA requirement is weak since it requires identification only from first-time voters who registered to vote by mail and did not provide identification when they registered to vote. Another weakness stems from HAVA listing "a copy of a current utility bill" as an acceptable form of ID for such voters, when – as proponents of stricter requirements claim – "anyone with a computer and a color printer" can produce a utility bill.[119]

Soon after HAVA, some states began to pass laws requiring identification from all voters. Some states require photo IDs, while others accept a Social Security card, birth certificate, or utility bill. There are two types of voter ID laws, "strict" and "nonstrict," partially based on the alternatives the states provide if a voter fails to show the ID required by the law.

The first voter ID law dates back to 1950 (South Carolina; no photo was required, just a document bearing the voter's name). By 2000, still only fourteen states asked voters to present an identification document.[120] However, the number of states with voter ID laws increased greatly after HAVA and after the 2005 report of the so-called Carter–Baker Commission.

[117] Jeff Guo, "It's Official: New Oregon Law Will Automatically Register People to Vote," *Washington Post*, March 17, 2015.

[118] Wendy Underhill, "Voter ID Laws," September 26, 2016, www.ncsl.org/research/elections-and-campaigns/voter-id.aspx.

[119] Fund, *Stealing Elections*, 66.

[120] NCSL, "Voter ID History," October 16, 2014, www.ncsl.org/research/elections-and-campaigns/voter-id-history.aspx.

In September 2005, the Commission on Federal Election Reform chaired by former President Jimmy Carter and former Secretary of State James A. Baker III recommended REAL ID–compliant driver's licenses as election credentials. Eighteen out of twenty-one commissioners approved; three dissented.[121] Soon after the commission made a bipartisan recommendation for voter identification at the polls, voter ID laws became more common.

In 2005, Georgia and Indiana passed new, "strict" voter ID laws. Instead of requesting identification documents, these states required government-approved photo identification documents to cast ballots. If a voter did not have the required ID at the polling place, such person voted on a provisional ballot that officials would count only after the voter returned to the elections office with proper identification within the next few days.

Opponents of voter ID laws challenged many of the laws in courts. In 2008, the Supreme Court upheld Indiana's law in *Crawford v. Marion County*, after finding the state's interest to detect voter fraud to outweigh any burden on voters. Georgia and Indiana implemented their voter ID laws in 2008. After Republicans won control of more states during the 2010 elections, numerous legislatures passed voter ID laws. States without ID requirements continued to adopt them, and states that had less-strict requirements adopted stricter ones.[122] Momentum accelerated even more after the June 2013 Supreme Court ruling *Shelby County v. Holder*, which effectively nullified the preclearance requirement (Section 5) of the VRA, freeing states, mostly in the South, to change their election laws without advance federal approval.

By 2016, more than thirty states passed laws requiring voters to show some form of identification at the polls, with sixteen of them requiring a photo ID, though some of the laws were struck down after passage or are subject to ongoing litigation. The remaining states and the District of Columbia use other methods to verify the identity of voters (e.g., through signature match).[123] States such as California, Massachusetts, and Maine do not have documentary identification requirements. Colorado, Oregon, and Washington are vote-by-mail states and do not require voters to provide identification when casting a ballot by mail.[124]

[121] Jimmy Carter and James A. Baker III, "A Clearer Picture on Voter ID," *NYT*, February 3, 2008.

[122] NCSL, "Voter ID History."

[123] Underhill, "Voter ID Laws."

[124] GAO, "Elections. Issues Related to State Voter Identification Laws," September 2014, 15–16.

In 2011, Texas passed one of the nation's strictest photo voter ID laws. In 2012, with the preclearance requirement in effect, the DOJ denied Texas permission to put the law into effect, fearing a retrogressive effect on voting by Latinos and African-Americans. However, when the Supreme Court effectively nullified the preclearance requirement in 2013, Texas officials immediately announced they would put the law into effect. The DOJ responded with a suit seeking to block the law under the VRA's general prohibition against racial discrimination (Section 2).[125] Many additional trials followed. In July 2016, the Fifth Circuit Court of Appeals ruled that the Texas law discriminated against minorities who lacked the IDs and could not easily get them. The court declined to strike down the Texas law completely but said provisions must be made to allow those who lack the specific ID the law requires to be able to cast a vote. A lower court later ordered state officials to let people without IDs vote by signing a statement that they "cannot reasonably obtain" one – and told the state to spend $2.5 million to educate voters and local election officials on the relaxed requirement. But in voter-education material, Texas omitted the word "reasonably," suggesting that only people unable to get an ID by any means could take the oath.[126]

North Carolina passed its voter ID law in August 2013. The law created a photo identification requirement, scheduled to take effect in 2016, for casting a ballot in person. The law also reduced early voting days and ended same-day registration and out-of-precinct voting. Opponents immediately argued that the voter ID law would make it difficult for African-Americans to vote, since many of them do not have acceptable identification documents or access to birth certificates. Multiple suits challenging the law were filed at the federal and state levels. In June 2015, just weeks before the trials on the law, the North Carolina General Assembly passed H.B.836, which eased the original provision by introducing a modification for voters who lack current photo identification. Such voters will be able to cast a provisional ballot after providing either an acceptable identification document (including an expired driver's license) or their date of birth and the last four digits of their SSN. They will also need to sign an affidavit stating that there is a "reasonable impediment" to their ability to present a photo ID, such as a lack of transportation, disability or illness, work schedules or family

[125] Kenneth Jost, "Voting Controversies." *CQ Researcher*, February 21, 2014, 173.
[126] Michael Wines, "Court Filing Accuses Texas of Misleading Voters Without IDs," *NYT*, September 7, 2016.

responsibilities, lost or stolen photo ID, or a lack of a birth certificate or other documents needed to obtain a photo ID. Some critics of the voter ID law welcomed the change, saying that it allowed qualified voters who lack photo identification to affirm their identities and exercise their constitutional right to vote. However, some, such as Rep. Henry Michaux, D-Durham, noted that the modification merely "makes a bad bill a little less worse."[127] Meanwhile, supporters of the voter ID bill argued that the provisional ballot addition effectively demolishes the voter ID law. Susan Myrick, elections policy analyst for the conservative Civitas Institute, said that, with this change, "There's no voter ID in North Carolina. It's over."[128] She claimed that the new requirement is "a joke" that goes like this: "You must show ID unless you say that you don't have one, then you don't have to show an ID."[129] Despite opposition from fellow conservatives, Governor Pat McCrory (R) signed the new bill into law on June 22, 2015.

The multiple trials that followed considered whether the North Carolina voter ID law unconstitutionally burdens voters of color. In April 2016, a federal judge upheld the law. However, in July 2016 a three-judge panel of the Fourth Circuit Court of Appeals reversed that decision. Rather than allow the law to function with the reasonable impediment exemption, the court rejected the entire law not only for having discriminatory effects but also for having been passed with a racially discriminatory motive. The court found that lawmakers had requested data on African-Americans before crafting rules to limit their franchise. This data showed that African-Americans disproportionately lacked photo IDs issued by the DMVs. The court wrote that, with race data in hand, the legislature amended the original bill to exclude many of the photo IDs used by African-Americans and retain the kinds of IDs that white North Carolinians were more likely to possess. The judges wrote that the voting provisions in North Carolina targeted African-Americans "with almost surgical precision."[130] In August 2016, the Supreme Court denied an emergency appeal to reinstate the North Carolina voter ID law before the November election.

[127] Sarah Moncelle, "Changes Made to North Carolina Voter ID Requirements," June 18, 2015, www.southerncoalition.org/changes-made-to-north-carolina-voter-id-requirements/.

[128] Richard L. Hasen, "Civitas Very Unhappy with Voter ID Changes in NC," June 20, 2015, https://electionlawblog.org/?p=73641.

[129] Susan Myrick, "Bad Bill of the Week: Ending Voter ID Before It Began?," June 22, 2015, www.nccivitas.org/2015/bad-bill-of-the-week-ending-voter-id-before-it-began/.

[130] Christopher Ingraham, "The 'Smoking Gun' Proving North Carolina Republicans Tried to Disenfranchise Black Voters," *Washington Post*, July 29, 2016.

Supporters of voter ID laws argue that the laws safeguard the integrity of elections, prevent voter fraud (specifically, in-person voter impersonation, but also voting by noncitizens, voting under false registration, or voting in more than one state), and improve public confidence in the electoral process in an era when photo identification is routine for many other activities.

Opponents of voter ID laws argue that voter fraud is rare. In truth, it is incredibly difficult to know the extent of voter fraud, not least because both successful fraud and deterred fraud may go undetected.

A 2014 GAO report explains that no single source or database captures the universe of allegations or cases of in-person voter fraud across federal, state, and local levels, in part because responsibility for addressing election fraud is shared among federal, state, and local authorities. In addition, federal and state agencies vary in the extent they collect information on election fraud in general and in-person voter fraud in particular, making it difficult to estimate the incidence of in-person voter fraud.[131]

Studies conducted by individual states are helpful, but limited. According to a report by the North Carolina State Board of Elections, a search of registration rolls in the run-up to the November 2014 General Election revealed more than 1,000 people in North Carolina whose eligibility to vote was put in question. The vast majority of those individuals did not turn out to vote, but eleven noncitizens did attempt to vote. The election officials successfully challenged them. In total, 2.9 million people voted in that election. North Carolina had 6.6 million registered voters in October 2014.[132] In Ohio, an investigation by the Secretary of State Jon Husted found that 436 noncitizens were registered to vote in Ohio and that 44 of them had voted recently, including 27 in 2014. Ohio had 7.7 million registered voters at the time.[133]

Many election experts, such as Minnite and Richard Hasen, argue that "almost no one knowingly and willfully casts an illegal vote in the United

[131] GAO, "Elections," 71.

[132] Mark Binker, "NC Rejected 11 Voters in 2014 Due to Citizenship Questions," February 10, 2015, www.wral.com/nc-rejected-11-voters-in-2014-due-to-citizenship-questions/14438306/; Letter from Kim Westbrook Strach, North Carolina State Board of Elections to North Carolina Rep. Chris Millis, February 6, 2015, www.wral.com/asset/news/state/nccapitol/2015/02/10/14438308/Correspondence_2_6_2015.pdf; North Carolina State Board of Elections, "Board of Elections Finalizes Citizenship Audit," October 24, 2014, www.ncsbe.gov/ncsbe/press-releases?udt_2226_param_detail=15.

[133] Darrel Rowland, "Husted Finds 44 Non-U.S. Citizens Who Voted in Recent Elections," *Columbus Dispatch*, March 12, 2015.

States today"[134] and that "there are virtually no recent cases of voter impersonation fraud." There are, however, incidents of voter *registration* fraud, and supporters of voter ID laws like to point to those as a sign that fraudsters are stealing elections.[135]

Minnite argues that there is a difference between *voter fraud*, committed by voters, and *election fraud*, committed by officials. Minnite argues that the latter is more consequential.[136] In fact, many election experts are most concerned with election crimes committed not by voters but by election officials, poll workers, or party officials supervising the vote. In contrast, many supporters of voter ID laws do not focus on election worker crime or absentee ballot fraud. Hasen says that they are "obsessed with *impersonation* fraud, the idea that people will go to the polling place pretending to be someone else – either a voter listed on the rolls or someone who has registered with a false name – to throw the results of an election."[137]

As Minnite points out, journalist John Fund, supportive of voter ID laws, wrote, in the first edition of his book *Stealing Elections*, that at least eight of the 9/11 hijackers were *able* to register to vote in either Virginia or Florida and not that they *did* register to vote or *were* registered to vote. However, in a TV interview in October 2004, Fund said that the hijackers "*did* register to vote." Minnite investigated this claim and found that "it is highly unlikely that any of the hijackers was registered to vote."[138]

While supporters of voter ID laws argue that there is voter fraud, and opponents of voter ID laws argue that there is not, one longtime US elections expert, Curtis Gans, openly faulted advocates on both sides. "Those who say there's no fraud are just wrong," said Gans. "Those who say there's huge fraud in elections are also wrong."[139]

Public opinion shows broad support for voter ID laws as a way to safeguard the integrity of the ballot box. Opinion polls between 2006 and 2009 showed that often more than 80 percent of respondents supported voter ID laws; between 2012 and 2014, it was often between 70 and 75 percent.[140] An August 2016 Gallup poll found that 80 percent of

[134] Minnite, *The Myth of Voter Fraud*, 6.

[135] Richard L. Hasen, *The Voting Wars: From Florida 2000 to the Next Election Meltdown* (New Haven: Yale University Press, 2012), 61, 65.

[136] Minnite, *The Myth of Voter Fraud*, 19.

[137] Hasen, *The Voting Wars*, 60–61.

[138] Minnite, *The Myth of Voter Fraud*, 7–9.

[139] Jost, "Voting Controversies," 175.

[140] Paul Gronke, William D. Hicks, Seth C. McKee, Charles Stewart III, and James Dunham, "Voter ID Laws: A View from the Public," April 11, 2015, 28–30, http://ssrn.com/abstract=2594290.

respondents supported photo ID laws (63 percent of Democrats, 95 percent of Republicans, and 83 percent of Independents).[141]

Those who champion stricter voter ID laws are largely Republicans. As Minnite writes, including a more restrictive federal voter identification mandate in HAVA was not possible due to Democratic opposition in Congress. However, because HAVA required the states to amend their electoral codes, officials made changes at the state level. Most states that passed stricter voter ID laws since the passage of HAVA did so under unified Republican Party control over state governments. This included Indiana and Georgia. However, there were exceptions. In Washington, Democrats were in control of the governor's office and the state legislature. Alabama passed a moderate voter ID law in 2003 when Democrats controlled the state legislature and a Republican was governor.[142] Still, at the national level voter ID is almost entirely a partisan issue, and it is also a racialized issue on which civil rights groups are the chief opponents and Republican Party officials are the chief proponents.

Opponents of voter ID laws say that the laws will lead to widespread disenfranchisement of voters who do not have identification documents: not only the minorities, but also the elderly, the young, and the poor.[143] Some studies in the mid-2000s suggested that 12–13 percent of voting-age Americans, or 22 million people, did not have a driver's license or a state-issued photo ID.[144]

The precise numbers are difficult to obtain. One good data set comes from the Federal Highway Administration; however, it covers only data for driver's licenses and does not include data for state-issued photo IDs. According to the data for 2014, 84.4 percent of US residents of the driving age (sixteen years old or over) were licensed drivers. Utah had the lowest rate at 66.9 percent. New York (70.7 percent), the District of Columbia (75.8 percent), Texas (75.9 percent), West Virginia (77.4 percent), Minnesota (77.8 percent), Hawaii (79 percent), and Nevada (79.8 percent) were all under 80 percent.[145]

[141] Gallup, "Four in Five Americans Support Voter ID Laws, Early Voting" August 22, 2016, www.gallup.com/poll/194741/four-five-americans-support-voter-laws-early-voting.aspx.

[142] Minnite, *The Myth of Voter Fraud*, 153, 282–283.

[143] "Symposium on Voter-ID Issues in Politics and Political Science," *PS: Political Science and Politics* 42, 1 (January 2009): 81–130.

[144] Peter P. Swire and Cassandra Q. Butts, "The ID Divide," Center for American Progress, June 2008, 12, 38, www.americanprogress.org/issues/civil-liberties/report/2008/06/02/4520/the-id-divide/.

[145] DOT, "Highway Statistics 2014."

A 2014 GAO report identified ten studies of driver's license and state ID ownership, which showed that ownership rates among *registered voters* ranged from 84 to 95 percent. Three of the ten studies also estimated ownership of selected IDs among individuals *eligible to vote*, but not necessarily registered to vote. One of the three studies reported the same ownership rate for both groups (91 percent), while two of three studies reported slightly lower ID ownership rates among individuals eligible to vote as compared with registered voters (81 vs. 84 percent and 86 vs. 87 percent).[146]

The North Carolina State Board of Elections conducted one of the studies cited by the GAO report. It showed that an estimated 3 percent of the state's 6.3 million voters may lack government-issued photo identification prescribed by the voter ID law. According to GAO, North Carolina may be better off than many other states that have implemented voter ID requirements. With at least 95 percent of voters having appropriate ID, North Carolina voters are better equipped than the national average and other states that were part of the report.[147]

Opponents of voter ID laws say the laws are unduly burdensome. They argue that if IDs are expensive and are required to exercise the franchise, they threaten to operate as a form of poll tax.[148] They cite examples of elderly people who might have been born at home and delivered by midwives in early twentieth century and never obtained birth certificates. At the time, no one regularly generated birth certificates, particularly for African-Americans in the South. In addition, midwives often improperly spelled names of babies and parents on birth documents.[149] Opponents of voter ID laws claim that forcing such people to obtain a birth certificate now, in order to apply for a government-issued identification document in order to be able to vote, is burdensome and creates a poll tax. However, states have the option to exempt elderly voters from voter ID requirements. Also, most states with "strict" voter ID requirements made some exceptions for people who are indigent (Indiana, Tennessee), "have a

[146] GAO, "Elections," 21–25.

[147] Ibid., 21–22; Mark Binker, "State to Send Voter ID Reminder to 200,000 This Month," March 2, 2015, www.wral.com/state-to-send-voter-id-reminder-to-200-000-this-month/14484939/.

[148] A. Michael Froomkin, "Identity Cards and Identity Romanticism," in *Lessons from the Identity Trail: Anonymity, Privacy and Identity in a Networked Society*, ed. Ian Kerr et al. (New York: Oxford University Press, 2009), 260.

[149] "Why New Photo ID Laws Mean Some Won't Vote," NPR, January 28, 2012, www.npr.org/2012/01/28/146006217/why-new-photo-id-laws-mean-some-wont-vote.

reasonable impediment" to getting an ID (South Carolina), do not have an ID because of a recent natural disaster (Texas), or are victims of domestic abuse or stalking (Wisconsin). There are also exceptions for people who have religious objections to being photographed (Arkansas, Indiana, South Carolina, Texas, and Wisconsin). In addition, voter ID requirements generally apply to in-person voting, not to absentee ballots or mailed ballots.[150]

The GAO report provides information on the costs, as of 2014, of a driver's license and a nondriver ID in selected seventeen states that passed voter ID laws. The cost of a driver's license ranges from $0 in Oklahoma (for drivers over sixty-five) to $58.50 in Rhode Island. The cost of a nondriver ID ranges from $0 in South Carolina to $32 in Georgia. Moreover, sixteen of the seventeen states provide a free voter ID for those who do not have a driver's license or a nondriver ID. Florida does not, but it allows as acceptable identification photo ID that may be nongovernment issued.[151]

The report also provides information on the costs of a birth certificate, which is the most common type of document individuals present to obtain a driver's license, nondriver ID, or free voter ID. Some states provide a birth certificate at no cost for the purposes of obtaining required voter ID (Alabama, Kansas, North Carolina). In other states with voter ID laws, the cost of a birth certificate ranges from $7 (North Dakota) to $25 (Georgia).[152]

In North Carolina, where the voter ID law briefly went into effect during the spring 2016 primaries, the law from the beginning contained important exceptions to the photo ID requirement for in-person voters. Exceptions existed for people over seventy, victims of recent natural disasters, those with religious objections to being photographed, and those qualified to vote curbside. The DMV ID card for voting purposes was available without a fee. If someone needed a copy of a North Carolina birth certificate to obtain acceptable photo identification or to vote, they could obtain one free of charge. DMVs were even scheduling home visits for people with medical conditions who were unable to get to the DMV to obtain a No-Fee DMV ID card for voting purposes. These exceptions existed even before the June 2015 law modification that allowed voters who lack current photo identification to be able to cast a ballot after providing their birthdates, the last four digits of their SSN, and an affidavit stating that there is a "reasonable impediment" to their ability to present a photo ID.

150 Underhill, "Voter ID Laws." 151 GAO, "Elections," 126–127. 152 Ibid., 32–33.

Finally, there has been little evidence presented in courts during the various voter ID trials that showed that there are US citizens who tried to obtain a government-issued identification documents but could not. Challengers of voter ID laws have not been able to prove in courts that these laws will injure people. Hasen points out that in the Indiana case, challengers explained well how the law *might* injure voters: some could be so old that they could not track down a certified copy of a birth certificate, which they would need to get a government-issued voter ID card; others might be unable to pay for a copy of their birth certificate. However, challengers did not find voters who actually could testify about their difficulties in obtaining an identification card. Instead, the challengers brought a "facial" challenge to the law, saying that it was unconstitutional for everybody – and because of that, they did not need to produce any actual disenfranchised voters to win their case.[153]

While the challengers to the Indiana law said it could disenfranchise up to one million Indiana voters, in her 2006 decision in the case Federal District Judge Sarah Barker was dismissive of the challengers' skimpy evidence of the law's burden. It turned out that some of the plaintiffs in the case actually had identification cards that would allow them to vote; others could easily get them; and still others were exempt from the law because they were older than sixty-five and could vote using an absentee ballot without an excuse and without identification.[154]

Judge Barker rejected the constitutional challenge, saying:

> Despite apocalyptic assertions of wholesale voter disenfranchisement, Plaintiffs have produced not a single piece of evidence of any identifiable registered voter who would be prevented from voting pursuant to [the law] because of his or her inability to obtain the necessary photo identification. Similarly, Plaintiffs have failed to produce any evidence of any individual, registered or unregistered, who would have to obtain photo identification in order to vote, let alone anyone who would undergo any appreciable hardship to obtain photo identification in order to be qualified to vote.[155]

The Supreme Court, in the *Crawford* case, agreed with Judge Barker that there was not enough proof of injury to justify striking down the Indiana law. As Hasen explains, Justices Alito, Scalia, and Thomas said that it would not matter even if there were evidence of some people disenfranchised by the law, so long as *most people* would not face a serious burden. However, the controlling opinion, written by Justice

153 Hasen, *The Voting Wars*, 82–83. 154 Ibid., 83. 155 Ibid.

Stevens and joined by Chief Justice Roberts and Justice Kennedy, was narrower. Justice Stevens wrote that the "facial" challenge failed because the law was not very burdensome for most people and was justified to prevent fraud and preserve voter confidence. Still, as Hasen notes, Stevens left the door open for a follow-on lawsuit brought by Indiana voters who could show that the voter identification law imposed a big burden *as applied to them*.[156]

In Georgia, as in Indiana, the plaintiffs' lawyers were unable to produce a single voter disenfranchised by the voter ID law, though they claimed that there were hundreds of thousands of voters in that situation.[157] Harold Murphy was a federal judge presiding over the Georgia voter ID case. Though he is considered liberal, Judge Murphy dismissed the plaintiffs' claims. He approvingly cited the Indiana case and agreed that

> voters who lack Photo ID undoubtedly exist somewhere, but the fact that Plaintiffs, in spite of their efforts, have failed to uncover anyone "who can attest to the fact that he/she will be prevented from voting" provides significant support for a conclusion that the photo ID requirement does not unduly burden the right to vote.[158]

Judge Murphy also agreed with the court in the Indiana case that "elections laws will invariably impose some burden upon individual voters" and that "the imposition of tangential burdens does not transform a regulation into a poll tax." Moreover, "the cost of time and transportation cannot plausibly qualify as a prohibited poll tax because those same 'costs' also result from voter registration and in-person voting requirements, which one would not reasonably construe as a poll tax."[159]

Efforts to prevent disenfranchisement and discrimination are crucial, but they rarely seem to go hand-in-hand with American policymakers advocating, or at least considering, long-term solutions to ensure the legitimacy of the voting process. After all, as Fund says, "The integrity of the ballot box is just as important to the credibility of elections as access to it."[160] He proposes that state election officials

> should be authorized to establish a national central death registry that would collect information on all deaths from state vital records agencies and provide each state with the information needed to purge deceased voters. Even states that have good record-keeping systems do not receive data on registered voters

[156] Ibid., 85. [157] Fund, *Stealing Elections*, 71, 80. [158] Ibid., 76.
[159] Ibid., 77–78. [160] Ibid., 12.

who have died outside the state. A central death registry would allow election authorities to check multiple registrations.[161]

Some academics propose their own solutions. Historian Alexander Keyssar asks: "How might we usher in a new era in which voting will be more open, accessible and democratic?" He answers that "it could become the responsibility of government, not individuals, to make sure everyone has an appropriate ID (as is the case in many countries)."[162] Richard Hasen argues that problems with registration and voting could be solved by a federal overhaul of the election system, such as "a national voter identification program run by the federal government which paid for all the costs associated with establishing identity and citizenship." Hasen adds that he would couple national voter ID with a unique voter ID number and universal voter registration proactively implemented by the federal government. However, due to state resistance to federal intrusion in elections – especially among conservative lawmakers – Hasen added, "I don't expect we will see this program in my lifetime."[163]

Politicians and policymakers rarely argue for a truly comprehensive solution to solve problems with registration and voting. The most important exception comes from former President Carter and former Secretary of State Baker, who emphasize the benefits of standardized, government-issued identification documents as a way of increasing voter participation and eliminating electoral fraud.[164]

Also rare are voices such as those of late Curtis Gans, who worked with the Carter–Baker Commission. He wrote that a solution can come only from a national ID card system:

> To maximize potential turnout, to eliminate virtually all possibility of electoral fraud, to make it profoundly easier for citizens to cast their ballots and to restore citizen faith in the integrity of the election process, the United States needs to adopt a mandatory, government-provided, distributed and paid for biometric identification card and system. Under such a system, every citizen (including the 50 million who are now unregistered) would be automatically enfranchised. There would be no invalid names on registration lists. With the exception of vote buying and election official chicanery, electoral fraud would cease to exist.

161 Ibid., 206.

162 Alexander Keyssar, "Who Gets to Vote?," *NYT*, September 30, 2016.

163 Richard L. Hasen, "About That Monkey Cage Item on Non-Citizen Voting, Calm Down," October 26, 2014, http://electionlawblog.org/?p=67451.

164 Jimmy Carter and James A. Baker III, "Voting Reform Is in the Cards," *NYT*, September 23, 2005.

The system, Gans argued, would have upfront costs of $14 billion, but benefits that would extend beyond election administration and into national and homeland defense, immigration, identity theft prevention, and other areas.[165]

Andrew Young, a civil rights leader, proposed bridging the divide over ballot security by putting photographs on Social Security cards. Young, who has been working on the proposal for about a year with the American Enterprise Institute scholar Norman Ornstein, made the recommendation in April 2014. Former Presidents Bill Clinton and Jimmy Carter also endorsed the idea. Young said he is not against photo identification, "but only as long as the cards are free and easily accessible. Providing eligible voters the ability to obtain a photo on a Social Security card eliminates any genuine concern." Young added, "It's just an idea whose time may have come." He called on President Obama to issue an executive order making such photos available. President Clinton did not go so far as to urge executive action. However, Clinton said, putting photos on Social Security cards would represent "a way forward that eliminates error and makes the best possible decision that we can all live with," without having to "paralyze and divide a country with significant challenges." The White House did not endorse the idea after Young presented it to President Obama. Press secretary Jay Carney said: "We haven't had a chance to review it."[166]

Top-level politicians and policymakers are not particularly proactive when it comes to proposing or reviewing possible solutions. Also, few people point to a possibility of a much larger disenfranchisement occurring in the American society. If government-issued identification documents are increasingly required to be able to take a college entrance exam, get a job, open a bank account, enter a federal building, donate blood, and obtain a library card, and yet millions of people do not have such documents, then the country faces a problem. Linda Kearns, deputy counsel to the Philadelphia Republican City Committee, put it this way: if there are people who do not have IDs, then voter ID opponents should spend their "talent and resources bringing those people into the fold of the majority of citizens who enjoy the

[165] Curtis Gans, "A Proposed Solution to Voter ID Controversy," December 28, 2011, www.huffingtonpost.com/curtis-gans/voter-id-laws_b_1172468.html.

[166] Peter Baker, "Obama, Citing New Laws, Says the G.O.P. Is Moving to Restrict Voting Rights," *NYT*, April 11, 2014; Juliet Eilperin and Karen Tumulty, "Democrats Embrace Adding Photos to Social Security Cards," *Washington Post*, April 10, 2014.

convenience of using checking accounts, entering office buildings and obtaining marriage and fishing licenses."[167]

A national voter ID system would resolve the issues raised by voter ID laws, yet there are only a few voices in the national debate talking about a solution based on identity policing. This is yet another example of this book's main theme, that policymakers will do just about anything to resolve certain issues except consider a national ID card, despite evidence that such a solution is popular with the American public. This pattern is predictable given so many other episodes in which policymakers have failed to consider national ID cards and instead have proceeded with smaller policy changes to existing systems of identification.

State Legislation

Faced with significant numbers of illegal immigrants, many states across the country attempt to crack down on illegal immigration through state enforcement of federal law. States across the country have proposed thousands of bills addressing immigration since 2007, when a federal effort to reform immigration law collapsed. While in 2006 legislators in states across the country introduced 570 immigration bills (84 laws were enacted), in 2007 legislators introduced 1,562 immigration bills (240 laws were enacted). In the first quarter of 2010 alone legislators introduced 1,180 bills and resolutions (107 laws were enacted and 87 resolutions were adopted).[168]

Arizona's controversial S.B.1070 law ("Support Our Law Enforcement and Safe Neighborhoods Act"), passed in April 2010, was the most contentious in a long line of efforts to regulate immigration at the state level. The law requires local and state law enforcement to question people about their immigration status, if officers suspect the person is in the country illegally, and if they have stopped them for a legitimate reason. It also makes it a state crime to be in the United States illegally. The follow-on bill clarifies that racial profiling is illegal and adds restrictions against using race or ethnicity as the basis for questioning by police. It states that immigration-status questions would follow a law enforcement officer's stopping, detaining, or arresting a person while enforcing another law. The initial law had referred to a simple "contact" with

[167] Linda A. Kearns, "Pa. Should Tighten Up on Voter Security with Simple ID Requirement," LancasterOnline, April 26, 2015.

[168] NCSL, "Immigrant Policy Project," April 27, 2010, www.ncsl.org/portals/1/documents/immig/immigration_report_april2010.pdf.

police.[169] The law would make the failure to carry immigration documents a crime. Importantly, it is a federal requirement that those legally in the United States must carry a proof of their lawful status at all times.

S.B.1070 unleashed immediate protests and reignited the divisive battle over immigration reform nationally. Supporters of the law point out that Arizona is simply the first state to demand that immigrants meet federal requirements to carry identification documents legitimizing their presence in the United States. Opponents have called it an open invitation for discrimination against anyone "foreign-looking," especially Hispanics, regardless of their citizenship status.

In addition, in the United States, the regulation of immigration is exclusively a federal power, and the Supremacy Clause of the Constitution (Article VI, Paragraph 2) prevents Arizona, or any other state, from taking federal immigration enforcement into its own hands. The federal government can permit states and localities to act on its behalf in immigration matters, but it must expressly delegate that authority. To that end, in 1996 Congress passed legislation that allows the federal government to make agreements with states and localities – called 287(g)s for the applicable code section – to assist in immigration enforcement. DHS has signed more than seventy such agreements, including with the state of Arizona and some of its municipalities. As former INS commissioners Doris Meissner and James Ziglar point out, this program, while controversial, appears to be constitutionally sound because it supplements – not supplants – federal authority based on a specific delegation. However, Arizona's law "appears to go well beyond the intent of 287(g), asserting for itself even greater powers to fashion immigration policy. Its approach invites a patchwork of inconsistent state policies, with results as untenable as having states set their own defense or foreign policies."[170]

Opponents of S.B.1070 predicted that it would suffer the same fate as California's Proposition 187, passed in 1994 but never carried out because of legal setbacks and political opposition. Susan Bolton, a federal judge for the US District Court for the District of Arizona, suspended parts of S.B.1070 in July 2010. In April 2011, the Ninth Circuit Court of Appeals ruled against Arizona and let stand a lower court decision blocking the most contentious parts of the state's immigration law from going into effect.[171]

169 "Ariz. Gov Signs Bill Revising New Immigration Law," Associated Press, May 1, 2010.

170 Doris Meissner and James W. Ziglar, "Why the U.S. Had to Challenge Arizona on Immigration," *Washington Post*, July 22, 2010.

171 Marc Lacey, "Appeals Court Rules against Arizona Law," *NYT*, April 11, 2011.

In June 2012, the Supreme Court unanimously sustained the most hotly debated provision of S.B.1070, the one critics have called its "show me your papers" provision. The provision requires state law enforcement officials to determine the immigration status of anyone they stop or arrest if they have reason to suspect that the individual might be in the country illegally. The court emphasized that state law enforcement officials already possessed the discretion to ask about immigration status. The Arizona law merely makes that inquiry mandatory if the police have reason to suspect a person is an illegal immigrant. However, the Supreme Court blocked other provisions, arguing that they interfered with the federal government's role in setting immigration policy. For instance, it rejected measures that would have subjected illegal immigrants to criminal penalties for activities such as seeking work.[172]

In September 2012, Judge Bolton cleared the way for police to carry out the 2010 law's requirement that officers, while enforcing other laws, may question the immigration status of those they suspect are in the country illegally.[173] In September 2015, Judge Bolton upheld the so-called "show me your papers" provision.[174]

Local ID Schemes

While many states and municipalities across the country attempt to crack down on illegal immigration, other states and municipalities try to make the lives of illegal immigrants easier. Much of that help focuses on the issuance of driver's licenses and/or municipal ID cards to illegal immigrants. Following President Obama's 2012 Executive Action on the Deferred Action for Childhood Arrivals, which deferred the deportation of young people brought to the United States illegally as children, all states now allow young people who have been granted "deferred action" – the so-called Dreamers – to get driver's licenses.

In addition, as of 2016, twelve states and the District of Columbia allow illegal immigrants to obtain driver's licenses.[175] One of them is California,

[172] Adam Liptak, "Blocking Parts of Arizona Law, Justices Allow Its Centerpiece," *NYT*, June 25, 2012.

[173] "Federal Judge OKs Section of Arizona Immigration Law Allowing Police to Question Status of Suspected Illegals," Associated Press, September 5, 2012.

[174] "U.S. Judge Dismisses Challenge of Arizona's S.B.1070 Immigration Law," Associated Press, September 6, 2015.

[175] NCSL, "States Offering Driver's Licenses to Immigrants," www.ncsl.org/research/immigration/states-offering-driver-s-licenses-to-immigrants.aspx.

which started issuing driver's licenses for illegal immigrants in January 2015 and projected that 1.4 million illegal immigrants will apply for them by 2018. These licenses are not REAL ID–compliant and have to be visually distinct from regular California licenses, with the phrase "Federal Limits Apply" on the front and a more detailed explanation on the back.[176]

Some municipalities are offering local identification documents to illegal immigrants. New Haven began offering a municipal ID card to all residents, including illegal immigrants, in 2007. More than 5,600 people have obtained them in the first ten months, and the cards have generated both passionate support and passionate opposition. The *New York Times* claims that the positive benefits the card's supporters predicted have materialized, and more immigrants have emerged from the shadows and are participating in city life. It says that the ID card "has made opponents angrier – no matter that it has made the city a safer, better place for all."[177]

There are similar schemes in San Francisco and in other municipalities. In January 2015, New York City began issuing much-anticipated municipal ID cards, which are available to all city residents who are at least fourteen, but are especially intended to make life easier for illegal immigrants and the homeless. The cards confer discounts for prescription drugs, access to city buildings, and free memberships to museums. They are accepted as public library cards and recognized as identification to open accounts at several banks and credit unions.[178]

SUMMARY

This chapter outlined the political history of the 2005 REAL ID Act. It also outlined other post-9/11 identity policing schemes, emphasizing the notion of patchwork in identity policing in the United States. The next chapter focuses on the drivers of new identification schemes and the obstacles to these schemes.

[176] Patricia Leigh Brown, "Talk of 'El D.M.V.' as Licensing Expands to Cover Undocumented Immigrants in California," *NYT*, December 19, 2014.

[177] "Courage in Elm City," Editorial, *NYT*, May 22, 2008.

[178] Matt Flegenheimer, "New York City to Formally Start Its Municipal ID Card Program," *NYT*, January 11, 2015.

5

Identity Policing in the Post-9/11 United States

Drivers and Obstacles

INTRODUCTION

This chapter focuses on the drivers of new identification schemes, especially illegal immigration and terrorism, in the post-9/11 United States. It then focuses on obstacles to these schemes: financial, technological and practical, constitutional and legal, relating to civil liberties and individual freedoms, and stemming from public opinion and resistance.

Even though there was some renewed interest in national ID cards after 9/11, no true national debate took place on the overall desirability of such documents. There was a lot of talk about the appropriate balance between maintaining personal freedom and protecting national security, and there was a plethora of loud voices critical of national ID cards. What was lacking was a loud voice in support of an improved identification regime, and a clear explanation for the American people of how benefits of such a regime could outweigh the costs. Nevertheless, although critics remain vocal, some policymakers and many members of the public continue to believe that the country deserves better than the existing patchwork of identification policies.

CRISES AS DRIVERS

Unpacking motivations for policy decisions can be problematic. Nevertheless, it is clear that in the United States, terrorism and illegal immigration are the primary drivers of identity policing schemes. Advocates of a national identification system assert that it would serve as a tool to track the movement of known, suspected, or potential terrorists, helping to prevent a terrorist attack. Such a system would also facilitate a more accurate view of the number of immigrants and might help facilitate tracking of illegal immigrants. While some people are unwilling to admit that there is a nexus between homeland security (especially terrorism) and illegal immigration, others are more willing to link the two. A lobbyist at an influential conservative advocacy group told me that given the importance of and the potential linkage between terrorism and illegal immigration, the issue of identification documents is "a very important issue. It is a very, VERY important issue."[1]

Illegal Immigration

While Rep. Sensenbrenner says his main concern in creating REAL ID was preventing attacks on the United States, he admits he created REAL ID partly as an obstacle to illegal immigrants.[2] The Act prohibits states, when issuing driver's licenses, from accepting for purposes of identification foreign documents other than valid passports, if officials are to accept such state driver's licenses for federal purposes. While REAL ID-compliant licenses cannot be issued to illegal immigrants, states can still issue them licenses that are not REAL ID-compliant.

That federal law in the United States allows such flexibility is a testament to the respect it has for states' rights, but also to the conflicting nature of the political, social, and economic priorities this country faces. The issuance of driver's licenses to illegal immigrants presents an important dilemma for the United States. On the one hand, if illegal immigration is to be discouraged, then illegal immigrants should not be receiving the same rights and privileges as those who are lawfully present. On the other hand, social, cultural, and economic contributions of illegal immigrants will cease if they cannot drive and use their documents to participate in other areas of life. When security is added to the equation, then, on the one hand, it is inconceivable to be issuing legitimate documents to illegal immigrants when that means that terrorists and other criminals could also get them. But, on the other hand, safety and security may actually be enhanced when all those on the road have proper driver's licenses and auto insurance, and when they do not "live in the shadows." Herein, in fact, lays one of the paradoxes of American politics: many US citizens and

[1] Interview with a lobbyist at an influential conservative advocacy group, Washington, DC, June 2013.

[2] Katel, "Real ID," 393.

policymakers recognize that illegal immigrants broke US laws to be here, and many continue to break additional laws while here, but many are also valuable members of their communities and are vital to the economy. Therefore, policymakers alternate in creating proposals to deal with this situation, and the result is a patchwork of regulations with often conflicting provisions.

However, we cannot ignore the problem of crimes committed by those using fraudulent identification. A REAL ID policy expert told me:

> Ninety-nine percent of those illegal immigrants will not use that driver's license to commit a terrorist attack ... One of the challenges we see is communicating that people don't fraudulently obtain driver's licenses for fun. They are using the commission in a multitude of crimes. Terrorism is just one. We see it in mortgage fraud, identity theft, purchasing firearms. Very wide ranging catalogue.[3]

DHS says REAL ID "prevents illegal immigrants from using your identity to violate immigration laws." In 2010, DHS listed this as one of the top five reasons to adopt REAL ID.[4]

Many of the estimated 12 million illegal immigrants in the United States have bought fake IDs with stolen names and SSNs. In addition to making driver's licenses more difficult to obtain for illegal immigrants, authorities have advanced identity policing in the realm of employment verification. There have also been attempts to make Social Security cards and SSNs more secure, but those saw little progress.

While these efforts go back to the 1970s and 1980s, they have been particularly pronounced since 9/11 when the issue of illegal immigration became increasingly linked with the issue of terrorism. In fact, in the United States the contrast between those who link illegal immigration and terrorism and those who argue that illegal immigrants do not pose a terrorist threat is perhaps one of the more defining features of the post-9/11 America. While these conflicting positions are being debated – or, as the case often is, as they are *not* being debated – another patchwork of programs and identity policing schemes is being proposed or expanded.

In the realm of employment verification, the E-Verify system is of particular interest. Its origins lie in legislation from the 1980s and 1990s, but the program started functioning in 2001. E-Verify is an Internet-based system that allows an employer, using information reported on an employee's Form I-9, Employment Eligibility Verification,

[3] Interview with a REAL ID policy expert, Washington, DC, March 2014.
[4] Kephart, "REAL ID Implementation," 9.

to determine the eligibility of that employee to work in the United States. For most employers, the use of E-Verify is voluntary and limited to determining the employment eligibility of new hires only. There is no charge to employers to use E-Verify, operated by DHS in partnership with the SSA. Companies access E-Verify to compare an employee's Form I-9 information with more than 455 million records in the SSA database and more than 80 million records in DHS immigration databases. Twenty-eight million queries were run through the system in 2014. E-Verify is mandatory only for those employers with federal contracts with the E-Verify clause.[5] In addition, state laws mandate using E-Verify for all new hires in Alabama, Arizona, Mississippi, and South Carolina, though in some states there are exemptions for small firms. Georgia, Utah, and North Carolina require E-Verify checks for all new hires in firms with at least ten, fifteen, or twenty-five employees, respectively.[6] Despite steps taken by USCIS to strengthen E-Verify's accuracy, the current voluntary system remains vulnerable to identity fraud and employer misuse and is not able to detect off-the-books employment. These problems likely would be exacerbated if all employers were mandated to use E-Verify.[7]

Unfortunately, the problem of identity theft is a huge one; illegal immigrants perpetrate much of it (though certainly not all of it); and E-Verify is not able to fully address it. A 2015 SSA report found that 6.5 million SSNs that were issued to Americans born 112 years ago or earlier do not have a death date listed in the SSA's computer database. Alex Nowrasteh and Jim Harper, authors of a 2015 report critical of E-Verify, note that employers can enter such SSNs into E-Verify and the system would not recognize that they belong to deceased persons. Individuals using 66,920 of those 6.5 million SSNs had approximately $3.1 billion in wages, tips, and self-employment income for the 2006–2011 tax years. Between 2008 and 2011, SSA received 4,024 E-Verify inquiries using the SSNs of 3,873 number holders born before

5 USCIS, "What Is E-Verify?," June 25, 2015, www.uscis.gov/e-verify/what-e-verify; USCIS, "E-Verify Overview Presentation," January 9, 2015, www.uscis.gov/sites/default/files/USCIS/Verification/E-Verify/E-Verify_Native_Documents/e-verify-presentation.pdf.

6 Alex Nowrasteh and Jim Harper, "Checking E-Verify: The Costs and Consequences of a National Worker Screening Mandate," Cato Institute, July 7, 2015, 3, http://object.cato.org/sites/cato.org/files/pubs/pdf/pa775_1.pdf.

7 Marc R. Rosenblum, "E-Verify: Strengths, Weaknesses and Proposals for Reform," MPI, February 2011, 1, www.migrationpolicy.org/research/e-verify-strengths-weaknesses-and-proposals-reform.

June 1901.[8] However, it is not just deceased people whose SSNs are used fraudulently. Children are fifty-one times more likely to be victims of identity theft than adults.[9]

Though it is very difficult to estimate, possibly as many as 75 percent of illegal immigrants use unlawfully obtained SSNs.[10] The SSA estimates that illegal immigrants make up a majority of SSA's "earnings suspense file," which is a record that the SSA keeps when it cannot match the name and SSN on the submitted W-2 forms (Wage and Tax Statement) to information in SSA's records (the Numident). SSA's chief actuary, Stephen Goss, estimated in 2005 that 75 percent of illegal immigrants pay payroll taxes through withholding, which requires a SSN.[11] Since illegal aliens are not eligible for SSNs, the implication is that most illegal aliens are doing this using unlawfully obtained SSNs (SSNs that do not belong to them). Some of those unlawfully obtained SSNs are stolen.[12]

Identity theft is not a victimless crime. Potentially millions of Americans, including an untold number of children, are victims of identity theft when illegal immigrants use their SSNs. Identity theft costs victims hundreds of hours and thousands of dollars to undo the damage and recover their names and lives. However, while politicians and the media pay some attention to the plight of illegal immigrants, they do not pay much attention to the plight of victims of identity theft.[13] In fact, many people increasingly refer to illegal immigrants as "undocumented" rather than illegal, ignoring the fact that many illegal immigrants have fraudulent documents such as counterfeit Social Security cards, forged driver's licenses, fake Green Cards, and phony birth certificates. In fact, those illegal immigrants are committing multiple federal and state felonies including forgery, Social Security fraud, perjury on I-9 forms, and identity theft. Moreover, some illegal aliens also sell such identification to other illegal aliens.

As Chapter 3 showed, there have been proposals, starting in the 1970s, to make Social Security cards harder to counterfeit, not only to resist use

[8] Nowrasteh and Harper, "Checking E-Verify," 6–7.

[9] Richard Power, "Child Identity Theft," April 2011, www.cylab.cmu.edu/files/pdfs/reports/2011/child-identity-theft.pdf.

[10] Ronald W. Mortensen, "Illegal, but Not Undocumented: Identity Theft, Document Fraud, and Illegal Employment. Backgrounder," Center for Immigration Studies, June 2009, www.cis.org/sites/cis.org/files/articles/2009/back809.pdf.

[11] Eduardo Porter, "Illegal Immigrants Are Bolstering Social Security with Billions," *NYT*, April 5, 2005; SSA, Office of the Inspector General, "Informational Report: Status of the Social Security Administration's Earnings Suspense File," September 2015, https://oig.ssa.gov/sites/default/files/audit/full/pdf/A-03-15-50058.pdf.

[12] Mortensen, "Illegal, but Not Undocumented." [13] Ibid.

by fraudsters and illegal immigrants but also to prevent discrimination against "foreign-looking" job seekers who are in the United States legally. In March 2010, Senators Chuck Schumer (D-NY) and Lindsey Graham (R-SC) outlined a plan that would require all workers, including legal immigrants and American citizens, to present a tamper-proof Social Security card when they apply for jobs. Biometric identity information would be stored on the card and not in a government database.[14] Dubbed "Biometric Enrollment, Locally Stored Information, and Electronic Verification of Employment (BELIEVE)," the card would be required to verify permanent residence when starting a new job. It would replace E-Verify. Funding for the BELIEVE system would be obtained by collecting various fees and fines; however, US citizens would not be charged for the card.[15]

While nothing came out of the proposal in 2010, some talk of it reemerged in 2013, during a bipartisan effort of eight senators to reform immigration laws. Schumer and Graham were part of the group, and three other senators in the group, John McCain (R-AZ), Jeff Flake (R-AZ), and Dick Durbin (D-IL), expressed at least some support for requiring such cards either at the time or before.[16] The final Senate bill (S.744) proposed by the "Gang of Eight" gained most attention for its provision that would make it possible for many illegal immigrants to gain legal status and eventually citizenship. The bill did not mention biometric Social Security cards, but it mandated the Social Security Commissioner to begin work to administer and issue "fraud-resistant, tamper-resistant, wear-resistant, and identity-theft resistant" Social Security cards. Five years post-enactment, the SSA would issue only such cards. There would also be increased penalties (up to five years in prison) for knowingly using a false SSN or another person's SSN. The individual House bills marked up in House Judiciary and Homeland Security Committees contained no mention of an improved Social Security card. Both the Senate and the House bills contained disclaimers, by now somewhat standard, that nothing in the law can be construed to authorize the issuance of a national ID card.[17] S.744 passed the Senate in June 2013, but the House never acted on it.

[14] Julia Preston, "2 Senators Offer Immigration Overhaul," *NYT*, March 18, 2010.

[15] Zack Martin, "Democrats: BELIEVE in Biometric Social Security Cards," May 3, 2010, www.secureidnews.com/news-item/*democrats-believe-in-biometrics-social-security-cards/.

[16] Danny Yadron, "Senators in Immigration Talks Mull Federal IDs for All Workers," *Wall Street Journal*, February 20, 2013.

[17] "Side-by-Side Comparison of 2013 Senate Immigration Bill with Individual 2013 House Bills," MPI, August 2013, www.migrationpolicy.org/research/side-side-comparison-2013-senate-immigration-bill-individual-2013-house-bills.

Terrorism

"Every lawmaker would love to find the silver bullet" that defeats terrorism, according to NGA federal relations director David Quam. "It doesn't exist."[18] Opponents of the national ID card argue that it would not help catch would-be terrorists. A card that confirms identity and history may not be effective in anticipating intent to commit a terrorist act. Many of the 9/11 terrorists were not on government watch lists or wanted for the kinds of violations that a national ID system might catch, and thus would not have been stopped.[19] After all, the positive identification of individuals does not equate to trustworthiness or lack of criminal intent.

National ID card advocates argue that it could help deter terrorists while catching plotters before they do harm. Since some of the 9/11 terrorists were violating immigration laws, they might have been caught when they tried to board a flight. A national ID card also might have made it more difficult for the terrorists to use false identities to obtain SSNs and driver's licenses.[20]

There is also the issue of effectiveness. Opponents argue that hardening identification credentials matters less than developing informants, conducting surveillance, and infiltrating terrorist organizations. "The notion that IDs will somehow magically fix the problem is very dangerous," according to security expert Bruce Schneier. "The real tools are intelligence, investigation, and emergency response."[21]

While a national ID card system has the potential to catch would-be terrorists, it certainly would not catch them all. It is unclear how many of the 9/11 terrorists would have been apprehended before carrying out their plans, but some might have been. Therefore, while a national ID card system is certainly no complete panacea to the problem, it could be part of the solution. Well-functioning identity policing schemes can become a part of a "layered security" approach, a practice that combines different security layers to find networked solutions to security problems.

While a national ID system is not in the cards for the United States, policymakers who are proponents of REAL ID and other policing initiatives tout these programs as helping to make terrorist actions less likely. In March 2007, Secretary Chertoff said:

> The REAL ID Act aims to make it harder for dangerous people to obtain licenses fraudulently and to make it easier for law enforcement and counterterrorism

[18] Katel, "Real ID," 388. [19] Wang, "The Debate," 2. [20] Ibid.
[21] Katel, "Real ID," 393.

authorities to detect documents that have already been falsified. In doing so, the REAL ID Act gives law enforcement and counterterrorism officials a critical new tool to prevent terrorism and to protect our homeland.[22]

In February 2011, House Judiciary Chairman Lamar Smith, Homeland Security Chairman Peter King, and Crime, Terrorism, and Homeland Security Subcommittee Chairman James Sensenbrenner, all Republicans, sent a letter to Secretary Napolitano in which they argued that any further extension of the deadline for REAL ID Act compliance threatened the security of the United States. Smith, King, and Sensenbrenner claimed that the recent arrest of Khalid Ali-M Aldawsari in Texas on a charge of attempted use of a weapon of mass destruction underscored the importance of the immediate implementation of REAL ID. When the FBI searched Aldawsari's residence, they found his journal in which he wrote of the need to obtain a forged US birth certificate, multiple driver's licenses, and a US passport. He planned to use those driver's licenses to rent several cars, each with a different license, specifically to avoid detection. Smith, King, and Sensenbrenner wrote, "Nearly a decade after the terrorist attacks of September 11, 2001, the loopholes exploited by the 9/11 hijackers still exist. And those, like Aldawsari, who want to do us harm, understand that. History is only repeating itself because we are letting it."[23] Others, however, argue that Aldawsari was nowhere near slipping through the net, and having a false driver's license would have made no difference after a chemical supply company reported to the FBI his suspicious attempt to purchase the chemicals.[24]

In addition to policymakers who are proponents of REAL ID and other policing initiatives, there is also support for these initiatives from the companies that stand to benefit from increased use of high-tech identification methods. One of the most prominent supporters has been Larry Ellison, CEO of Oracle Corporation, the leading maker of database software. Right after 9/11, Ellison offered to the administration free software to run a national ID card system as a means of bolstering national security.[25] Importantly, he has offered to donate the software for the creation of the system, but not the maintenance or upgrades. His idea was for a national ID card that would be mandatory for foreigners

[22] DHS, Remarks by Secretary Chertoff, March 1, 2007.

[23] "Smith, King and Sensenbrenner: Further REAL ID Extension Threatens National Security," February 28, 2011, https://judiciary.house.gov/_files/news/2011/feb/110228REALID.html.

[24] Jim Harper, "Terror Arrest Does Not Justify REAL ID Revival," March 2, 2011, www.cato-at-liberty.org/terror-arrest-does-not-justify-real-id-revival/.

[25] Lyon, *Identifying Citizens*, 72.

and voluntary for citizens.[26] It is telling that despite his offer of free software and his meetings with several Washington officials to discuss the idea, both at a time when America was only starting to come to terms with the 9/11 tragedy, the administration officials did not take him up on it. The opposition to national ID cards does indeed run deep in the psyche of American policymakers, if arguments against national ID cards outweigh arguments in favor even in the face of a national emergency.

A senior DHS official told me:

> Right after 9/11, if, at the highest level, there would have been a very well-articulated campaign that showed that 18 of the 19 hijackers used these forms of ID ... and that's what facilitated their movement throughout the country and was a huge contributor to what they were planning, if that link was made clear and crystallized, there might have been more of a chance [to implement a national ID card]. But whether the country was willing to accept something called a national ID, that is hard to say.[27]

OBSTACLES

Opponents of national ID cards in the United States base their opposition partially on pragmatic and partially on principled arguments. Just as in the United Kingdom, there is opposition to the high financial costs of identity policing schemes. There are pragmatic and technical arguments that ID cards will not work, concerns about the danger of data loss and abuse of centralized and comprehensive databases storing sensitive data, and fears of an increase in identity theft. However, unlike in the United Kingdom, opponents of national ID cards in the United States spend relatively little time discussing pragmatic arguments. The bulk of the opposition is based on principled arguments. American opponents of national ID cards perceive them as profoundly altering the established balance between freedom and control. There is great concern about the constitutionality of identity policing and anything that resembles a national ID card, the growing powers of the federal government, and the impact any such scheme would have on civil liberties. Opponents worry about privacy, the specter of a "Big Brother" state, and possibility of a "slippery slope" path or "function creep" (the incremental use of ID cards for various and originally undeclared purposes). There are also

[26] Wang, "The Debate," 10. [27] Interview with a senior DHS official, May 2015.

arguments that national ID cards would lead to increased ethnic profiling and racial discrimination and that they will complicate the relationship between the police and minority groups.

Voicing these concerns and opposing national ID cards is an incredibly varied group of organizations and individuals. Among them are liberal civil libertarians of the ACLU, conservative libertarians of the Cato Institute, religious conservatives, gun rights groups, some immigration advocates, privacy advocates, and small government and antigovernment conservatives – all very outspoken and frequently talking and writing about their opposition to national ID cards.[28]

Former Speaker Newt Gingrich was probably right when he said that "the people most opposed to a national ID card are dramatically more passionate than the people who have some vague general support for a national ID card."[29] This works in favor of national ID card opponents, since the American political system favors committed, well-organized, and energized voices.

Voices of those advocating for better identity policing and national ID cards are rare and not particularly loud. Yet, that group is quite varied too, ranging from Republican politicians (James Sensenbrenner and Lamar Alexander) to Democratic ones (Chuck Schumer and Dianne Feinstein) – though only some of those politicians are comfortable using the term "national ID card" for the documents they support. In fact, Republican Lamar Alexander is one of the few high-profile politicians who openly says that the United States needs a national ID card, but he qualifies his support by saying that he also hates it.[30]

Support for national ID cards in the United States, or at least for more secure identification documents, also comes from some police forces, corporations, organizations (Coalition for a Secure Driver's License; some analysts at the Heritage Foundation), and journalists and commentators (Nicholas Kristof and Bill Keller of the *New York Times*, Kevin Drum of the *Mother Jones* magazine, David Frum of CNN, and Bill O'Reilly, then at Fox News). In February 2013, the editorial board of the *Washington Post* expressed its support for a tamper-proof, biometric national ID

[28] See, for instance, multiple writings by Jim Harper at the Cato Institute, www.cato.org/people/jim-harper.

[29] "Does America Need a National Identifier?" Hearing, Subcommittee on Government Efficiency, Financial Management and Intergovernmental Relations, Committee on Government Reform, House of Representatives, 107th Congress, November 16, 2001.

[30] Lamar Alexander, "As Much as I Hate It, We Need a National ID," *State News*, May 2005.

card.[31] Support for national ID cards also comes from some academics and public intellectuals (Alan Dershowitz, Curtis Gans, and communitarian Amitai Etzioni).

This chapter examines the key contentious points in the debates, as seen through the five key obstacles to the schemes: financial, technological and practical, constitutional and legal, relating to civil liberties and individual freedoms, and stemming from public opinion and resistance.

Financial Costs

Financial costs are an issue for those opposing national ID cards, enhancing Social Security cards, or implementing REAL ID. In particular, those who oppose national ID cards say that such system would cost billions of dollars to administer. The costs of a national system would include paying for cards, card readers, staff, and overhead, as well as the integration of the databases of the various government agencies. There would also be the costs of creating a vast new bureaucracy to administer the system. Even a partial identity policing scheme would be costly: in the aftermath of 9/11, the SSA estimated that creating counterfeit-resistant Social Security cards would cost $4 billion.[32] Others, including the ACLU, countered that such a system would cost as much as $9 billion. In a February 2002 letter to President Bush, the ACLU and other organizations "representing a broad and diverse coalition of national organizations" opposed a national ID and argued that "a national ID would be expensive and direct resources away from other more effective counterterrorism measures."[33] A 2012 study from the University of California–Berkeley estimated that establishing a biometric employment card (in line with the 2010 BELIEVE proposal of Senators Schumer and Graham) would cost the government $22 billion at the outset, with ongoing maintenance costs of $2 billion per year. The study noted that accounting for costs to employers and costs from projected productivity loss would make the system much more expensive (almost $40 billion at the outset, with maintenance costs of $3 billion per year).[34]

[31] "The Case for a National ID Card," Editorial, *Washington Post*, February 2, 2013.

[32] "Does America Need a National Identifier?," November 16, 2001.

[33] Letter to President Bush, February 11, 2002, https://epic.org/privacy/id_cards/presidentltr2.11.02.html.

[34] A. Michael Froomkin and Jonathan Weinberg, "Hard to BELIEVE: The High Cost of a Biometric Identity Card," Chief Justice Earl Warren Institute on Law and Social Policy, University of California–Berkeley, February 2012.

However, supporters say that an expense for a national ID card system is a reasonable expense for greater security. The cost of the effects of a terrorist attack should also be included when undertaking any analysis of the cost issue. The World Trade Center attack cost New York City dearly; while the true cost is still not known, it is certainly in the many billions of dollars.[35]

However, public conversations about the financial costs and financial benefits of a national ID scheme in the United States have been rare. Much more common have been conversations about the financial costs surrounding REAL ID. According to many advocacy groups, state officials, and members of Congress, REAL ID imposes an unconstitutional "unfunded mandate" on the states. Governor Mark Sanford (R-SC) called REAL ID an "unfunded mandate," as did Senator Lamar Alexander (R-TN), who nevertheless supported it.

The term "unfunded mandate" refers to requirements that one unit of government imposes on another without providing funds to pay for costs of compliance. In this case, the argument has been that the federal government has imposed the requirements of REAL ID on the states without providing adequate funding to cover the implementation costs. Arguments related to "unfunded mandates" typically take two forms. The first is that unfunded mandates are unconstitutional as violations of the Tenth Amendment. As the CRS points out, jurisprudence with respect to the Tenth Amendment is limited, and the federal courts have not to date specifically addressed the "unfunded mandate" issue. The second argument refers to the statutory requirements of the Unfunded Mandates Reform Act of 1995 (UMRA), which contains provisions designed to limit the number of unfunded mandates adopted by Congress. Although REAL ID requires significant expenditures by the states to comply with its requirements, UMRA arguably exempts the REAL ID regulations from the statute's requirements, since UMRA excludes regulations that are "necessary for the national security." DHS relied on this provision in its explanation as to why REAL ID is not an unfunded mandate.[36] Some REAL ID supporters point out that REAL ID is not a mandate on states; rather, it seeks to ensure that every state's process for issuing driver's licenses – including the documents themselves – meets specified minimum security standards.[37]

35 Wang, "The Debate," 7. 36 Tatelman, "REAL ID," 14–16.

37 Janice L. Kephart, "Identity and Security: REAL ID in the States," April 2007, 3, 14, www.cis.org/sites/cis.org/files/articles/2011/IDSecurityStateWhitePaper0407.pdf.

In September 2006, NCSL, NGA, and AAMVA projected a cost of $11 billion for the first five years of REAL ID. Their study argued that all 245 million driver's license and ID card holders would be required to make an in-person visit to their DMV to obtain a REAL ID–compliant license. States would need to hire more employees and expand business hours.[38] The $11 billion estimate dwarfed the Congressional Budget Office estimate of $100 million. While Rep. Sensenbrenner dismissed the $11 billion estimate as fanciful, in March 2007 Secretary Chertoff agreed that the cost could be as high as the states estimate, and he acknowledged that every cardholder would have to pay some $20 more for a REAL ID–compliant license.[39]

Janice Kephart argues that what is most remarkable about REAL ID implementation to date, from the states that have made public their REAL ID expenditures, is that the costs for compliance are coming in nowhere near the $11 billion price tag. By January 2011, Congress had appropriated, and DHS had allocated, $176 million in federal grants to the states, some of which went unused and was returned to the US Treasury.[40]

Technological Obstacles and Practical Constraints

Critics of identity policing schemes voice concerns about the danger of data loss and abuse of centralized and comprehensive databases storing sensitive data, as well as the prospect of an increase in identity theft because of official reliance on a card that can be forged. Every database is prone to error and breakdown. In hearings before Congress, computer scientist Ben Shneiderman stressed that a national ID system is based on a combination of humans who enter and verify data, and hardware and software that store and transmit data. "Such socio-technical systems are always vulnerable to error, breakdown, sabotage, and destruction by natural events for any people with malicious intentions."[41] Hackers have breached both government and private databases around the world; criminals have subsequently used some of the information gained from hacks in fraud schemes. The fear of data loss is valid, and one would be hard pressed to find an expert who would not acknowledge this as a significant risk.

[38] NCSL, "The History of Federal Requirements."
[39] Katel, "REAL ID," 400; DHS, Remarks by Secretary Chertoff, March 1, 2007.
[40] Kephart, "REAL ID Implementation," 2, 7.
[41] "Does America Need a National Identifier?," November 16, 2001.

Less clear-cut is the issue of the reliability of identification technologies. Those who are fearful of current identification technology object to more reliance on identification technology and to more comprehensive identity policing schemes. However, supporters of more comprehensive identity policing schemes point out that identification technology is being used effectively by private industry and in other countries. While none of the technologies are foolproof, some are clearly better than others.[42]

Contrary to the frequent assertion of REAL ID opponents, REAL ID contains no requirement for cards to have an RFID chip or other device that can scan data from a distance. The final rule requires two-dimensional barcodes on all compliant IDs, a technology that is already used by most states.[43]

Constitutional and Legal Obstacles

In a testimony before Congress, Jonathan Turley, a professor of public interest law, argued:

> The imposition of a national identification card would not violate the United States Constitution. Congress can require every citizen to participate in a national registry and to acquire both a number and a card as part of that registration. Any constitutional or legal problems would arise in the details of how such a card is used and how such a system is maintained ... it would be difficult to design a system that would pass constitutional muster.[44]

According to Alison Smith, legislative attorney at the CRS, "Congress could permissibly legislate a national identification card under a number of its powers enumerated in Article I, Section 8, of the Constitution." For example, Congress has plenary power over naturalization and citizenship. Assuming that a national ID system was instituted to track aliens, "the enactment of such a system would appear to fall within Congress' authority," according to Smith. In addition, under the Commerce Clause, Congress has the power to regulate international and interstate commerce. If the purpose of a national ID system would be to facilitate better security for international and interstate travel, then such a system "would appear to be sufficiently related" to interstate commerce to fall within Congress's Commerce Clause authority. Furthermore, the Constitution authorizes Congress to use federal monies to provide for the common

[42] Wang, "The Debate," 2.
[43] DHS, Regulatory Evaluation, Final Rulemaking, January 17, 2008, 110–111.
[44] "Does America Need a National Identifier?," November 16, 2001.

defense and the general welfare. As such, Congress could legislate a national ID card by providing funds to states and attaching conditions to these funds without violating the Constitution due to the voluntary nature of states' participation. States would remain free to reject the federal monies, but if accepted they would be taken subject to the conditions imposed by Congress.[45]

While Congress would have the authority to enact a national ID system, "constitutional and legal concerns could presumably arise in the implementation and enforcement of such a system." For instance, enforcement of a national ID system could conceivably implicate the right to travel and privacy rights.[46]

Court rulings and the American public have long recognized freedom to travel throughout the United States as a basic right under the Constitution. In 1958, in *Kent v. Dulles*, the Supreme Court asserted, "The right to travel is a part of the 'liberty' of which the citizen cannot be deprived without due process of law under the Fifth Amendment." In 1966, in *United States v. Guest*, the Supreme Court held that there is a constitutional right to travel from state to state. In 1969, in *Shapiro v. Thompson*, the Supreme Court noted that the Constitution does not explicitly mention the right to travel because "a right so elementary was conceived from the beginning to be a necessary concomitant of the stronger Union the Constitution created." In 1999, in *Saenz v. Roe*, the Supreme Court reaffirmed *Shapiro v. Thompson*'s opinion that the right to travel is a "virtually unconditional personal right, guaranteed by the Constitution to us all." In 1991, in *Cramer v. Skinner*, the Fifth Circuit Court of Appeals argued: "Although no clause in the Constitution specifically provides a right to interstate travel, the Supreme Court has inferred this right from various constitutional provisions and from the structure of the federal system itself."[47]

Smith points out that a law implicates the right to travel when it actually deters such travel, or when obstructing travel is its primary objective. A law that infringes the right to travel is subject to strict scrutiny by the courts, under which a compelling state interest must be shown and the government's purpose "cannot be pursued by means that broadly stifle fundamental personal liberties when the end can be more narrowly achieved." Thus, as Smith points out, the question of whether a national ID system would impermissibly infringe upon the right to travel

[45] Alison Smith, "National Identification Cards: Legal Issues," CRS, January 7, 2003, 2–3.
[46] Ibid., 3. [47] Ibid.

would ultimately depend upon the nature and effect of the system adopted. Where the system, as implemented, deters the ability to travel, a court would likely inquire whether the objective underlying the system is sufficiently "compelling" to justify the restriction on travel.[48] To avoid the constitutional concerns presented by a mandatory identification system, law professor Alan Dershowitz has suggested utilizing a voluntary system.[49]

Implementation and enforcement of a national ID system could also implicate privacy rights relating to the collection and dissemination of information, especially if national ID cards were to contain sensitive information. Even though the Constitution does not explicitly provide a right to privacy, the Supreme Court has found some right to informational privacy. These rights, however, are limited by judicial deference to the government's need to acquire information. This would mean that federal or state collections of information may receive some constitutional or statutory protection, but the collection and use of information by private organizations would not be covered.[50]

In addition, while the Constitution does not explicitly provide a right to privacy, in 1965, in *Griswold v. Connecticut*, the Supreme Court held that "various guarantees create zones of privacy." The right of association contained in the First Amendment, as well as the Third, Fourth, Fifth, and Ninth Amendments, were held to give people a right to privacy, and this doctrine has been used in many cases since. However, there has been some debate over whether the constitutional right to privacy includes the right to anonymity. Dershowitz argues that the right to privacy is solely the right to control one's personal information and its dissemination, not hide one's identity. He says, "American taxpayers, voters, and drivers long ago gave up any right of anonymity without loss of our right to engage in lawful conduct within zones of privacy."[51] However, in several cases, the Supreme Court has at least hinted that there is a right to anonymous political speech under the First Amendment.[52]

Moreover, although the right to anonymity is protected in the context of political and religious rights, US citizens are required to identify themselves in a wide range of encounters with their government. Identification

48 Ibid., 3–4.
49 Alan Dershowitz, "Why Fear National ID Cards?," *NYT*, October 13, 2001.
50 Smith, "National Identification Cards," 4.
51 Dershowitz, "Why Fear National ID Cards?"
52 Wang, "The Debate," 5.

is required to receive almost any recurring government benefit and to make substantial campaign contributions.[53]

The right to travel and the right to privacy also often come together. Law professor Michael Froomkin points out that today the legal regulation of driving starts from the premise that driving an automobile is a "privilege," not a "right." This is true in both federal and state law. It was not always thus: fifty to one hundred years ago, courts repeatedly wrote of an individual's "right to travel" by automobile and struck down regulations limiting the liberties of automobile drivers. In contrast, since 1950, no court has described driving an automobile as a "right."[54] In fact, Froomkin points out that the "collision between the romantic vision of freedom of movement and the legal regulation of it" took place in a recent Supreme Court case involving, of all things, "a motionless cowboy." The "cowboy," as Froomkin says, "surely the embodiment of the romantic ideal of the wandering American," was Dudley Hiibel, a rancher from Nevada. In the account of his legal team, on May 21, 2000, Hiibel was standing around minding his own business when a police officer pulled up and demanded that Hiibel produce his ID, which he declined to do. This refusal led to his arrest on charges of failure to cooperate for refusing to show ID on demand.[55] Nevada has a "stop-and-identify" law that allows a peace officer (a police officer, sheriff, or marshal) to detain any person he encounters "under circumstances which reasonably indicate that the person has committed, is committing or is about to commit a crime." The officer may detain the person only to ascertain his identity and the suspicious circumstances. In this case, the officer was responding to a caller who reported seeing an assault inside a truck traveling down the road. Police located the truck, which had by then pulled off the road. A man was standing by the vehicle and a woman was inside. After repeatedly refusing to identify himself, the man was arrested, charged with obstructing a public officer, and convicted. Hiibel appealed his subsequent conviction, and the case ultimately reached the Supreme Court. In 2004, in *Hiibel v. Sixth Judicial District Court of Nevada*, the Supreme Court held that nothing in the Fourth or Fifth Amendments (protection against unreasonable search and seizure, and right against self-incrimination) prevents a state from requiring a suspect to disclose his name in the course of a justified investigative ("Terry")

53 A. Michael Froomkin, "Anonymity and the Law in the United States," in *Lessons from the Identity Trail*, ed. Kerr et al., 458.

54 Froomkin, "Identity Cards," 248–249.

55 Ibid., 250.

stop. The Court read the Nevada statute as being satisfied with verbal self-identification: a detainee was not required to produce written identification, but could satisfy the requirement merely by stating his name. It is important to note that different obligations apply to drivers of motor vehicles. State vehicle codes require drivers to present a driver's license to police upon request.[56]

Arguments made on constitutional grounds against national ID documents and identity checks have also been made in the same or similar way against REAL ID. The first argument made against REAL ID on constitutional grounds is that REAL ID cannot be premised on Congress's power to regulate interstate commerce, and it is hence a violation of states' rights as protected by the Tenth Amendment. As Todd Tatelman points out, although Congress's power to regulate matters affecting interstate commerce is broad, it has limits. In fact, it has been constrained in recent years by the Supreme Court's interpretation of the Tenth Amendment (on state sovereignty), which the Court has invoked as a limit on Congress's Article I domestic powers. In 2000, however, the Supreme Court decided *Reno v. Condon* and upheld as constitutional provisions of the Driver's Privacy Protection Act of 1994, which regulated the ability of the states to disclose and resell information collected from state DMVs. The Court wrote that the Act "does not require the [states] to enact any laws or regulations and it does not require state officials to assist in the enforcement of federal statutes regulating private individuals." Whether limiting the standards to federal acceptance – as opposed to direct federal requirements on the states – prevents federalism concerns under Supreme Court jurisprudence remains to be seen. Tatelman points out, however, that one could argue that because the issuance of driver's licenses remains a function of state law, the minimum issuance and verification requirements established by REAL ID, even if limited to federal agency acceptance, constitute an effective commandeering by Congress of the state process, or a conscription of the state and local officials who issue the licenses.[57]

The second argument made against REAL ID on constitutional grounds is that the requirement that REAL IDs be used to board federally regulated aircraft impermissibly encroaches on citizens' right to travel. The argument has developed along two strands: one regards burdens

[56] Ibid., 250–251, 253; Beverly A. Ginn, "Chief's Counsel: Stop-and-Identify Laws," *The Police Chief* 71, 9 (September 2004).

[57] Tatelman, "REAL ID," 6, 8.

imposed by state governments and involves the Fourteenth Amendment, and the other regards federally imposed burdens and involves the Fifth Amendment.[58]

Under the Fourteenth Amendment cases, the right to travel from one state to another has been considered a fundamental right under the Constitution. There have also been cases where the state has placed burdens on the act of travel itself, and the court has held that burdens on travel are justifiable as long as they are uniformly applied and support the safety and integrity of the travel facilities. Thus, courts have upheld highway tolls and airport fees, but a general tax imposed on all individuals leaving a state may impermissibly restrict travel.

Conversely, in right-to-travel cases involving federally imposed burdens, which implicate the Fifth Amendment, courts appear to reject the Fourteenth Amendment fundamental rights analysis and apply a less stringent rational basis test, which requires that laws be rationally related to a legitimate government interest. Here the government is not required to show a compelling interest to justify a uniformly applied, nondiscriminatory travel-related restriction.[59]

Tatelman points out that the airlines have authorization to refuse service to anyone who fails to present proper identification. Therefore, one can make an argument that REAL ID imposes an additional burden on citizens who wish to travel by federally regulated aircraft. That said, it appears difficult to argue that ensuring the security and validity of identification documents will fail to increase passenger safety and transportation facility security, which are compelling governmental interests. Tatelman writes that the government may be in a strong position to argue not only that the identification requirements are justifiable, but also that their burden on the right to travel is minimal and, considering the present conditions, entirely reasonable. Moreover, it is important to note that not having a REAL ID-compliant document will not prevent individuals from flying. Rather, the lack of a REAL ID, whether by personal choice or state noncompliance, will mean that a citizen will have to produce alternative identification accepted by the TSA or will have to undergo additional security screening.[60]

The third argument made against REAL ID is that it potentially violates the Free Exercise Clause of the First Amendment. Since REAL ID requires a digital photograph on each document, it may violate the religious

[58] Ibid., 9. [59] Ibid., 9–10. [60] Ibid., 10.

beliefs of some Amish and others, and thus may unconstitutionally affect the free exercise of religion.[61] The Supreme Court has consistently affirmed that the Free Exercise Clause protects religious beliefs, but protection for religiously motivated conduct has waxed and waned over the years.[62] In post-9/11 cases, courts generally have not required exemptions for photo requirements in identification laws. However, courts have not summarily dismissed the possibility of exemptions. Voter ID laws in many states contain exemptions for people with religious objections to being photographed, and it is possible that exemptions from the REAL ID photo requirement will be required for citizens whose religious principles forbid compliance. Importantly, however, US passports must include a photograph, and the DOS does not permit exemptions from this requirement based on religious objections.[63]

The final argument made against REAL ID is that it infringes upon a citizen's right under the First Amendment to freely assemble, associate, and petition the government. The ACLU has made this argument,[64] and others have linked this right to the right to anonymity. The argument is that linking a state's issuance of identification documents to its citizen's ability to board a federally regulated aircraft prevents the full exercise of an individual's First Amendment rights that depend on a citizen's ability to move freely throughout the country. In 1964, in *Aptheker v. Secretary of State*, the Supreme Court decided that freedom of movement "is akin to the right of assembly and to the right of association." Tatelman writes that by imposing burdensome requirements on interstate travel, the government has arguably prevented persons who wish to refrain from identifying themselves and/or submitting to enhanced security screening from exercising their constitutional rights.[65]

Although it appears that neither the Supreme Court nor any lower federal court has seen an analogous situation, the Court has indicated that anonymity is a concept protected by the First Amendment. For instance, in 1944, in *Thomas v. Collins*, the Supreme Court invalidated a Texas statute requiring labor organizers to register and obtain an organizer's card before making speeches to assembled workers as incompatible with

[61] Ibid., 10–11; ACLU, "Scorecard on Final Real ID Regulations," January 17, 2008, 20, www.aclu.org/images/general/asset_upload_file162_33700.pdf.

[62] Tatelman, "REAL ID," 11–13.

[63] Cynthia Brougher, "Legal Analysis of Religious Exemptions for Photo Identification Requirements," CRS, September 5, 2012.

[64] Tatelman, "REAL ID," 13; ACLU, "Scorecard," 21–22.

[65] Tatelman, "REAL ID," 13.

the guarantees of the First Amendment. Tatelman claims that although there may be a general right of anonymity, it is difficult to connect the implication of this right to the purpose of REAL ID. A strong argument exists that the regulations are in no way intended to impact a person's First Amendment rights; rather, the regulations are aimed at preventing and deterring the use of fraudulent identification documents for federal purposes. Thus, these regulations can arguably have, at most, an indirect effect on rights protected by the First Amendment. Given that, it is unlikely that challengers could establish the significant impact on their right to associate or petition the government that would be required to trigger First Amendment scrutiny.[66]

Civil Liberties and Individual Freedoms

A threat of erosion of civil liberties and individual freedoms is an issue for those worrying about national ID cards, enhancing Social Security cards, and implementing REAL ID. The most widely cited fears are the encroachment of freedom and privacy, the specter of a "Big Brother" state, and possibility of a "slippery slope" path or "function creep." While some arguments are concrete (e.g., security breach of an ID database), others are based on an opposition to a national ID card system per se.

Privacy advocates and civil libertarians oppose a national ID card system, citing the loss of privacy and fear of misuse.[67] They worry that such a system would enable the government and private companies to collect and disseminate personal information and that government employees who would have access to that information might deliberately or accidentally release or abuse it. Katie Corrigan, legislative counsel at the ACLU, argued during a 2001 Congress hearing: "One mistake by a government employee could result in disclosure of personal information that could follow you around the rest of your life ... With an ID system, one accidental keyboard stroke could put a person's most sensitive information into public distribution." She then added that "one of the biggest protections of privacy is actually the decentralized nature of the data."[68]

The precedent of misuse of SSNs demonstrates the potential for national ID cards to be used in ways that extend beyond their original

66 Ibid., 13–14.

67 Adam Thierer, "National ID Cards: New Technologies, Same Bad Idea," September 28, 2001, www.cato.org/tech/tk/010928-tk.html.

68 "Does America Need a National Identifier?," November 16, 2001.

purpose. While created to track the earnings of workers to calculate their Social Security contributions, SSNs have since been used ubiquitously in private transactions, and the easy access to SSNs contributes to fraud and identity theft. Although the 1974 Privacy Act protects the use of personal information by the government, it places no restrictions on private companies or individuals. The SSN precedent makes opponents of national ID cards worry that such a system might quickly evolve beyond terrorism prevention. Government agencies, employers, banks, and insurance and health care companies might want more information added to the cards. One concern is that health care information might become traceable through the card in order to help emergency responders after a terrorist attack, and this may enable insurance companies to use that information in determining whether to cover an individual or how to price a policy.[69]

Supporters of national ID cards respond that such privacy issues exist anyway and a new system would not exacerbate them. After all, driver's licenses and other forms of identification are already required to cash checks, get a post office box, buy alcohol, and register to vote in some states. Private industry and government already gather so much personal information that they would not learn much more than they already do. Appropriate (possibly European-style) protections could help secure privacy, and inappropriate misuse of records could be made a felony with very stiff penalties.[70]

Ethnic minorities and civil libertarians fear that ID cards will complicate the relationship between the police and ethnic minorities. They fear that law enforcement authorities would abuse a national identification system and that those individuals who do not produce an ID card when stopped on the street by law enforcement officers might become subject to a search or even arrest, and not having the card would make the person an immediate suspect. Some also argue that a national ID system would increase the incidence of ethnic and racial profiling. Authorities might be more likely to stop people who look Middle Eastern or Hispanic to ask them for their ID, therefore subjecting certain minorities to having to constantly prove their citizenship or immigration status. Barry Steinhardt of ACLU has said:

> Rather than eliminating discrimination, as some have claimed, a national identity card in any form would foster new forms of discrimination and harassment of anyone perceived as looking or sounding "foreign" … A super driver's license

[69] Wang, "The Debate," 4. [70] Ibid., 4–5.

would have the same effect on a massive scale, as Latinos, Asians, Muslims, and persons of Middle Eastern descent become subject to ceaseless status and identity checks from police, banks, merchants and others. Failure to carry a national ID card would likely come to be viewed as a reason for search, detention or arrest of minorities. The stigma and humiliation of constantly having to prove that they are Americans or legal immigrants would weigh heavily on such groups.[71]

In contrast, supporters of a national ID system respond that it actually would reduce profiling, since an encounter would immediately halt upon production of the card. In his testimony before Congress, Rudi Veestraeten, Consul at the Belgian Embassy, argued:

In case of police checks, if some things happen and people are stopped in the street in a car, the fact that we have the identity cards and a very efficient database does save a lot of time. People can be released after only two minutes, just checking if this person is really who he is. So it's a matter there in our view of civil liberty that we can release people immediately if there is no need to keep them. We don't need to take them to the ... police office.[72]

Nevertheless, arguments such as that presented by Veestraeten do not find understanding with most Americans, who often believe that European societies with mandatory IDs are "Your Papers Please!" societies, where citizens are constantly stopped in the street and asked for identification. American organizations such as the ACLU contribute to this image by using the phrase "Your Papers Please!" whenever discussing identification documents.[73] Interestingly, Froomkin points out that Americans have in mind a popular image – probably in black and white – of a Nazi in a film, perhaps with a big German Shepherd at his side, demanding "Papers, please" in a German accent, but they cannot identify a movie in which it appears. *Stalag 17* (1953) has moments that come close ("Anybody asks for your papers, you're French laborers"). The film that probably launched the image is *The Great Escape* (1963), but neither film has the actual image that people seem to refer to.[74]

So while some arguments criticizing identity policing and identification documents are concrete, others are based on an opposition to a national identification card system per se. Critics say REAL ID is a euphemism for a national ID card and that it has been mislabeled in an effort to fool the

71 "The Uniform Driver's License as a National ID," Address by ACLU Associate Director Barry Steinhardt to AAMVA, February 10, 2002.
72 "Does America Need a National Identifier?," November 16, 2001.
73 Ronald Bailey, "Your Papers Please," *Reason Magazine*, October 19, 2006.
74 Froomkin, "Identity Cards," 246–247.

country. "If it walks like a duck and quacks like a duck, it's a duck," according to Timothy Sparapani, legislative counsel at the ACLU. "What we're building, database by database, is a national identification system, which is the next critical step for the government's efforts to establish the total surveillance society, where our entire lives are subject to scrutiny and reinterpretation by government bureaucrats."[75]

In American culture, opposition to a national identification system runs deep. "If you've suggested a national ID, you're doomed," says former Senator Alan Simpson, recalling the demise of a provision in IRCA in 1986. "We never suggested a national ID. We called it a "more secure identifier," but the right was calling it the mark of Cain, and the left was talking about retina scans and Nazi Germany."[76]

As Simpson alluded to in his comment about the "mark of Cain," one element of America's antipathy to ID cards has a religious basis – and this is, in fact, an element particular to America. Other countries with devout religious populations – Poland, Italy, or Spain – do not exhibit a similar fear. This is perhaps because it is segments of the evangelical Protestant movement, particular to America, who fear enumeration. They believe that mandatory IDs are a precursor to the second coming, or the end of times, foretold in Revelations 13:16–18. They see a national ID card as the next step toward the imposition of the biblical "mark of the beast" that Christians will be forced to have to buy and sell during the "Last Days." Therefore, they see it as their religious duty to oppose the cards. As Froomkin points out, this view that enumeration is ungodly is as old as the Republic. George Washington feared that the first census in 1790 would "greatly" undercount the population because so many would refuse to be counted due to "religious scruples," although he also noted that others would evade the census for fear "it was intended as the foundation of a tax." Froomkin argues that doubts about ID cards today "are found both in the leadership of the Christian Coalition and all over the wilder parts of the Internet." He adds that since religious movements, and especially Protestants, are organized political forces in the United States, "the opinions of the leaders of advocacy groups such as the Christian Coalition carry weight, especially within the Republican Party."[77]

Speaking further about America's fear of national ID cards, former Senator Simpson stated in 2001: "you do a disservice to the country when you use the phrase national ID." A national ID is "a diversion for people

[75] Katel, "Real ID," 387. [76] Ibid., 388. [77] Froomkin, "Identity Cards," 247–248.

who like to talk about tattoos and Nazi Germany ... We're not talking about that. Every time we tried to do something in this area, it was filled with emotion, fear, guilt, and racism."[78]

In particular, critics accused REAL ID of being a national ID in disguise. The Electronic Privacy Information Center argues that REAL ID creates a de facto national ID card.[79] ACLU argues that the final regulations do nothing to prevent REAL ID from becoming a de facto national ID card.[80] Opponents argue that the uniform issuance and verification standards imposed by the federal government will result in turning state workers into immigration enforcement officials by forcing them to check the citizenship status of each applicant. Opponents also point to the machine-readable technology requirements and state data-sharing proposals as evidence of substantially increased federal government involvement in the traditionally state-run issuance of identification documents. Finally, opponents note that there appears to be an unlimited number of activities for which REAL ID–compliant licenses could be required. These could potentially include voting, firearm registration, employment, and receipt of subsidies and other federal or state benefits.[81]

In the final rule, DHS specifically indicates that it "does not intend that REAL ID documents become a *de facto* national ID and does not support the creation of a national ID." In addition, DHS notes that it has limited the potential uses of REAL IDs to accessing federal facilities, boarding federally regulated aircraft, and entering nuclear power plants, thereby limiting the functionality of the card. DHS also notes that it does not intend to own or operate a database on holders of driver's licenses and ID cards.[82]

Despite the variety in features that could define national ID cards, at a minimum, such cards tend to be uniform and are issued by the same national governmental entity. Tatelman writes that it is difficult to argue that REAL ID is, or could lead to, a national ID card since REAL ID participation by the states and individuals is voluntary, not mandatory. Moreover, the Act contains specific restrictions on DHS's ability to regulate the design and/or appearance of the card, and the issuance will continue to take place on the state level, not the federal level.[83]

78 "Does America Need a National Identifier?," November 16, 2001.

79 "National ID and the REAL ID Act," http://epic.org/privacy/id-cards/.

80 ACLU, "Scorecard," 8.

81 Tatelman, "REAL ID," 28.

82 DHS, "Minimum Standards."

83 Tatelman, "REAL ID," 29.

Writing in 2007, Janice Kephart made the following argument:

> REAL ID was passed in part to do away with any notion of a national ID card. By seeking to set out minimum standards for the ID card already the ID of choice by financial, airline, entertainment and other sectors – the state-issued driver's license or personal ID card – Congress made clear their intent to refrain from creating a national ID card. The only aspect of REAL ID that is national is the national interest that all states be set on a foundation of minimum standards; states can choose to meet none of them and not comply or they can choose to exceed those standards. Examples already exist on both sides of compliance, with states like Maine and Idaho currently opting out, and states like Washington already passing laws to exceed REAL ID minimum standards. Far from calling for a national ID, fully implementing REAL ID is the best chance we have as a nation to prevent future calls for a national ID.

Kephart, however, followed this with a warning that "a national ID could become the default policy if REAL ID compliance does not occur in a comprehensive way. That makes the stakes a lot higher for all of us if states who say they will opt out actually do opt out."[84]

Public Opinion and Resistance

Resistance of many states and politicians to REAL ID has been clear. Governor Mike Huckabee (R-AR) was opposed to what he called the Bush administration's encroachment on states' rights. Governor Bill Richardson (D-NM) said he would challenge REAL ID on constitutional grounds. Since 2005, at least two dozen states have at one point or another opposed the implementation of REAL ID. Political scientists Priscilla Regan and Christopher Deering find that relatively less populous and less wealthy states, which are likely to be more impacted by unfunded mandates, and more conservative states, which are more likely to be concerned about retaining state control, were more likely to oppose REAL ID. States with stronger privacy orientations also were more likely to pass statutes or resolutions in opposition.[85]

However, not all responses have been negative, and many states have passed laws enabling REAL ID compliance. Maryland, for instance, originally vocal in opposition to REAL ID, decided in 2008, with a push from Governor Martin O'Malley (D) in a late-night legislative session,

[84] Kephart, "Identity and Security," 8.

[85] Priscilla M. Regan and Christopher J. Deering, "State Opposition to REAL ID," *Publius: The Journal of Federalism* 39, 3 (2009).

to force REAL ID compliance language through the Maryland General Assembly.[86]

The Fraternal Order of Police (FOP) supports implementation of the REAL ID Act, calling it "a common sense system that takes the right approach to ensuring the security and authenticity of the most commonly used identity document in the United States – a driver's license."[87] As a REAL ID policy expert told me, "FOP is very supportive of REAL ID because they view driver's licenses on a regular basis."[88] Chuck Canterbury, FOP National President, told Senate Majority Leader Harry Reid that REAL ID is "very much an officer safety issue." He continued:

> Law enforcement officers need to have confidence that the documents presented to them to establish the identity of a given individual are accurate. Officers rely on these documents during traffic stops and other law enforcement actions to access information related to that individual's criminal history. No police officer wants to be in the dark about the fact that he may have detained a wanted or violent criminal who has simply obtained false identification. This places both the officer and the public he is sworn to protect in greater danger. For this reason, the FOP will strongly oppose any bill or amendment that would repeal the REAL ID Act.[89]

In 2005, the National Sheriffs' Association (NSA) discussed "at length" whether it should take a position on REAL ID, and while the Association did not take an official position on the Act itself, it did support the concept of the need to develop a national standard for identification security. Later, NSA recognized "the significant problems associated with REAL ID and the looming deadline for full compliance," and the Board of Directors officially endorsed the PASS ID proposal. NSA argued that under PASS ID, "the requirements necessary for obtaining state identifications and driver's licenses remain as strong as they were with REAL ID," but PASS ID avoids "the systematic malady of REAL ID including cost and privacy concerns." NSA became the first national law enforcement organization to endorse PASS ID.[90] Subsequently, the National Association of Police Organizations and Major Cities Chiefs

86 Kephart, "REAL ID Implementation," 9.

87 "Understanding the Realities of REAL ID: A Review of Efforts to Secure Driver's Licenses and Identification Cards," Hearing, Subcommittee on Oversight of Government Management, the Federal Workforce, and the District of Columbia, Committee on Homeland Security and Governmental Affairs, Senate, 110th Congress, March 26, 2007, 54.

88 Interview with a REAL ID policy expert, March 2014.

89 Chuck Canterbury, Letter to Majority Leader Reid on REAL ID Act, February 21, 2007.

90 Leroy D. Baca (Sheriff, Los Angeles County, California), Testimony, "Identification Security: Reevaluating the REAL ID Act," Committee on Homeland Security and Governmental Affairs, Senate, July 15, 2009.

Association have also endorsed PASS ID, which was to amend the REAL ID Act to enhance the security and integrity of driver's licenses and identification cards "while maintaining flexibility for states and reducing the costs of implementation."[91]

Opinion polls reveal that a cross-section of American residents believes that the country needs a national ID card. Gallup polls taken in 1983, 1993, and 1995 consistently showed that a majority of respondents favored a national ID card. Polls taken in the decade following 9/11 show similar support.

A Pew Research Center poll conducted between September 14 and 17, 2001, just a few days after the attacks, found that 70 percent of respondents were in favor of "the following measure to curb terrorism: requiring that all citizens carry a national identity card at all times to show to a police officer on request." In a June 2002 Fox Broadcasting Company poll, 62 percent of respondents said it would be a good idea to require "U.S. citizens to carry national identification cards." In a September 2002 Pew Research Center poll, 61 percent of respondents were in favor of "the following measure to curb terrorism: requiring you to carry a national identity card at all times to show to a police officer on request." In a September 2002 Harris Poll, 60 percent of respondents were in favor of "adoption of a national ID system for all U.S. citizens." In a January 2006 Pew Research Center poll, 57 percent of respondents were in favor of "the following measure to curb terrorism: requiring that all citizens carry a national identity card at all times to show to a police officer on request." In a May 2010 CNN/Opinion Research Corporation poll, 70 percent of respondents were in favor of "creating an ID card issued by the federal government that all U.S. citizens and legal immigrants would be required to show to an employer when applying for a job." In an August 2011 Harris Poll, released in September 2011, 61 percent of respondents were in favor of "adoption of a national ID system for all U.S. citizens."[92]

In 2010, both the McClatchy–Ipsos poll and the Pew Research Center set out to take the national pulse on Arizona's controversial S.B.1070. In each poll, more than six in ten Americans supported the law. In addition, roughly seven in ten said they would not mind if police stopped them to

[91] NGA, "PASS ID," www.nga.org/files/live/sites/NGA/files/pdf/0907PASSIDTALKINGPOINTS.PDF.

[92] Records from "Polling the Nations," gathered by the author at the Library of Congress, June 4, 2013.

ask for proof of citizenship, and two-thirds supported police detaining people who could not provide one. Even among Democrats, evenly split over the law, nearly two-thirds supported the provision requiring people to produce documents verifying legal status, and 55 percent supported detaining those who could not.[93]

SUMMARY

The recent political history of national ID card proposals and other identity policing schemes in the United States is a complicated one. In the past, Congress has expressly rejected proposals that would have banned the use of the SSN as a national identifier, yet it has also opposed the creation of a national ID card. Post-9/11, Congress held hearings entitled "Does America Need a National Identifier?," but although figures such as former Senator Alan Simpson and Professor Jonathan Turley have proposed a creation of a federal commission on a potential for a national ID card, policymakers have not created one. In fact, Turley could not be closer to the truth when he stated that "this is a subject where generally more heat than light is generated." Turley further argued before Congress, "Whether one views a national identification card as a necessary security measure or Big Brother's little helper, it is a subject on which the United States must reach some consensus."[94]

Yet consensus on identity policing is not likely. The subject is rife with passion and controversy, and voices opposing national identification documents and REAL ID are much louder than those supporting such schemes. Then there are those who vehemently oppose a national ID system for Americans, but want it for foreigners living here. For instance, former House speaker Newt Gingrich said that he thinks most Americans would agree that for foreign visitors, "you could have a nationwide system of identifiers [written as "identifying" in another transcript] – because that's not part of what we think of as our civil liberties." And ultra-conservative Phyllis Schlafly, the late president of the Eagle Forum, wrote that a national ID card is a "thoroughly un-American idea," but went on to argue for an ID card for aliens. She wrote, "We are not going to tolerate a system that treats U.S. citizens and aliens the same; all aliens are not terrorists, but nearly all terrorists are aliens. We do not want to

[93] Bruce Maiman, "Immigration Reform Should Include National ID Cards," *Populist Examiner*, January 20, 2011.

[94] "Does America Need a National Identifier?," November 16, 2001.

live in a police state where every American is treated like a terrorist, drug trafficker, money launderer, illegal alien or common criminal."[95]

In light of views like that, it is not surprising that the topic stirs controversy. Add the fact that in the popular American imagination ID cards are identified as tools of oppression and totalitarianism, some religious groups identify ID cards with the anti-Christ, and in many peoples' minds ID cards conflict with the popular myth, but declining reality, of the right to move about freely, and the topic becomes truly explosive, even before practical concerns over data protection and privacy come into play.

Few politicians wish to confront these issues, yet some recognize the lack of sustainability of certain US identity policing practices in the changing world. The satisficing that takes place helps create a genuine patchwork in American identity policing.

The United States never had a concerted effort to develop a policy on identification documents. Whatever efforts existed were piecemeal. As with much else in American political development, identity policing efforts have built up on previous efforts and developed sporadically and patchily. In recent years, one clear example of this is the confusing, near-simultaneous development of REAL ID–compliant driver's licenses and WHTI-compliant EDLs. There is also a confusing patchwork of state responses to REAL ID, ranging from states that fully comply to those that forbid their DMVs from participating.

The satisficing that takes place in US identity policing is evident in the way some politicians and policy experts approach identity policies. While they may not be happy with the satisficing, they learn to be pragmatic and see positives in selecting the option that seems to address at least some needs rather than attempt to seek an optimal solution. Therefore, politicians such as Chuck Schumer, who in fact may be in favor of a more comprehensive identity policing scheme, may decide that the most they will push for is a proposal to improve Social Security cards. In addition, policy experts such as Janice Kephart may decide to agree that some improvement in identity policing is better than no improvement. Despite her avid support for REAL ID, she acknowledged that a partial system in which only some states participate in REAL ID, while "not optimal," is "still going to be better than what we had before." In fact, when facing a charge from REAL ID opponents that state defections from the REAL ID

[95] Ibid.

network have already dealt a fatal blow to the law, Kephart replied, "Anytime you have two states sharing information – not to mention five or ten – that's better than no sharing."[96]

Still other policy actors exhibit concern that satisficing will not suffice, but a patchwork system can work if it is one of the security layers. Richard Barth, Assistant Secretary for Policy Development at DHS, testified before a Senate subcommittee that a state or territory "identified as being the weak-link in the chain will draw terrorists and other bad actors to its territory, resulting in less security for all of us." However, a "more stringent process in place for obtaining a driver's license will add a layer of defense in the fight against identity theft."[97]

The 114th Congress (2015–2017) did not amend the REAL ID Act. The law survives, Sensenbrenner says, "because it's not the police-state law its opponents say it is. This is one of the few issues that people who are on the left and on the right agree on. I'm on the right, and I agree with people on the left on this."[98] He may be too optimistic about the Act's ability to survive, but he is right when he talks about the law's supporters – they, too, like the opponents, are a diverse group.

In 2004, the *New York Times* argued that it is time to begin "a serious discussion on how to create a workable national identification system without infringing on the constitutional rights of Americans."[99] While no major national discussion on national ID card system and identity policing is likely to emerge in the near future, controversies over immigration, Arizona S.B.1070 and similar immigration enforcement laws, voter ID laws, and REAL ID are all likely to keep identity policing and identification documents at the forefront of developments. Whatever those developments are, one would hope that the words of late Stephen Horn (R-CA), then Chairman of the House Subcommittee that looked into national identifiers, will ring true:

> One small but important example of the Nation's strength is the ability to conduct this calm, civil but vigorous discussion of whether America needs a national identification system and, if so, how to go about creating it. Ultimately, we can trust the American people and their representatives to make the right decision.[100]

[96] Katel, "Real ID," 389.
[97] "Understanding the Realities of REAL ID," March 26, 2007, 53–54.
[98] Katel, "Real ID," 389. [99] "A National ID," Editorial, *NYT*, May 31, 2004.
[100] "Does America Need a National Identifier?," November 16, 2001.

Conclusion

The need for identity policing rises and falls with various threat levels, producing historical ebbs and flows in identity policing, yet the overall trend is toward more identity policing. Identity policing helps build state power, and states often take advantage of technological innovations, but a trend toward more identity policing does not apply evenly across countries or is met everywhere with approval. While identification documents are an enduring aspect of the modern state, obstacles like public resistance and built-in constraints make it hard for liberal democratic states to increase their identity policing efforts.

This chapter summarizes the findings about the past and present of national ID cards and identity policing in the United States. It also talks about the United Kingdom, which is another country that, just like the United States, does not currently have national ID cards. The chapter outlines the main differences in national reactions to identity policing and national ID cards between the two countries. It also briefly considers the following question: can identity policing and national ID cards be beneficial to individuals or, as often portrayed by opponents, are they just a threat to individual freedom? In addition, this chapter considers the future of identification documents and identity policing, concentrating on the biometric revolution and its costs. The chapter reviews the book's findings, outlines avenues for future research, and spells out the implications of this research for the study of liberal democratic states.

I base my comprehensive study of the political history of British and American national ID card and identity policing proposals and controversies on archival research; interviews with politicians, policymakers, and ID card technology experts; and public opinion data. The research focuses especially on crises, such as wars and terrorist attacks, which have been instrumental in bringing national ID cards to life in the United Kingdom and have played a role in inspiring national ID card proposals in the United States.

It is crucial to understand this link between wars, threats to national security (real and perceived), immigration, and national ID debates. Most of the debates on national ID cards occurred during wartime. The ones that occurred in peacetime were still linked to threats to national security and borders. Appreciating the link between wars, terrorist attacks, immigration, and national ID cards is valuable given that national security and immigration are crucial issues in the twenty-first century. This makes the possibility of a national ID card in the United States today viable, though not likely.

Studying the political history of identity policing informs our understanding of democratic political processes, governmental responses to threats, and the trade-offs between civil liberties and security. My focus is not only on national ID cards but also on constraints to adopting or enhancing national ID cards – something of particular importance in the case of the United Kingdom. My focus is also on functional equivalents of national ID cards, such as driver's licenses, new uses for older documents, and a more general patchwork of methods that liberal democratic states use to police identity – something of particular importance in the case of the United States.

The evidence presented in this book reveals that national ID cards have a complicated history in the United States. Over the last 100 years, American policymakers and members of the public made multiple proposals for national ID cards, but national ID schemes never got off the ground, though various identity policing initiatives have been and are being implemented, with varying degrees of success.

The book began by showing that the resentment toward German-Americans, Japanese-Americans, and Italian-Americans during WWI and WWII led the government to create special identification documents for these groups. Some opinion-makers feared that the government would extend registration to the entire population. In the mid-1920s, the government began to extend fingerprinting beyond the criminal population to include civilians. During WWII, policymakers and members of the public made multiple proposals for universal fingerprinting and national ID cards. Despite the public support for national ID cards for all Americans, the government did not introduce them. Yet the 1930s and 1940s saw the evolution of two basic forms of identification: driver's licenses and Social

Security cards. Many of the subsequent proposals for national ID cards have focused on utilizing driver's licenses and Social Security cards as a basis for a new scheme. In the 1970s, Frances G. Knight, the Director of the Passport Office, supported national ID cards with fingerprints, and in the 1980s, Theodore Hesburgh, the Chair of SCIRP, supported biometric ID cards. President Reagan was close to agreeing to the proposal made by his Attorney General, William French Smith, for a national ID card in 1981, but many of his advisers were critical, causing the issue to be dropped. Immigration reforms of the 1980s and 1990s kept bringing up ID cards, as some policymakers argued that the absence of a reliable ID system for verifying employee eligibility made it easy for illegal aliens to evade detection at the workplace. Some policymakers – Alan Simpson, Barbara Jordan, and Daniel Patrick Moynihan – promoted stricter identity policing. However, the lobbying of national ID card opponents – a multifaceted coalition of libertarians, civil libertarians, religious conservatives, those in big business, and privacy advocates – ensured that national ID cards were not implemented. Meanwhile, states and localities across the United States have been considering their own proposals for identification documents and increased identity policing.

In the wake of 9/11, there was a renewed interest in national ID cards and a debate about the appropriate balance between personal freedom and national security. In 2005, Congress addressed the issue of national standards for driver's licenses by passing the REAL ID Act. Since then, REAL ID has been highly contested among state legislatures, governors, and advocacy groups, who criticize it, among other things, for being an unfunded mandate. Opponents also argue that the Act will create a national ID card. Bills to repeal REAL ID have been introduced and failed multiple times. Despite this opposition, most states are implementing the law. This shows that the goal of securing identification documents and increasing identity policing is being achieved through multiple means and on multiple levels, not always along a single path. The notion of patchwork is even more evident when one considers other identity policing schemes that sprung up after 9/11: WHTI-compliant EDLs, biometric passports and passport cards, and Trusted Traveler Programs. In addition, the United States has been a forerunner in recording face and fingerprint biometrics from foreign nationals entering the country.

In the United States, as in the United Kingdom, the key obstacles to the schemes are financial, technological and practical, constitutional and legal, relating to civil liberties and individual freedoms, and stemming from public opinion and resistance. In American culture, opposition to a national identification system runs particularly deep. Many regard ID cards as a tool of oppression; some religious groups identify them with the anti-Christ; and for many they conflict with the popular myth, but declining reality, of the right to move about freely. The topic becomes truly explosive even before practical concerns over data protection and privacy come into play.

Voices of supporters of increased identity policing are heard less often than voices of their opponents, and even rarer are those calling for national ID cards. Yet that group is quite varied too, ranging from Republican politicians (James Sensenbrenner and Lamar Alexander) to Democratic ones (Chuck Schumer and Dianne Feinstein) – though only some of those politicians are comfortable using the term "national ID card" for the documents they support. In fact, Lamar Alexander is one of the few high-profile politicians who openly says that the United States needs a national ID card. Supporters of increased identity policing and national ID cards also include some corporations, police forces, and public intellectuals, such as Alan Dershowitz and Amitai Etzioni.

History shows that the United States has been ambivalent about legislating on immigration in general, and on identity policing in particular, and ambivalent about enforcing its laws. As a REAL ID policy expert told me: "Politically, [a national ID card] is not going to happen. I don't think it is something that will ever get through the political process."[1] However, while no major national discussion on identity policing is likely to emerge in the near future, controversies over immigration, Arizona S.B.1070 and similar laws, voter ID laws, and REAL ID are all likely to keep identity policing and identification documents at the forefront of developments.

In the United Kingdom, national ID cards have come and gone despite state-builders' enthusiasm for them as planning tools, and the latest ID scheme failed due to cost and efficiency concerns. Historically, British state elites played a critical role in embracing ID cards. Moments of crisis, in particular, provide decision-making points, or critical junctures, where individuals can push forward their ideas in an unsettled territory. Especially during WWI, civil servants and reformers were able to exert influence on ID card policymaking because the Cabinet was preoccupied with the more direct conduct of war. Those state-builders carefully organized the scheme and were relatively successful in implementing a large logistical project under war conditions, even though it had not been

[1] Interview with a REAL ID policy expert, March 2014.

planned before the war broke out. The public showed respect for the registration efforts, especially initially. Many people genuinely treasured their ID cards. The newspapers' attitudes ranged from criticism to die-hard support.

In WWII, the task was much greater than in WWI because everyone was to be enumerated, not just people between fifteen and sixty-five. Those administering the system secured its success by analyzing the problems of the WWI system. Institutional memory was not lost. Since it was tied not only to conscription, but also more firmly to food rationing, the WWII ID card was valuable to the public. Authorities secured compliance by appealing to self-interest. Authorities have also placed the emphasis on dissolving the effects of war, rather than on arguing that the ID card would make the United Kingdom more secure.

The WWI and WWII debates raised issues of liberty, state control, and cost, which foreshadowed post-9/11 debates. Shifting alliances and political drama marked these earlier conflicts. National ID card supporters and opponents in WWI and WWII were not split among party lines. Even those who disagreed with the principle at least argued for the method to be effective. During national mobilization, and when state resources were at stake, opponents of the national ID scheme were not trying to sabotage it.

Seeing the success of ID cards during WWII, some British officials wished to see the system continue after the war. However, not all officials were keen on a peacetime national ID card. Even the Home Office argued that the public would not support it. During WWII, press reaction against ID cards was muted, but from 1945, the press asserted that national ID cards were a wartime necessity and not acceptable in peacetime. In 1952, the Conservative government scrapped ID cards entirely.

Since the 1980s, both the Conservatives and Labour have, on occasion, advocated for national ID cards. In the aftermath of 9/11, Home Secretary David Blunkett revived a proposal for national ID cards. It was only initially that the Labour government presented the idea as a way of combatting terrorism. As time went by, the government started portraying ID cards as way to combat benefit fraud and employment of illegal immigrants.

After a few turbulent years of parliamentary debates, political wrangling, and press scrutiny, the Identity Cards Act became law in March 2006. The National Identity Scheme was to affect all those over the age of sixteen residing in the United Kingdom for more than three months. The United Kingdom started issuing ID cards for some foreign nationals in 2008 and for some British citizens in 2009.

One of the most controversial issues was the cost of the scheme, both to the budget and to individual cardholders. Government-provided estimates differed wildly and changed often. Some groups campaigning against ID cards focused on pragmatic and technical arguments. Other groups focused on principled arguments. Some groups were keen to disrupt the scheme, within the law. And some Conservative politicians even attempted to sabotage the government project.

The Conservatives and the Liberal Democrats viewed the ID database as intrusive and costly. They defeated Labour at the polls in May 2010, and the new government immediately announced it would scrap ID cards. Commentators saw it as fitting that the coalition's first bill involved the repeal of ID cards, a measure that is emblematic of the Labour government's time in office. National ID cards became invalid in January 2011.

The story of the National Identity Scheme is a perplexing one. Despite widespread realization in industry and academia that any large-scale scheme would likely face problems, "the government presented its proposals using the language of technological certainty."[2] In addition, it did not disclose some key information about the scheme. Yet it would be unfair to argue that it was hiding its rationale for the increased emphasis on identity policing, even as, over the years, it went through distinctive justifications for introducing ID cards. The shifts in publicly articulated motivations are a possible sign of the genuine belief by Labour politicians that ID cards could address multiple problems. They are also a possible sign that government discourse is responsive to challenges and incorporates arguments being made against ID cards.

British authorities during WWI and WWII organized their schemes carefully, but they were also divided on the best way to proceed and were not ready to push forward their state-building activities at any cost. In contrast, the most recent scheme was more sophisticated but less carefully designed, and its proponents were determined to push it forward even in light of problems and opposition.

The cases of the United States and the United Kingdom may indicate that in countries that have not had national ID cards in peacetime, such documents can be accepted in wartime, and perhaps only in wartime. Still, such a conclusion can be drawn only about the United Kingdom, and not about the United States, where neither WWI nor WWII saw an introduction of national ID cards for US citizens. In both countries, ID

[2] Whitley and Hosein, *Global Challenges*, 217.

cards for foreign citizens were more readily accepted. In peacetime, in both countries, countervailing pressures, contesting priorities, and other obstacles and costs heavily restrict the expansion of identity policing. Nonetheless, it would be erroneous to assume that the dangers from terrorism and illegal immigration are not strong enough to persuade policymakers and the public that identity policing is warranted. Despite common misconceptions that national ID cards are universally opposed in both the United Kingdom and the United States, part of the public opinion in both countries as well as some policymakers (more in the United Kingdom than in the United States) are in favor of introducing national ID cards or enhancing identity policing. Those who have doubts tend to be worried about the costs and effectiveness of identity policing. Outright opposition tends to come from those opposed on ideological grounds.

In the United States, the conventional wisdom is that the American people and policymakers are staunchly opposed to national ID cards and that American policymakers never propose national ID cards, but the historical evidence I examined revealed a more complicated story. I showed that policymakers and the public often support the proposals for introducing national ID cards and for improving existing identification documents. This is particularly the case in times of war, when the country is under attack, or when it is experiencing a crisis. Passionate opposition to national ID cards has been and remains present in the United States, but many policymakers and members of the public see national ID cards more positively than conventional wisdom would let us believe.

This book shows that popular support for national ID cards has been significant over the last 100 years. It also shows that when American policymakers were confronted with the need to strengthen identification, a number of individual policymakers did propose national ID cards. However, the proposals did not get very far. This is in contrast to pretty much every other nation in the world, including the United Kingdom, which during national crises first created and then repealed national ID cards.

British policymakers and the public often embrace proposals for national ID cards and, if introduced, the cards themselves, especially in times of war, when under attack or experiencing a crisis, even if the cards eventually get repealed. As in the United States, passionate opposition to national ID cards has been and remains present in the United Kingdom, but many Brits see national ID cards more positively than conventional wisdom would let us believe.

There are, however, also differences between the United States and the United Kingdom. In the United Kingdom, there is a tendency to address issues of identity policing through a single, centralized system, comprehensively built from scratch. The United Kingdom introduced such ID card systems on three separate occasions. In the United States, in contrast, identity policing measures tend to be adopted ad hoc, sometimes locally, and sometimes only for targeted segments of the population. There, as elsewhere in the world, many identification systems were at first partial, designed to control specific segments of the population, suspicious to the state and potentially beyond its reach. In the United States, the policymaking process has been piecemeal and has taken place over different stages, creating a patchwork of identity policing measures.

In both countries, proponents of contemporary identity policing schemes tend to emphasize prevention of terrorism and illegal immigration as the rationale for the schemes. Proponents also emphasize employment verification and crime and fraud prevention. But only Brits place emphasis on convenience and enabling access to entitlements, public services, and e-government. Hence, the argument that terrorism and illegal immigration are the primary drivers of ID policies, while crime and fraud prevention, e-government, convenience, and establishing employment verification and access to entitlements are specific selling points and desired outcomes of these policies, seems to hold truer for the United Kingdom than the United States.

Another difference concerns what the American and British opponents of national ID cards and identity policing primarily focus on in their opposition. There are two types of concerns about national ID cards and identity policing: pragmatic concerns (cost, efficiency, data security) and principled (often ideological) opposition. People who oppose national ID cards may do so because of pragmatic concerns, principled opposition, or both. Some people without the experience of ID cards and databases may initially support them, only to decrease their support as they learn about practical concerns, yet they may not develop any principled opposition. Others may oppose ID cards and databases only on principled grounds.

In both countries, there is a large opposition to the high financial costs of identity policing schemes. However, the relative emphasis opponents place on other issues differs. In the United States, national ID cards tend to be perceived as profoundly altering the established balance between freedom and control. There is great concern about the constitutionality of identity policing and anything that resembles a national ID card, the growing powers of the federal government, and the impact any such scheme would have on civil liberties. Opponents worry that national ID cards would lead to increased ethnic profiling and racial discrimination. In the United Kingdom, issues of constitutionality and government powers are less pronounced, and while civil liberties are important, it is striking that the possibility of increased ethnic profiling does not feature prominently in the British discourse. Instead, opposition to national ID policies is primarily based on their costs and perceived ineffectiveness. There are also substantial concerns about the security of centralized databases, especially given the poor data safety record of contemporary British governments. Practical issues tend to feature more in British than in American opposition. This can be partially explained by the fact that in the United Kingdom national ID card schemes have actually been implemented, whereas in the United States they have never advanced beyond proposal stage, although the ongoing implementation of REAL ID and other identity policing measures is likely to bring practical issues to the front.

There is a striking difference between the two countries in the way British opponents frequently use humor to discredit ID cards, but the American opponents have a more serious attitude. In the United Kingdom, the use of mocking ranged from the occasional ridiculing of ID cards in newspapers in WWI, the lampooning of identity papers in film *Passport to Pimlico* (1949), to the use of parody in the case of the latest scheme. In the United States, in contrast, the attitude of those opposing identity policing has always been more serious. This could perhaps be because in the United States some of the opposition to enumeration is religion-based, hence increasing the sensitive nature of the topic. Other than the rare article by playwright Arthur Miller ridiculing national ID cards or the one-off remark by Reagan advisor Martin Anderson in a meeting with the president, few American opponents of identity policing have chosen to discredit national ID schemes with the use of humor.

In the myriad of reasons why many Americans and Brits oppose identity policing, one argument is often brought up with respect to Americans, but not with respect to the British. This is the argument that Americans have always reserved the right to reinvent themselves. Novelist Walter Kirn characterized it best:

> The cult of unending self-improvement, our informal national religion, takes as its primary article of faith the idea that who a person was yesterday or happens to be

today doesn't determine who he'll be tomorrow ... In America to be ID'd – sorted, tagged, and permanently filed – is to lose a bit of one's soul. To die a little.[3]

But if Americans have always reserved the right to reinvent themselves, why do they consistently support national ID cards in opinion polls? Cultural explanations for policy outcomes are attractive, but they are also ad hoc, and in this case they run up against the polling data that I assembled. Moreover, it seems just as likely that the lack of an existing (and well-managed) national ID card system might be influencing cultural attitudes toward national ID cards. Policies often create political culture and that is very likely the case here.

The attitudes toward national ID cards in the United States and the United Kingdom stand in contrast not only to each other, but also to other countries where identity policing is nowhere near as controversial, and where identification documents are ubiquitous and rarely given a second thought. Even countries where national ID cards were first introduced in nondemocratic ways have long come to support them. Despite Nazi, communist, or socialist origins, national ID cards in Germany, Poland, Italy, and Spain are accepted by contemporary societies. It is debatable, and would deserve a separate study, whether national ID cards in these countries became customary only through usage or because of genuine public support. What is clear is that in these countries national ID cards became part of the political culture in a different era. Somewhat counterintuitively, however, this has probably only enabled their steady transition from simple paper documents to laminated ones to plastic cards, which are now machine-readable, RFID-enabled, and biometric, and connected to sophisticated databases, which concern many people more than the cards themselves.

Overall, it seems that those who live in countries with national ID cards see no problem with them, and those who do not are most dubious. An international survey in 2006 showed that 78 percent of respondents in France, 77 percent in China, 53 percent in Canada (62 percent in Quebec), and 42 percent in the United States agreed that everyone should have a government-issued ID card that they must carry at all times.[4] It is important to note that the figure for the United States in this international survey is much lower than the figures in the domestic polls quoted in this book.

[3] Walter Kirn, "The Mother of Reinvention," *Atlantic Monthly*, May 2002.

[4] David Lyon, "National ID Card Systems and Social Sorting," in *Surveillance, Privacy, and the Globalization of Personal Information*, ed. Elia Zureik, L. Lynda Harling Stalker, Emily Smith, David Lyon, and Yolande E. Chan (Montreal; Ithaca: McGill-Queen's University Press, 2010).

Even in countries where the society in general accepts identification documents, people may have different reasons for carrying the documents. Some may carry IDs with pride, others with indifference, and yet others with fear, depending on the political conditions. The same attitudes may apply to the databases. In the 1930s, Nazi Germany used IBM technical infrastructure on census materials to enable identification during the Holocaust, and IBM had a role in supplying the passbook computer infrastructure in South Africa from 1953 onward.[5] But the same technology was also used in the United States for nonsinister purposes: for the census since the 1890s and for the administration of the Social Security Act since 1935.[6]

Many Americans genuinely worry that identity policing and national ID cards may infringe on individual liberties. They associate national ID cards with totalitarianism and worry that in the conflict between national security and individual liberties, the latter will lose. Although in some countries national ID cards had origins in totalitarian regimes, their contemporary societies accept identity policing measures. While opponents of national ID cards see them as a major threat to individual freedom, identity policing and national ID cards do not have to be inherently dangerous and can, in fact, be beneficial to individuals. Just because ID cards and an interconnected network of searchable databases can facilitate the tracking down of minute details of personal life does not mean that they will do so, or that if they do that these will necessarily have a negative impact on the individual.[7] We have to remember that individual identification procedures can ease mobility and communication as well as control these activities; and they enhance public security at the same time as they expose everyone to the "dispassionate eye of official surveillance."[8]

While some authors believe all enumeration and ID documents are inherently evil,[9] the use and abuse of ID cards as a tool for ethnic cleansing has been a rare exception. ID cards may have enabled the carrying out of some atrocities, but they have not caused them. Historian Simon Szreter argues that all tools can be used for both positive and negative

[5] Lyon, *Identifying Citizens*, 3, 25.

[6] Sybil Milton, "Registering Civilians and Aliens in the Second World War," *Jewish History* 11, 2 (fall 1997): 84.

[7] Lyon, *Surveillance Studies*, 10. [8] Caplan and Torpey, "Introduction," 6.

[9] Watner and McElroy, eds., *National Identification Systems*.

purposes, and the more powerful and important the tool, the greater its potential impact. He states:

> The fact that the Nazi regime tragically was able to exploit the national identity information system of Holland to locate Jews ... does not mean that an identity registration system is so intrinsically dangerous that it should not be constructed – any more than the Nazis' use of Europe's rail system to expedite the Jews in large numbers to their fates means that railway technology is an intrinsically sinister threat.[10]

Opposition to ID cards today should not be based on the fact that ID cards were used by the Nazis. In the United Kingdom, it was cost and ineffectiveness, rather than a fear of ethnic persecution, that caused the latest ID program to be scrapped. Democratic states can and do make use of ID documents and identity policing without deteriorating into totalitarian states.

Groups that wish to strengthen their sense of national identity – in Palestine or Quebec – welcome markers such as ID cards. For people affected by the Israeli-Palestinian conflict the forms of legal identification they hold are central to their life chances. In Palestine, holding an ID is the prerequisite for a work permit in Israel, thus people long for a card and make considerable efforts to accumulate documents for political and economic advantage.[11]

Some advocates argue that in certain countries ID cards are vital for upholding human rights. Szreter points out that although identity registration at birth is a human right proclaimed by the United Nations, it is not available in many poor countries. This is a major development obstacle. Szreter adds that identity registration systems must be created principally for the liberty and the use of individuals, and not to serve the purposes of states or companies.[12] Sonia Pierre, human rights activist working on behalf of Haitians in the Dominican Republic, argues simply: "Fundamentally, for us, having an ID card is the beginning of the right to have rights."[13]

Philosopher Charles Taylor argues that identification and recognition are inevitably conjoined in the modern world and are the prerequisite for

[10] Simon Szreter, "The Right of Registration: Development, Identity Registration and Social Security – An Historical Perspective," *World Development* 35, 1 (January 2007): 80.

[11] Tobias Kelly, "Documented Lives: Fear and the Uncertainties of Law during the Second Palestinian *Intifada*," *Journal of the Royal Anthropological Institute* 11, 1 (2006): 89.

[12] Szreter, "The Right of Registration," 81.

[13] PBS NewsHour, December 17, 2010. www.pbs.org/newshour/bb/international-july-dec10-haiti_12-17/.

individual and collective claims against the state.[14] It is often in the interest of the individual to be recognized: individuals cannot expect government protection if they cannot prove, through the system of identification, that they are affiliated to the given community. National communities may be imagined but are also dependent on codified ID documents.[15] ID documents have beneficial functions for the state, but they also have beneficial functions for the holder.

We should not discount the possibility that democratic states may be able to develop ID systems that are fair, efficient, and secure – and that take the interests of the cardholder, not the system operator, to be paramount. Regardless of whether such systems are possible or not, the way citizen registration is conducted and identity policing is debated are important indicators of the health of a given democracy. The challenge is to establish systems that enforce rigorous safeguards and avoid exclusionary bias, and in which accountability for handling personal data is paramount. There should be mechanisms for monitoring the voracious appetite for data exhibited by policymakers and system administrators. Lyon warns that the driving force behind the adoption of many ID systems is not the notion of "risk" but "precaution." This leads to preemptive action (garnering data "just in case"), which can harm civil liberties.[16]

Problems with identity policing existed in the past, but have been augmented in the world of biometrics. Although biometric technologies were being developed before 9/11, it was the last decade that brought them into the forefront of developments. The industry is booming, though projections for growth, and estimates of the current market size, vary widely. The global biometrics market was estimated at $10.3 billion in 2014 and is projected to reach $30 billion by 2020.[17] Just the government portion of the market (concerned primarily with e-passports and

[14] Charles Taylor, *Sources of the Self: The Making of Modern Identity* (Cambridge, MA: Harvard University Press, 1989).

[15] Benedict Anderson, *Imagined Communities: Reflections on the Origin and Spread of Nationalism* (London; New York: Verso, 1991); David Lyon, "The Border Is Everywhere: ID Cards, Surveillance and the Other," in *Global Surveillance and Policing: Borders, Security and Identity*, ed. Elia Zureik and Mark B. Salter (Portland, OR: Willan Publishing, 2005), 74.

[16] Lyon, *Identifying Citizens*, 46, 56–57, 59–61.

[17] "Biometrics – A Global Market Overview," January 2015, www.researchandmarkets.com/research/5dqltd/biometrics_a.

national ID cards) was estimated at $3.6 billion in 2014 and is projected to reach $6.9 billion by 2024.[18]

In law enforcement, commerce, and employment, identification is increasingly associated with biometrics. Many policymakers see biometrics as the silver bullet, the ultimate solution to a range of problems. Despite shortcomings in biometric technologies, there is great confidence in biometric products on the part of corporations and governments. British Home Secretary David Blunkett claimed that biometrics would make identity theft and multiple identities not nearly impossible but actually impossible,[19] and others have argued that biometric ID cards could be made foolproof. Yet studies show that such confidence depends on high rates of success in isolated trials rather than in practice. Most of the trials have had limited profiles ("frequent travelers" who are typically white males) and carefully arranged setups (controlled lighting).[20] It is not clear that such studies will be applicable to the more heterogeneous population. In fact, biometrics systems as currently calibrated might privilege whiteness. Because of reliance on bodily characteristics, biometric systems need to be refined so that they do not marginalize those whose lives are already marginalized in society by color or ethnicity.[21]

In addition, just as older identification technologies have been erroneous, for instance, by making spurious matches due to data-input errors or failure to update records, the biometric ones have yet to be refined to a point where they can be said to have proved their reliability. Even industry experts I interviewed admit that "biometrics as a technology is just starting off . . . there's a long way to go from a technology perspective."[22] Biometric ID systems are neither entirely beneficial nor fully sinister, but to utilize them to the citizens' best advantage, the policymakers and the public need to be aware of the good, the bad, and the ugly that comes with the territory.

However reliable modern identification technologies and biometrics are, and however effective they are in dealing with problems of terrorism,

18 Zack Martin, "Report: Biometric Market Worth almost 7 Billion by 2024," January 21, 2014, www.secureidnews.com/news-item/report-biometric-market-worth-almost-7-billion-by-2024/.

19 "Mission Impossible?," November 11, 2003, www.theregister.co.uk/2003/11/11/mission_impossible_blunketts_big_biometric/.

20 Whitley and Hosein, *Global Challenges*, 148.

21 Lyon, *Identifying Citizens*, 119, 129, 154.

22 Interview with a senior director at one of the strategic suppliers of the British national ID scheme, London, September 2009.

illegal immigration, and identity fraud (and the jury is still out on issues of reliability and effectiveness), the use of modern identification technologies and biometrics introduces a whole new set of problems. Unfortunately, policymakers' keenness to find new solutions has not been matched with the knowledge of technological issues involved. In addition, policymakers often lack the foresight into the types of social problems that may result. After all, the fast-moving scientific landscapes alter not only the nature of available technologies, but also the nature of the problems that the identity policies are trying to solve.

The politics of identification documents can be just as fierce as the politics of taxation, according to scholars Edgar Whitley and Gus Hosein. Both types of policies call on political ideologues to question the very foundations of the relationship between the individual and the state. However, unlike with taxation, few policymakers have an idea about legislating policies on identification documents. Many do not understand the complexity of the problem or appreciate the alternative solutions. The policy processes need to incorporate fast-moving scientific landscapes that alter not only the nature of available technologies, but also the nature of the problems that the policies are hoping to solve.[23]

Both in the United States and in the United Kingdom, identity policing has been, is, and will be – at least in the foreseeable future – a controversial issue, and one that does not easily sit along the same fault lines as other issues with which people are more accustomed to deal. One high-level policymaker told me:

> It's not a simple left-right view . . . If there is a dividing line in modern public policy on [information technology and identity cards], it is between libertarians and totalitarians on how to use technology; it is not between Luddites and modernists. [It is about freeing up data and using it in a progressive way versus using it in a more sinister way.][24]

In the United States, in particular, the policy discourse on identity policing and national ID cards is one of the rare political debates that transcends the political divisions between the left and the right on the political spectrum. There are even actors from both sides of the political spectrum becoming "strange bedfellows" in the process.

[23] Whitley and Hosein, *Global Challenges*, 5.

[24] Interview with a high-ranking member of the Conservative Party, London, September 2009.

At the same time as identity policing does not fit neatly into a simple left-right view of politics, the issue of identity policing is very much about politics. A senior director at one of the strategic suppliers of the British national ID scheme told me:

> It's just politics. The whole [UK National Identity] Scheme, and everything, has been driven by politics. This is about Home Office gaining control ... They don't really care about the plastic document. It's the database they are interested in. It's what they've always been interested in, but they've sugarcoated it with those citizenship benefits.[25]

Historically, the fear of authorities has played a significant role in the resistance of some people to the carrying of ID cards. For many, though, it has been a matter of principle. In the United Kingdom, the best-known case is that of Harry Willcock, who refused to produce an identity card when stopped by police for speeding in 1950. Willcock, a parliamentary candidate, planned to get himself prosecuted for not producing an identity card, to launch a cause célèbre. In the United States, Dudley Hiibel, a rancher from Nevada, refused to identify himself to a police officer during a justified investigative stop in 2000. Both Willcock and Hiibel were defending a point of principle, the right to tell a police officer to back off. Both had their cases considered by the courts, eventually reaching the High Court in the United Kingdom and the Supreme Court in the United States, respectively. Those courts ruled against Willcock and Hiibel, though in the Willcock case, the court gave him a kind of moral victory.

Interestingly, there have not been other high profile cases like these two, so perhaps the opposition in the general public is not as strong. But opposition, and even hostility, exists. Michael Froomkin suggests that the American hostility to national ID cards is based on a romantic vision of free movement, and the English hostility is tied to a concept of the rights of Englishmen. These views distract from the real issues raised by contemporary ID plans, which "have little to do with romantic stories of cowboys and motorists talking back to policemen, and a great deal to do with data storage and access."[26]

However, the more practical issues matter too. In both countries, the financial costs of identity policing measures have been a significant point of opposition. In the United States, states oppose the REAL ID because they see

[25] Interview with a senior director at one of the strategic suppliers of the British national ID scheme, September 2009.

[26] Froomkin, "Identity Cards," 245.

it as an unfunded mandate. The British debate has been focused on the increasingly large cost estimates. A senior director at one of the strategic suppliers of the British scheme told me that Liberty and NO2ID, two groups that were opposed to the 2006 Identity Cards Act, based their argument

> on the infringement on civil liberties, and ... that line of argument had very little impact. The whole business case cost justification [which was the argument of scholars from the London School of Economics] has had bigger impact. The climate – jobs being lost, budget cutbacks – means every budget is scrutinized ... that's had more effect on the design of the scheme.[27]

In fact, even while the IT industry favored the scheme, some key industry players were voicing concerns about the cost and shape of the scheme. The same senior director stated:

> for a citizen to voluntarily enroll and to carry an ID card, they have to have a derived benefit from what they are paying to receive a card and have a benefit of using it but the card itself, the technical design of it, was dumbed down ... [now it has] no more value than a business card.[28]

It is unclear whether the future of identity documents will be that of mere (but expensive) business cards. At worst, national ID cards can be tools of discrimination. At best, they can be tools for fostering fulfilled human life. Their impact will be determined in part by how policymakers and the public approach identity policing. The signs are both encouraging and discouraging.

On the one hand, some people around the world have successfully mobilized to thwart the identity policing schemes they have considered undesirable. In Australia, organized opposition stopped national ID schemes on two occasions. In 1985, the government proposed the Australia Card, and in 1986, the public opposition helped defeat it. In 2007, the Access Card, a multipurpose identifier that appeared to its opponents as a backdoor national ID, became the focus of bitter political wrangling and was ultimately shelved. Worldwide, activists and scholars have been providing criticisms to proposed schemes and suggesting alternatives. In the United Kingdom, a well-publicized 2005 report from the London School of Economics made constructive suggestions on how an ID card system can be set up in less contentious and more secure ways than the one legislated.[29]

[27] Interview with a senior director at one of the strategic suppliers of the British national ID scheme, September 2009.

[28] Ibid. [29] Lyon, *Identifying Citizens*, 149–150.

On the other hand, many debates have been based on simplistic and false arguments, and with little willingness to hear the other side of the story, something of which the governments, experts, the press, and the public have been guilty. Equally concerning have been the signs that the debate is being stifled by those who disagree with their opponents. In the United Kingdom, London School of Economics researchers, vocal in their opposition to the ID card scheme, have been subject to personal and professional verbal attacks by members of the government. In the United States, supporters of national ID card schemes have been under attack. Public intellectual Amitai Etzioni points out that national ID cards are so alien to Americans that they are "not considered fit for discussion. As a rule, think tanks do not study them, nor are they subject of public policy debates. A few advocates of ID cards have faced such strong criticism that they stopped speaking and writing about their merits." He argues that there exists a "chilling effect" whereby national ID cards have not been seriously examined as a public policy because those who have studied them, and the very few who have considered advocating their merits, know that doing so would arouse considerable criticism.[30] In 2002, the ACLU, the Free Congress Foundation, and dozens of other liberal and conservative groups took aim at a proposal to link the driver databases of individual states. In a letter to President Bush, the groups said the "administration should not take any steps to implement such a system or fund any proposals that would result in a national ID, *including the study* or development of standardized state driver's licenses."[31] While the objections to a proposal are understandable, any call for a ban on research and study of a social issue and policy is worrying. Governmental studies and commissions do, of course, often face criticism – British Prime Minister Harold Wilson once famously observed that commissions are bodies that take minutes but sit for years – but they can perform a valuable service, enabling a qualified body to examine an issue in detail and in public.

Froomkin argues that in the United States, "we are fated to have a national debate on ID cards if we are lucky; if we're unlucky we'll dispense with the debate and go straight to the cards and the databases." He makes a cautious and uneasy argument, that "once one gets past a certain visceral revulsion, the marginal harms caused by a national ID

[30] Etzioni, *The Limits of Privacy*, 103, 123–124.

[31] Amitai Etzioni, "It's Not Just a Driver's License Anymore," *Washington Post*, May 16, 2004. Emphasis added.

system are fewer than one might initially believe given the deteriorating state of personal privacy in the face of invasive technology." Ironically, though, Froomkin points out that the political justification for national ID cards is likely to be their supposed virtues as an antiterrorism measure, although the cards' true merits probably lie elsewhere.[32]

Overall, it is possible that a fruitful debate on identity policing will take place in the future in both the United States and the United Kingdom, and elsewhere in the world, and that democratic states will find ways to address problems of terrorism and illegal immigration – whether or not the solutions will involve identity policing. One of my interviewees said the following about the British scheme:

> Because there is no history of precedents and of what has worked or hasn't worked, it's almost like an open discussion forum for people to have a debate; there's been an awful lot of discussion, and there's been an awful lot of criticism.[33]

Opportunity for debate should be good news from the point of view of citizens and policymakers. An informed conversation is especially important when the issue at stake is so closely related to the latest technology. Technology can be a lever and a force multiplier in any process, but when it is a biometric one and has the potential to affect human beings, it should always be made subordinate to both democratic policy processes and protective measures.

Importantly, as with any other issue, the future of identity policing will be influenced by its past. What happens in the past influences the range of possibilities for the future, and structures the subsequent debate. One British policymaker told me: "I am sure ... that every single Home Secretary coming in gets a little dossier [from the civil servants] marked 'Identity cards' and up until now most incoming ministers have pushed it back, and obviously the Labour government [has not]." More importantly, the policymaker added:

> [Very often] a governing party does something because of path dependency. They've gone down routes, they've invested so much political capital, they can't quite do a U-turn because they are so committed. It does happen in politics ... and sometimes U-turns are a good thing ... ID cards are a good example [of a policy where] they've dropped so many things but are ploughing on regardless.[34]

32 A. Michael Froomkin, "The Uneasy Case for National ID Cards," unpublished paper, March 2004, 1, 3, 57.
33 Interview with a senior director at one of the strategic suppliers of the British national ID scheme, September 2009.
34 Interview with a high-ranking member of the Conservative Party, September 2009.

An article on ID cards in *The Economist* expressed a similar sentiment in a headline: "Ploughing On: Forcing through a Divisive Plan Is Judged Less Damaging Than Dropping It."[35]

In this case, it was the Labour Party politicians who decided to continue with the ID scheme in 2009. Still, the new government scrapped the scheme just a year later.

During the last 100 years, policymakers on both sides of the aisle in the United States and the United Kingdom have been making decisions regarding whether to introduce identity policing schemes, to continue, to scrap, or to enhance already existing ones. Some of these decisions may have been harder than others, for as political scientists and policymakers are well aware, once policies, schemes, and infrastructures become established, path dependency kicks in, with self-reinforcing mechanisms often preventing change. Once a policy is initialized, unless it is carefully designed, it is increasingly difficult to make changes to it. This is mainly so since "new policies create a new politics."[36] The policy generates new political institutions with practices and resources of their own, strengthening the policy and being strengthened by it. The cycle continues, as the policy provides actors with new capacities and generates new pressures from the public, thus influencing the range of possibilities in later rounds of policymaking, and so the "policy feedback" continues.[37] If rooted deeply enough, the policy and its attendant politics will outlast the circumstances that brought it into being and will take on a life and trajectory of its own – perhaps for generations.[38]

In American politics, in particular, the legislative process is fraught with veto points, making policy revisions difficult. In this system, characterized as "separated institutions sharing powers," there is probably no area of public policy where an authoritative decision can be made by a single institution. In addition, federalism requires that many actors agree on a policy action, and hence has been criticized for inhibiting change. Since state and federal governments are not monolithic, but are only

[35] "Ploughing On: Forcing through a Divisive Plan Is Judged Less Damaging Than Dropping It," *The Economist*, May 7, 2009.

[36] E. E. Schattschneider, *Politics, Pressures and the Tariff* (New York: Prentice-Hall, 1935), 288.

[37] Paul Pierson, "When Effect Becomes Cause: Policy Feedback and Political Change," *World Politics* 45, 4 (1993).

[38] Jennifer L. Hochschild, "International Migration at a Crossroads: Will Demography Change Politics before Politics Impedes Demographic Change?," Harvard University, June 2010.

the executors of the desires of a collection of diverse interests, each government pursues multiple, and often competing, objectives.[39] Consequently, conflicts abound. For example, while REAL ID licenses cannot be issued to illegal immigrants, states can still issue them licenses that are not REAL ID–compliant. That federal law allows such flexibility is a testament to the respect it has for states' rights, but also to the conflicting nature of the political, social, and economic priorities the United States faces. One of the paradoxes of American politics is that many US citizens and policymakers recognize that illegal immigrants broke US laws to be here, and many continue to break additional laws while here, but many are also valuable members of their communities and are vital to the economy. Therefore, policymakers alternate in creating proposals to deal with this situation, and the result is a patchwork of regulations with often conflicting provisions. The satisficing that takes place in identity policing is evident in the way some policymakers approach identity policies: settling for a satisfactory, rather than an optimal solution. The patchwork-like nature of identity policing in the United States is partially the result of federalism.

Federalism may well inhibit coordination of policies, but its multiple venues do not prohibit change by any means. States often serve as laboratories of democracy as they move ahead to solve problems that are not being solved at the federal level. Federalism and separation of powers add dynamism to policymaking and can be opportunities for change as much as inhibitors of change.[40] Still, often only an exogenous shock – a war or a social or economic crisis – can stimulate a policy revision or innovation.

Historical institutionalist literature teaches us that much institutional development is characterized by relatively long periods of path-dependent institutional stability and reproduction and is occasionally punctuated by brief phases of institutional flux, critical junctures, during which more dramatic change is possible. These choices close off alternative options and lead to the establishment of institutions that generate self-reinforcing path-dependent processes.[41] Paul Pierson argues that junctures are

[39] While this is true in the United States because of separation of powers, arguably, the British government *is* monolithic, or at least close to it, because of the Westminster system.

[40] Frank R. Baumgartner and Bryan D. Jones, *Agendas and Instability in American Politics* (Chicago: University of Chicago Press, 1993), 239–240.

[41] Capoccia and Kelemen, "The Study of Critical Junctures," 341.

"critical" because they place institutional arrangements on paths or trajectories, which are then very difficult to alter.[42]

Critical junctures are rare events: the normal state of an institution is either one of stability or one of constrained, adaptive change. Many scholars define critical junctures based on their outcome, namely, change. Tempting as it is to equate critical junctures and change, change is not a necessary element of a critical juncture. If an institution enters a critical juncture, in which several options are possible, the outcome may involve the restoration of the pre–critical juncture status quo. If change was possible, if it was considered, and was ultimately rejected, then there is no reason to discard these cases as "noncritical" junctures.[43]

Path dependence does not simply mean that "history matters." This is both true and trivial, according to political scientist Margaret Levi. Path dependence means that once a country has started down a track, the costs of reversal are high. A better metaphor may be a tree, not a path: while it is possible to turn around, the branch on which a climber begins is the one they tend to follow.[44]

However, paths can and do get changed, sometimes when we do not expect the changes, and sometimes for reasons we do not expect. The United Kingdom provides a good example: there, national ID cards have been introduced three times over the last 100 years, and they have been scrapped three times. In the last instance, it did seem for a while that the program would continue. In fact, this was an assumption as this research was initially taking its shape. But it was not an entirely misguided one, for it is possible that despite the opposition to the scheme, subsequent governments would have continued with the scheme, had it not been for the economic crisis. In interviews, conducted primarily in 2009, those involved with the program have often argued that the scheme's descaling or death would be "fundamentally as a consequence of the financial pressures and the economic climate ... It all has to do with budgets."[45]

In fact, the issue of costs is of key importance for analyzing path-dependent processes. Costs include the nonrecurring cost of the initial

[42] Pierson, *Politics in Time*, 135.

[43] Capoccia and Kelemen, "The Study of Critical Junctures," 352, 368.

[44] Margaret Levi, "A Model, a Method, and a Map: Rational Choice in Comparative and Historical Analysis," in *Comparative Politics: Rationality, Culture, and Structure*, ed. Mark Irving Lichbach and Alan S. Zuckerman (New York: Cambridge University Press, 1997).

[45] Interview with a senior director at one of the strategic suppliers of the British national ID scheme, September 2009.

investment associated with setting up a project (start-up costs) and maintenance costs that contribute to the creation of economies of scale and lead to increasing returns. In particular, it is the start-up costs that help determine the path a project will take. When organizers incur financial and social costs early on, it is difficult to justify a change later on, partly because of the costs already incurred and partly because of the costs that would have to be incurred to facilitate the transition and to implement the alternative project. It is thus easier to stay on the path already chosen. Large set-up costs are particularly critical. If initial costs are a high proportion of total expenses, there are likely to be increasing returns to further investment, providing individuals with a strong incentive to stick with a single option. Decisions generate sunk costs; they create commitments. By accelerating the momentum behind one policy path, they render previously viable alternatives implausible. The result is often not conflict over the foregone alternative, but the absence of conflict. "Lock-in" leads to "nondecisions."[46]

When the initial investment is insufficient, resulting in poor quality of the project, additional costs are needed to improve the project already in place. Often, a "Concorde Fallacy" is the result: costs are being incurred even after it becomes apparent that there is no longer an economic case for the project. It is simply a case of throwing good money after bad, but the project continues.

Alternatively, when an institution can maintain itself at low cost, the uncertainty and costs of transformation are too great for there to be a large lobby for change. Only when the costs of maintaining the institution increase, the uncertainty of change decreases, or enforcing the status quo becomes prohibitively expensive will actors have an incentive to change.[47]

Human resistance to change and the complex organizational changes required to support a new standard also impede adjustments. Since people tend to be risk averse, they often choose to maintain the known costs of the current configuration rather than encounter the unknown risks. This is so unless – and even sometimes when – the status quo becomes clearly indefensible. Often, policies begin with a choice that makes sense at a particular time, but survive despite the eclipse of the justification for that choice, because once established, external factors discourage other options. Given the sticky nature of institutions, only exogenous shocks

[46] Pierson, "When Effect Becomes Cause," 607–610.

[47] Helen Williams, "Towards a Coherent Theoretical Framework of New Institutionalism: Explaining Institutional Stability and Change," unpublished paper, 2011.

tend to be strong enough to create critical junctures, opening a window for actors to embark on an alternative path. Only emergencies induce significant new investments.

All the above applies both when a country already has a national ID card and when it does not. In the first case, the existence of a national ID card creates a strong policy on identification documents, powerful attendant politics, entrenched institutions, and interests. The longer the country has national ID cards, the harder it is to abandon them. In the second case, not having a national ID card also becomes a kind of policy on identification documents – whether the choice was consciously made or not. When a country functions without national ID cards, it relies on other identity policing measures (such as driver's licenses) and powerful lobbies form around these other measures, preventing change. It takes strong new threats, new expertise, changing interest group coalitions, and changing institutional opportunities and constraints to help drive the demise of older policies and the creation of new ones. Especially in the American system, which was designed with a formidable set of veto points to frustrate major policy departures, those rare moments in which new political and policy orders are founded often require the convergence of several forces at once.[48] All of this helps to explain why there have been some successful efforts in the United States to strengthen existing systems of identification, though often in the form of half-measures, but no national ID card.

Political scientist Graham Wilson argues that institutions change and yield when there is sufficient political will. When the United States has set its mind on a goal (winning WWII, putting a man on the moon), it has found the revenue and ways to do so.[49] But it would be unwise to assign too much weight to the argument that the United States lacks the political will to introduce a national ID card, let alone argue that this argument is more convincing than the argument that institutions get in the way. As I explained, path dependency raises the cost of changing paths, and institutional arrangements with many veto points can make policy change difficult. But the biggest challenge comes from trying to define what "political will" even means. Often equated with the determination of political actors to achieve some desired outcome, the term is a kind of

[48] Tichenor, *Dividing Lines*, 294.

[49] Graham K. Wilson, *Only in America? The Politics of the United States in Comparative Perspective* (Chatham, NJ: Chatham House, 1998), 39.

catch-all concept, the meaning of which is vague and does little to enrich our understanding of the political process.

Yet, as this book shows, one could argue that some political will – however defined – does exist to implement national ID cards in the United States, since, over the last 100 years, a number of individual policymakers have in fact proposed national ID cards and since the polling data shows that many members of the public support national ID cards. At the same time, many Americans are very troubled by national ID cards, and voices of those opposed are louder than voices of those who are in favor, which likely results in a lack of true determination on the part of most policymakers to introduce national ID cards. Why spend political capital on an issue that is opposed by concentrated and well-represented interests (in the case of the national ID cards: civil libertarians of the ACLU, conservative libertarians of the Cato Institute, religious conservatives, gun rights groups, some immigration advocates, privacy advocates, small government and antigovernment conservatives) and supported by diffused and not well-represented interests (in the case of the national ID cards: the public opinion)? Many policymakers assume that this is simply not worth the trouble. Of course, policymakers would need to spend a lot less political capital if they could prove that national ID cards would help prevent terrorism and if well-organized, well-represented, and well-respected groups existed that would successfully emphasize the importance of prioritizing security, even if at some expense of civil liberties and privacy.

This book explains the politics of identity policing in terms of the drivers and obstacles. Different historical experiences, differences in governmental structure, and even small differences in culture influence the relative emphasis placed on each of the drivers and obstacles in the two countries. However, it is difficult to separate the inherent and perennial orientations to authority from the more temporary attitudes about the government-of-the-day. The politics of national ID cards can become intertwined with a range of related and unrelated questions about the competence of those in power at the time. The latest British ID project is a case in point. The project was highly attractive, and the authorities easily made the choice, but after the excitement of deciding on new policies, costs crept in. Growing unpopularity of Labour governments and doubts about their trustworthiness helped discredit the policy on identification documents they were pushing. The recycling of arguments in favor of ID cards did not work in their favor, either. Although public policy scholars talk about "ideas whose time has come" – i.e., policy "innovations" that may be rehashed proposals that were tabled years earlier, but were not deemed politically feasible or practical at the time[50] – it seems that the time has not yet come for a national ID card in the United Kingdom.

Aristide Zolberg argued in 2002 that in the United States "despite the normative and political difficulties involved, it is likely that some form of reliable biometrically-based identification will emerge in practice, probably on a voluntary basis, to speed up processing through the country's proliferating public and private security checkpoints."[51] My book refrains from making too many predictions, but it is likely that debates will increasingly be more over the "how" of identity policing, rather than the "if." They are more likely to be about the safeguards and precautions, rather than about whether or not ID systems should be introduced or enhanced.

Wilson argues that path dependency ignores the tendency for nations to develop in similar ways at particular historical moments. Instead of imagining each nation as moving along a unique path, we might imagine advanced industrialized democracies as ships in a convoy. Some are ahead of others or off to either side; all are progressing in the same general direction.[52] In this case, the direction seems to be toward more identity policing, but the trend is not an inevitable one.

Social sciences have had at best a checkered history as predictive sciences. In comparison to the wealth of a social science scholarship on a range of topics, this book is only a modest attempt to elucidate certain historical and contemporary features of a topic not much researched in the past: identification documents and identity policing. Whatever is elucidated here may not greatly help us understand the future of identity policing, but it should help put identity policing in context and in some historical and comparative perspective.

The agenda for future research is likely to build on three puzzles. First, it will be important to analyze the relationship between identification documents and state-building, in particular whether national ID cards increase a sense of national unity for citizens. Second, it will be important to explore the relationship between the emancipatory and the repressive aspects of identification documents. Third, it will be important to explore whether the introduction of ID cards triggers a far-reaching shift in relations between governments and those governed. It will be helpful to study other advanced industrialized states, such as Poland and Germany. It will also be

50 John W. Kingdon, *Agendas, Alternatives, and Public Policies* (Boston: Little, Brown, 1984).

51 Zolberg, "Guarding the Gates," 297–298.

52 Wilson, *Only in America?*, 15.

important to include developing countries – especially India, which is now in the process of issuing national ID cards to its billion citizens.

Given that the dissemination of national ID cards speaks directly against the projected decline of nation-states and their citizenship policies, it would be fruitful to look at the alleged decline. In a supposedly borderless world, the reinforcement of borders and greater emphasis on domestic population policing may seem paradoxical, but it is not. It might be considered cynical, but what a British policymaker told me when asked about the Conservative Party's opposition to ID cards for British citizens and support for ID cards for foreign nationals is telling:

> It's a very different concept [from ID cards for British citizens]. It's not unreasonable to have some form of identity measure to help police that, to manage [foreign people living in the United Kingdom]; that's not an expression of citizenship per se; it is not an expression of controlling your citizens or monitoring your citizens; it is merely an expression of controlling your borders, and recognizing the need for controlled immigration policy.[53]

Wealthy countries are not immune from disasters, but natural and man-made crises, wars, and ethnic conflicts continue to plague especially the poorest inhabitants of our planet. In light of such adversities, many people seek refuge and a chance for a better life in the developed world. This has always been the case, but it most recently came to the world's attention during the 2015 influx of Syrian refugees and migrants into Europe. Economic disparities also breed resentment among some in the developing world. As a result, immigration and security will continue as the most important challenges facing developed and developing countries alike. Hence, identity policing will grow in importance, and although it may not be at the forefront of developments or proposed solutions, it is unlikely to be far behind.

It would be useful to examine how effective identification documents are in dealing with immigration or security violations. How about related practices, such as requiring foreign individuals to register their place of residence with the local authorities, as is the case in many European countries? The documents and the registration practices undoubtedly facilitate investigations of violations after the fact, but do they have any preventive power?

It would be valuable to look at public approval and resistance, and explore the notion that immigrants often favor ID cards at a higher rate

[53] Interview with a high-ranking member of the Conservative Party, September 2009.

than native-born citizens since they see it as "a symbolic reward of citizenship." Future work would look at groups that oppose ID cards and study them from a point of view of social movement theories to explore issues of resistance and civil disobedience. Examples abound: from opposition to ID cards in South Africa in 1906 to those Americans today who refuse to be counted or to carry government-issued ID documents. In fact, the themes of religious opposition to enumeration and identification are particularly interesting. It would also be important to examine what effect different forms of organized opposition have on the progress of ID card systems.

It would be interesting to examine how attitudes toward privacy, surveillance, and identity policing are changing as new generations grow up. Will young people brought up in the world of online social networks feel differently than their parents about ID documents? With their lives increasingly documented online, are Americans about to lose their ability to reinvent themselves? What would that mean for their attitudes toward identity policing?

It would also be useful to look at how policymakers from different countries learn from each other, or use each other's examples to highlight policy benefits and flaws. The British and Australian policymakers have found out that an unpopular policy on identification documents can become a political and electoral liability. Given the recent stormy experience of the British scheme, it will be interesting to see whether and how other countries that have yet to adopt national ID cards or debate identity policing will be taking note of the debate as it unfolded in the United Kingdom.

If identity policing and ID card schemes are to be introduced elsewhere, are all-out comprehensive and centralized schemes, such as the one that was intended for the United Kingdom, best from the points of view of states and their citizens? Or are piecemeal schemes, more in line with those in the United States, the future of identity policing worldwide? Do incremental initiatives facilitate public use and acceptance of identification documents, or do they increase the risk of fraud? Does having multiple, independent identity assurance providers increase the system reliability? Which systems are secure, and which lead to public distrust? If the perfect cannot be the enemy of the good, when is a system good enough?

In the future, it will be important to examine the "ID Divide," which exists between "credentialed" and "uncredentialed" Americans. As Chapter 4 noted, some studies in the mid-2000s suggested that 12–13 percent of voting-age Americans, or 22 million people, did not have a driver's license or a state-issued photo ID. The issue is particularly pronounced among African-Americans. While reliable studies are lacking, some studies estimate that 25 percent of African-American voting-age citizens have no government-issued photo ID, compared with 8 percent of white voting-age citizens. Although Americans of all backgrounds may find themselves on the wrong side of the ID Divide, there are disproportionate effects on the poor, the disabled, and communities of color.[54] It is necessary to examine the implications of that, and consider possible solutions.

As I stated earlier, few people point to a possibility of a much larger disenfranchisement occurring in the American society. It is possible to argue that having an identification document is not just a convenience but a necessity, and every American citizen should have a government-issued identification document. If government-issued identification documents are increasingly required to be able to take a college entrance exam, get a job, open a bank account, enter a federal building, donate blood, and obtain a library card, and yet millions of people do not have such documents, then the country faces a problem that needs to be fixed. I am not advocating for a national ID card as a solution, but for a recognition that a fix may be needed.

The relationship between any state and its people is inherently coercive, given sociologist Max Weber's widely accepted definition of a state as "a human community that (successfully) claims the *monopoly of the legitimate use of physical force* within a given territory."[55] State-formation is a force-based effort, given sociologist Charles Tilly's dictum that states make wars and wars make states.[56] Justice Louis Brandeis reminded us that even well-intentioned official actions in response to major dangers deserve scrutiny: "Experience should teach us to be most on our guard to protect liberty when the Government's purposes are beneficent ... The greatest dangers to liberty lurk in insidious encroachment by men of zeal, well-meaning but without understanding."[57] Future work on identification documents and identity policing would shed more light on the relationships between citizens and the state and on power relations more broadly.

[54] Swire and Butts, "The ID Divide," 12, 13, 38.

[55] H. H. Gerth and C. Wright Mills, eds., *From Max Weber: Essays in Sociology* (New York: Oxford University Press, 1958), 78. Emphasis in original.

[56] Charles Tilly, *Coercion, Capital, and European States, AD 990–1990* (Oxford: Basil Blackwell, 1990), 1–2.

[57] *Olmstead v. United States*, 277 U.S. 438 (1928).

Although this study could not have been fully comprehensive in examining the issues surrounding identity policing and identification documents in all western liberal democracies, let alone worldwide, it does place identity policing and identification documents in the United States in a much-needed historical and political perspective. In this concluding chapter, I also included some discussion of the United Kingdom. This book outlines the significance of identification documents and identity policing in the United States, carefully examines their history and present, and sheds some light on the future. This book also debunks some common myths by showing that Americans see national ID cards more positively than is popularly believed and that, despite the existence of some passionate opposition, some policymakers in the United States have in fact proposed national ID cards over the last 100 years, albeit unsuccessfully.

The successful and failed schemes; international, national, and local experiences; and historical and contemporary knowledge and debates all influence present-day and future developments. Whatever happens in the future, the exercise of governmental authority in the important area of identity policing will be a delicate balancing act for all involved. This book is only the necessary first step to examine the implications of identification documents and identity policing for the study of the United States and other liberal democratic states.

Index

Lightning Source UK Ltd.
Milton Keynes UK
UKHW011947300419
341903UK00009B/128/P

9 781316 510100